Modern World History 1919 onwards

Philip Sauvain

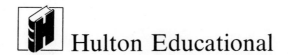 Hulton Educational

First published in Great Britain 1985
by Hulton Educational Publications Ltd
Raans Road, Amersham, Bucks HP6 6JJ

Text © *Philip Sauvain* 1985
Illustrations © *Hulton Educational 1985*

ISBN 0 7175 1312 2

Acknowledgements
Anglo-Chinese Educational Institute 90
J. Allan Cash Photolibrary 145
BBC Hulton Picture Library 9, 10(T, C, B), 12B, 15, 23L, 28, 30B, 31, 33, 38T, 44, 47(T, C), 49T, 50B, 51, 54B, 67, 79, 80R, 85, 92, 94, 97, 100T, 112, 116, 119, 121, 122T, 128, 129, 130, 138, 139, 142, 154, 155
Commission of European Communities 172, 174/5
FAO 194T
Imperial War Museum 4
Mansell Collection 5, 6, 11, 12(TL, TR), 16, 18, 21L, 26L, 29, 30T, 39(L, R), 40, 41, 42, 46, 47B, 48T, 48/9, 50T, 52, 59(T, B), 61B, 65B, (66T, C, B), 76, 86T, 87, 93T, 102, 108, 117B, 120, 122C, 123, 141
Novosti 56/57, 58, 61T, 62, 63, 64/5, 68, 69(T, B), 71, 72, 131, 190L
Popperfoto 14, 19, 20, 21R, 24, 38B, 53, 54T, 60, 78, 81, 82, 83, 86B, 94B, 96, 100B, 109, 110, 114, 115, 117T, 124, 126, 133, 134, 135, 136, 140, 144, 146, 148, 151(TL, B), 152B, 153, 158, 158/9, 161(TL, TR, B), 162(T, B), 163, 164, 165, 166, 167, 168, 169T, 170, 173, 176, 178(L, R), 180, 182B, 183, 185L, 186, 198/9, 200T, 201(L, R), 202, 204, 208, 209, 210/11, 212, 213, 214, 215, 216
Topham Picture Library 17, 23R, 26/7, 32, 34(L, R), 35, 36, 37(T, B), 73, 74, 84, 88, 95, 98, 99, 113, 118, 151TR, 152T, 160, 169B, 177, 182T, 184, 185R, 200B, 203, 206
UNESCO 194B
United Nations 190R, 191, 195, 196
UN Geneva 104, 106
WHO 188
'Brother can you spare me a dime' by Jay Gorney/E. Y. Harburg is published in the UK by Chappell Music Limited. Copyright: 1932 Harms Inc.

Phototypeset by Input Typesetting Ltd, London
Printed in Great Britain by R J Acford, Chichester

CONTENTS

CHAPTER 1

Europe in 1919

'The Menin Road', a painting of the horrors of trench warfare, by Paul Nash.

'Eleven o'clock today, November 11, troops will stand fast on the positions reached at the hour named. The line of outposts will be established, and reported to Army Headquarters. The remainder of the troops will be collected ready to meet any emergency. All military precautions will be preserved, and there will be no communication with the enemy. Further instructions will be issued. Acknowledge'.

In these words peace came to the armies in the field. The greatest war in history was brought to an end by a curt message for which a single pink slip sufficed.

The quote on the left shows how a British newspaper, *The Manchester Guardian*, recorded the last moments of the First World War, in its edition for 12 November 1918.

At the time, people used to call it the Great War, because no other war in history had involved so many soldiers, from so many countries, on so massive a scale. Over 8.5 million soldiers had been killed out of the total of over 70 million who fought in the War. The countries who had declared war on Germany and her allies came from all over the world, including the member nations of the British Empire and also countries as widely separated as Cuba, China, Liberia, Siam, Guatemala and Japan. Many people in the world had been affected in some way or other by the course of the War. All were soon to be affected by the peace settlement in Paris – and its consequences.

The Paris Peace Treaties

The peace settlement at the end of the First World War was drawn up by the five great Allied powers, without prior consultation with Germany or the other defeated Central Powers (Austria, Hungary, Bulgaria and Turkey). Nor was Russia invited to take part in the deliberations, which took place in Paris in 1919–20. Britain was represented by Prime Minister David Lloyd George, France by Prime Minister Georges Clemenceau, Italy by Prime Minister Vittorio Orlando and the United States by President Woodrow Wilson. Many other countries were also represented at the conferences, notably Japan, initially one of the five great powers making up the Council of Ten. In the final analysis, however, most of the important decisions were made by the United States, Britain, France and Italy.

Revenge

For much of the time, the Conference delegates argued amongst themselves. The French wanted revenge. They wanted to punish Germany and weaken the country so much that the German people would never again be strong enough to wage war against France. Much of the fighting during the War had taken place on the Western Front in northern France. By contrast British and American soldiers fought on foreign soil, as did the Italians for most of the War. Many French towns and villages had been reduced to rubble during four years of heavy fighting. Fields, woods and farmland had been pitted with craters and shell-holes, scored and lacerated with deep trenches, and left as a hazardous and desolate wasteland. Hundreds of thousands of French people had been made homeless and one and a half million French soldiers killed in action. Clemenceau spoke for the French people as a whole when he demanded peace terms which would use German money to help restore and rebuild France.

A just and lasting peace

But the Americans were more concerned about getting a just and lasting peace. President Wilson was opposed to colonialism and did not want the European powers enlarging their own frontiers and empires at the expense of the Central Powers (Germany, Austria, Hungary, Bulgaria and Turkey). On the other hand, he had no intention of letting the Germans escape without some form of penalty. Lloyd George also sought a satisfactory peace settlement which would hold; one that would exact fair compensation from the Central Powers without reducing them to poverty and anarchy. The British had no desire to see Germany, or the countries of the former Austro-Hungarian Empire, succumb to a new Bolshevik Revolution. And there were signs that it might do just that. Left-wing uprisings in Germany and Hungary had already shaken Europe – the Spartacist uprising in Berlin in January 1919 and the Communist rebellion in Hungary in March (see page 12).

Lloyd George, Orlando, Clemenceau and Woodrow Wilson at the Paris Peace Conference in 1919.

Berlin in June 1919. A vast crowd demonstrates against the terms of the Treaty of Versailles, which many Germans consider to be unfair.

Compromise

In the end the peace settlement was something of a compromise; neither as tough as that demanded by the French, nor as fair as that for which the British and Americans had argued. Only one Allied delegate, from China, eventually refused to sign, although the United States Senate later failed to ratify the treaties. Some delegates, such as Orlando of Italy, walked out of the Conference in disgust. Others, like Japan, expressed dissatisfaction with the terms of the agreement. China was unhappy because Japan was granted the rights and concessions in Shandong Province (in China) which had formerly been held by Germany. These had been promised to Japan by the Allies during the course of the War.

There were five peace treaties in all, of which the one signed at Versailles on 28 June 1919 was the most significant, and the best remembered, since it settled the War with Germany. Germany was forced to agree to the terms of the treaty imposed by the Allies. She was given little opportunity to dispute its clauses or to state the German case. So it was not, therefore, a negotiated treaty agreed by both sides. This imposition of the treaty by threat of force, rankled with many Germans, especially Hitler and the Nazis. It lit a fuse to the crises which exploded in the years immediately before the outbreak of the Second World War in 1939. A final straw was the Allied insistence that the Germans acknowledge that they alone were guilty of having started the War. This was not quite true, since the other European powers had also been guilty of building up their armed forces and expanding their empires in the years before 1914.

You can see the effects of the boundary changes, imposed by the Paris Peace Treaties, on the maps on pages 7, 8 and 9. A summary of the principal terms of the Treaty of Versailles can be seen in the panel on the next page and at the top of page 8.

Effects of Treaty of Versailles

The net effect of the treaty was:

(a) to 'rob' Germany of about one tenth of its territory in Europe;

(b) to take away all of Germany's colonies abroad;

(c) to impose severe restrictions on the composition, dispersal and future development of the German armed forces;

(d) to hinder German relations with neighbouring countries (such as German-speaking Austria, forbidden by the terms of the Paris Peace Settlement from forming a union, called *Anschluss*, with Germany);

(e) to burden future generations of the German people with a huge bill for the damage and destruction caused by the War. The Germans had to agree to pay the Allies a vast sum of money, called *reparations*, even though many of the German people were desperately poor and close to starvation at this time.

(f) One of the most promising features of the treaty was the Covenant which all the participating nations signed, agreeing to form and join the League of Nations (see Chapter 8).

(g) The resentment in Germany, caused by the signing of the Treaty of Versailles, later helped Adolf Hitler and the Nazi Party to sweep into power with the avowed intention of overturning many of the provisions of the Versailles peace agreement.

THE TREATY OF VERSAILLES

1. Military Provisions for Germany

Army: to be reduced to only 100,000 men. No conscription allowed. The number of guns to be strictly limited. No soldiers (or other armed forces) to be stationed in the Rhineland – to act as a buffer zone separating Germany from her neighbours France, Belgium and the Netherlands.

Navy: to be reduced to only 15,000 sailors, six battleships, six light cruisers, twelve destroyers and twelve torpedo boats. No submarines. The German fleet was later scuttled in the anchorage of Scapa Flow off the north coast of Britain.

Air: by October 1920 Germany to have disbanded her existing air forces. No air force allowed.

2. Reparations

Germany to pay a large sum in compensation, much of it in the form of goods, such as 40 million tonnes of coal to France and the Low Countries. The Treaty fixed a temporary sum, pending the calculation of the full amount of reparations claimed by the Allies. This was eventually settled at $32,000 million – a huge sum of money, obviously beyond the means of the Germans to pay, since they too had been drastically affected by the War. This was later a chief cause of the catastrophic inflation of the German mark in 1923 (see page 28).

3. Territorial adjustments

* Alsace and Lorraine to be given back to France, Eupen and Malmedy to Belgium, Hultschin to Czechoslovakia, Memel to Lithuania.
* The Saar coalfield to go to France; but the people of that region to vote by plebiscite in 1935 on whether they want to stay in France or not. (They did not.)
* Plebiscites also to be held in Allenstein (East Prussia or Poland), Schleswig (Germany or Denmark) and Upper Silesia (Germany or Poland), to determine whether the people there want to be German or part of the neighbouring state.
* Poland, formerly part of the Russian empire and now a separate nation once more, to be given part of West Prussia – as a corridor between East Prussia and Germany, giving her access to the new free port of Danzig.

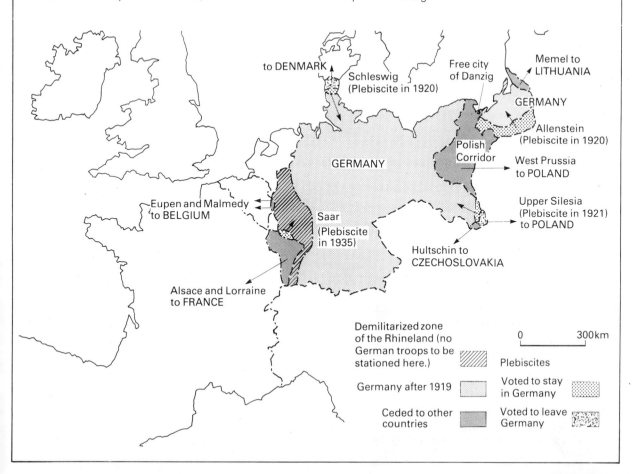

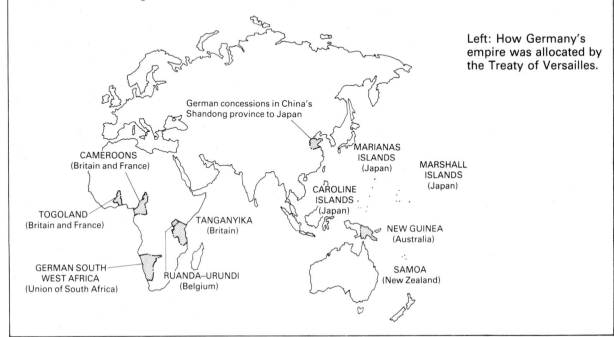

4. German empire

German overseas possessions to be administered as mandates of the new League of Nations:
* Tanganyika to go to Britain;
* the Cameroons and Togoland to Britain and France;
* Ruanda-Urundi to Belgium;

* German South West Africa to the Union of South Africa;
* Samoa to New Zealand;
* New Guinea to Australia;
* the Marianas, Marshall and Caroline Islands in the Pacific, and the German concessions in Shandong Province (in China), to Japan.

Left: How Germany's empire was allocated by the Treaty of Versailles.

German concessions in China's Shandong province to Japan

CAMEROONS (Britain and France)

MARIANAS ISLANDS (Japan)

MARSHALL ISLANDS (Japan)

CAROLINE ISLANDS (Japan)

TOGOLAND (Britain and France)

TANGANYIKA (Britain)

NEW GUINEA (Australia)

GERMAN SOUTH WEST AFRICA (Union of South Africa)

RUANDA–URUNDI (Belgium)

SAMOA (New Zealand)

Peace agreements were also negotiated in Paris with Austria, Hungary, Bulgaria and Turkey.

The Treaty of St Germain (with Austria)

This was signed on 10 September 1919. By this time the old Austro-Hungarian Empire had already disintegrated. During the last months of the War soldiers from the different nations, who formed part of the Empire, began to desert from the army and some fought for the Allies. Uprisings led to the creation of national councils in exile. In the summer of 1918 the Allies recognized Czechoslovakia as an independent state and on 21 October the Czechs officially proclaimed their independence. The Yugoslavs then followed suit a week later, as did Hungary on 1 November. Austria, too, became a republic on 13 November.

The new Austrian Government resented the fact that their new *republic* was held responsible for the misdeeds of the old Habsburg *empire*. But this argument carried little weight and the Austrians were made to pay reparations and to limit the size of their army. New boundary changes meant that substantial

*For ease of reference the name Yugoslavia is used here, although not given until 1929; previously the Kingdom of Serbs, Croats and Slovenes.

POLAND

CZECHOSLOVAKIA

AUSTRIA

HUNGARY

ROMANIA

ITALY

YUGOSLAVIA*

0   300 km

Austria–Hungary in 1914

numbers of German-speaking peoples were transferred from Austria to neighbouring countries as part of the peace settlement.

Part of the Austrian Tyrol was given to Italy whilst the German-speaking lands of Bohemia and Moravia were incorporated in the newly created **nation state** of Czechoslovakia (see Explanatory Notes, page 13). Other territorial changes affected some of the people of Slovenia and Croatia, who now became Italians rather than citizens of Yugoslavia.

The Treaty of Trianon (with Hungary)

This was signed on 4 June 1920. It was similar to the other peace agreements: reparations were agreed, the army was limited in size, and large portions of the old kingdom of Hungary were dispersed, mainly to Romania, Czechoslovakia and Yugoslavia. By this time the new republic had been replaced by a monarchy, headed by Admiral Horthy as regent; Hungary was left as only a shadow of the original kingdom – about a quarter the size with only a third of the population.

Below left: The Austro-Hungarian Empire after 1919.
Below: How the Ottoman Empire was allocated by the Treaty of Sevres.
Below right: Mustafa Kemal, centre, who became the new leader of Turkey in 1923, later renegotiated the Treaty of Sevres.

The Treaty of Neuilly (with Bulgaria)

This was signed on 27 November 1919. Its main provisions also included reparations, reduction in the size of the armed forces and loss of territory (chiefly Thrace to Greece).

The Treaty of Sevres (with Turkey)

This was signed on 10 August 1920 and redistributed Turkish territory in Europe (Eastern Thrace and part of the Aegean Islands to Greece). It placed various Middle East possessions in the care of Britain (Palestine, Transjordan, Iraq), and France (Syria, Lebanon), as mandates to be administered by the League of Nations. In addition the existence of the independent kingdom of Hejaz (later Saudi Arabia) was ratified by the treaty.

However the terms of the treaty were denounced by Mustafa Kemal, leader of the successful revolution in Turkey which eventually replaced the Sultan. After going to war with Greece, he was able to negotiate a new treaty at Lausanne in 1923.

The Treaty of Sevres had a dramatic effect on the geography of the Middle East, since it broke up the old Ottoman Empire. Turkey had long been regarded as the 'sick man of Europe'. The European provinces of the Sultan had been torn by revolution and violent reprisals ever since 1821. Lack of effective control meant that Turkey's grip on the outlying territories of her empire had been loosened in the years before the War. Now she paid the penalty.

French mandates

British mandates

0   480 km

TURKEY

PERSIA (IRAN)

SYRIA

LEBANON

IRAQ

PALESTINE

EGYPT

TRANSJORDAN

ARABIA

Old Empires and New Republics

In 1914 three out of the four Great Powers of continental Europe were ruled by powerful emperors, not by democratic governments. Indeed, one of the main reasons why the War was fought, and why millions of people died, was because Czar Nicholas II of Russia, Kaiser William II of Germany and the Emperor Francis Joseph of Austria-Hungary wanted to maintain the great power and influence of their empires.

But the War was their undoing. By 11 November 1918 all three had gone and their empires had either broken up (Russia and Austria-Hungary) or were soon to be dismembered by the peacemakers of Versailles (Germany).

* Czar Nicholas II abdicated in 1917 and was murdered by the Bolsheviks in 1918. Russia became a republic.
* Kaiser William II abdicated in 1918 and fled into exile in the Netherlands. Germany became a republic.

Left: Czar Nicholas II of Russia.

Below: Kaiser William II of Germany.

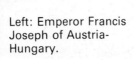

Left: Emperor Francis Joseph of Austria-Hungary.

* Emperor Francis Joseph died in 1916 and his successor, Charles, was unable to hold the empire together. Austria, Hungary, Czechoslovakia and Yugoslavia all became republics.

In addition, the Sultanate of Mohammed V of Turkey was replaced in 1923 by a republican government led by Mustafa Kemal, who was known as Kemal Ataturk.

The Seeds of Totalitarianism

The new republics – among them the USSR, Germany, Poland and Czechoslovakia – faced many problems in the next twenty years. But having rid themselves of one form of dictatorship (that of the monarchies), most soon acquired new forms of dictatorship and totalitarian systems of government.

As you will see in Chapter 5, many European countries attempted to intervene in the civil war which followed the Bolshevik Revolution in Russia in 1917. Fear of Communism and its consequences (for example, common ownership of the land and a dictatorship of the workers) led other European governments to take repressive measures to ensure there was no repetition of the Bolshevik Revolution in their own countries.

This reaction, and the fears that inspired it, were fertile grounds for the development of right-wing dictatorships and the establishment of totalitarian systems of government. Josef Pilsudski became the dictator of Poland, Admiral Horthy controlled Hungary and right-wing goverments dominated all of the countries of eastern Europe, with the exception of Czechoslovakia. One-party systems of government were normal. In no sense of the word were they democracies, like those of the United Kingdom or the United States.

Totalitarianism

This is the name given to states where the government is in the hands of a dictator and a single political party. Total control is exercised over the people; there are no opposition parties; no opportunities for the people to choose an alternative government.

Totalitarian governments often maintain control through terror (secret police, concentration camps, imprisonment of political prisoners), propaganda and control of the media (newspapers, radio, and now television).

Totalitarian governments can be Communist or Fascist. The term is used to describe the method of exercising power, not the principles or beliefs of these governments.

Riots, Strikes and Revolutions

The Bolshevik Revolution in Russia showed the poor and oppressed peoples of Europe one way of solving their problems. Many returning soldiers were unemployed after the War. Welfare benefits were meagre then and many people came close to starvation. Many could not understand why the War had been fought in the first place, or what lasting benefits it had brought ordinary working people. They could see that many wealthy factory-owners and industrialists had grown even richer on profits from wartime production. But there seemed to be no corresponding gain for the factory-worker or the farm-labourer. Much talk in wartime had been about heroes fighting for their country. But what did the country have to offer its heroes when the fighting stopped and they came home?

Discontented and disenchanted soldiers and workers foresaw a return to the old pre-war way of life, with the lives of the rich and well-to-do contrasting dramatically with those of the poor and needy. Politicians who offered extreme solutions to these problems were sometimes listened to rather than laughed at. Hitler's Nazis, Mussolini's Fascists and like-minded extremist groups on the far right promised a better life – as did Communists in Russia, Marxists, and extreme left-wing groups, throughout Europe.

Marxism

Marxism is a set of political ideas, originally devised by Karl Marx (1818–83) and later modified by his followers (including Lenin and Stalin in Russia, and Mao Zedong in China). Marxists believe that there is, and always has been, a class struggle between the poor and the rich – between the peasants and the landowners; between the workers and the factory-owners; and between the working class and the middle and upper classes.

Marxists believe that revolution is inevitable and that the workers will eventually seize power and govern the country. But this will only be the first stage on the road to true Communism – that of the dictatorship of the proletariat. The next stage, Socialism, will be reached when the people own the factories and farms. These are called the means of production. Communism will be achieved when there are no differences between people, when everyone accepts that all are equal, when people are paid according to their circumstances and not as a reward for the amount of work they have done. 'From each according to his abilities, to each according to his needs', said Marx.

Germany 1918. A speaker makes a violent revolutionary speech at the funeral procession of rioters who were killed during disturbances on 24 December 1918.

Above: Rosa Luxembourg in 1919.

Left: Spartacist revolt in Germany. German Government troops in action in 1919.

The Bolshevik Revolution in November 1917 gave Marxists a powerful new source of inspiration. Poverty, inequality and hatred of an unjust war had helped Lenin's Communists to seize control of the world's largest country. If this could be achieved in Russia, why not in Germany or Hungary as well?

The Spartacists

In Germany the Spartacists, a group of Marxists, led by Rosa Luxembourg and Karl Liebnecht, opposed the War in 1915. They urged the workers of Germany to overthrow the capitalists (ie the factory-owners and bosses). In January 1919 there was an uprising in Berlin when some of the Spartacists took to the streets. Armed Communists occupied key buildings, hoping to spark off a revolution among the workers of Germany. In the violence which followed, Rosa Luxembourg and Karl Liebnecht were both murdered by the *Freikorps* – a volunteer army of right-wing and extremist ex-soldiers.

The Freikorps

This 'Free Corps', consisting of ex-servicemen led by discontented ex-officers, posed a threat of its own to the legitimate government in Germany. They linked up with nationalist groups who bitterly resented the terms of the Treaty of Versailles. As patriots they could not accept that Germany had been defeated. So in March 1920 they attempted to seize power in Berlin with soldiers commanded by General von Luttwitz. Wolfgang Kapp was named Chancellor but the German workers called a general strike and the putsch (attempted takeover of the government) failed in only a matter of days. Many of these nationalists later became Nazis and one infamous group, the Erhardt Brigade, wore swastikas on their uniforms.

Bela Kun

In Hungary, a Communist leader, called Bela Kun, led a successful rebellion in March 1919. Kun had been captured by the Russians during the War and returned to Hungary after the Bolshevik Revolution. For several months Hungary had a Soviet government, like Russia, until it was overthrown by the right-wing leader Admiral Horthy, with Romanian help, in November of the same year.

Bela Kun, Bolshevik leader of Hungary in 1919.

Explanatory Notes

Nation state is the name given to countries whose people all belong to the same nation. The term is used because nation does not always mean the same thing, nor refer to the same boundaries, as country or state. For instance, a group of people sharing the same language or race, heritage, history, ancestry or tribal group, can be regarded as belonging to the same nation – even though they may live in different countries. This is why Hitler thought that German-speaking peoples were rightfully members of the German nation, even if they lived in Lithuania or Poland.

When the great powers re-distributed the boundaries of central Europe at the Paris Peace Conferences, they made some effort to define them so that they included peoples of the same nationality. It is these countries which are regarded as being nation states, as opposed to other countries (for example the United Kingdom) where peoples of many different races, beliefs and languages live. Unfortunately it is much easier to define what constitutes a nation than it is to separate one national group from another by drawing frontiers on a map. The idea of a nation state and the frontiers drawn in 1919 led to many of the controversial issues of the twentieth century.

Exercises

1. Marshal Foch is reported to have said of the Paris Peace agreements: 'This is not a peace. It is an armistice for 21 years.' What did he mean by this? What justification did he have for making this remark in 1919? How accurate was he in making this forecast?

2. Explain carefully the circumstances at the end of the First World War which lead to the break-up of the Austro-Hungarian Empire. How and why was it divided into separate nation states?

3. What was a nation state? Give examples and discuss the problems raised when trying to define what constitutes a nation. What importance do you think should be attached to characteristics such as language and the existence of the nation as a separate country at some stage in the past?

4. Write brief notes explaining the significance of each of the following:
(a) The Spartacist uprising in Germany
(b) Bela Kun
(c) The Freikorps

5. Examine carefully the maps on pages 7, 8 and 9. Which countries do you think gained most as a result of the terms imposed by the Paris Peace Treaties? Which of the participating countries on the Allied side gained least material benefit from the peace settlement?

Further Activities

1. Do you think the terms of the Paris Peace Treaties were fair? Were they wise? Discuss this topic with your friends. Some members of your group could put forward the opposing views and opinions of the different Allied delegates – one representing the French, another the Italians, and so on. Others could represent the Central Powers – German, Austrian, Hungarian, Bulgarian and Turkish representatives – arguing the case against the terms of the different treaties.

2. See if any of your older relatives and their friends can remember the inter-war years between 1918 and 1939. Write down a list of any of the things they can recall vividly, such as the outbreak of war in 1939, the Japanese invasion of Manchuria in 1931, or even the events immediately following the end of the First World War.

As you read through this book try to supplement the material you see here with comments and reminiscences from people who lived through these great events. You will find this especially valuable when studying the more recent history, since most older people will be able to recall clearly events like the Moon landing in 1969 or the assassination of President Kennedy in 1963.

Italy and the Rise of Mussolini

After the March on Rome in 1922 – Mussolini with other Italian Fascist leaders.

Monday, 21 October 1922, Noon, Rome

The Fascist revolution is triumphant today all over Italy. The Fascisti this morning, when marching into Rome, were acclaimed by tens of thousands of people, and Signor Mussolini, called by special telegram from the King, has come to undertake the task of forming a new government. Italy is thus on the threshold of a new period in its history, which, it is hoped, will lead her on to greater destinies. Mussolini, the man of iron nerve, of dauntless courage, of striking initiative and patriotic ardour, has imposed his will and personality upon the entire nation. Hundreds of thousands obey his beck and call.

His army of Fascisti, with their black shirts and strict military discipline, recall the red shirts of the days of Garibaldi and Mussolini himself is like a second edition of the great hero of Italy's 'risorgimento'.

The extract on the left shows how the *Daily Telegraph* in London announced the bloodless revolution which installed Mussolini as the new leader of Italy only three years after the founding of the Fascist Party. Two years later all pretence of a democracy was swept aside and Mussolini ruled Italy as a dictator, acclaimed by the Italians as *Il Duce* – the Leader. He remained in office until 1943 and left an indelible mark on modern Italy.

In a Nutshell

* Italian nationalists (patriots who put their nation first) are bitterly disappointed when the peace agreements fail to provide Italy with adequate territorial rewards at the end of the War.
* Weak governments, high unemployment, especially among ex-servicemen, a high level of inflation and poor living conditions lead to riots and unrest.
* Some workers, stirred by events in Russia and Berlin, join the Communists. Factory sit-ins and strikes worry small businessmen and landowners, who fear a 'Bolshevik' revolution in Italy.
* Mussolini starts the Italian Fascist movement in 1919 to combat the spread of Communism. His followers use violent strike-breaking methods; but, because they are successful, they win the approval of influential people.
* In 1922 Mussolini threatens to 'march on Rome' but is asked instead to form a government. Within two years he turns Italy into a Fascist dictatorship.
* Despite repression and censorship, Italians can point with pride to Mussolini's achievements before 1930. Agricultural and industrial production is increased, educational standards are raised and agreement reached with the Pope.
* Mussolini drains marshes and builds roads and hospitals but the Great Depression hits Italy hard in the 1930s.
* His expansionist foreign policy seeks to repair the damage done to Italian prestige after the First World War. When Italian troops invade the poor, but independent, African state of Abyssinia in 1935, the world disapproves.
* By 1937 Italy draws closer to Nazi Germany. Mussolini's earlier achievements are forgotten when Italy intervenes in the Spanish Civil War (1936) and starts to persecute Italian Jews (1938).

Italian Hopes at the End of the First World War

The Treaty of London

In the early years of the twentieth century Italy was a member of the Triple Alliance, together with Germany and the Austro-Hungarian Empire. But Italy resented the fact that many Italians were living in the South Tyrol and Trentino, then parts of Austria not Italy. So, at the outbreak of war in 1914, she remained neutral instead of coming to the aid of her two allies.

The Germans and the Austrians tried to persuade the Italians to enter the conflict but were upstaged by Britain, France and Russia. By the terms of the Treaty of London (26 April 1915), the Italians agreed to declare war on Austria-Hungary in return for a number of territories. These included the South Tyrol and Trentino, Trieste and part of the Dalmatian coastline. Italy was also promised enlarged colonies in Africa, if Britain and France took possession of Germany's colonies after the War.

During the War the Italian army got bogged down in an endless series of battles along the valley of the River Isonzo on the Austrian border. When Russian resistance collapsed in 1917, Germany sent reinforcements to help the Austrians break through the Italian defences. By this time the Italian army was tired and dispirited after two long years of pointless warfare. The resulting battle of Caporetto was a disaster and many Italian soldiers were killed, wounded or captured, or deserted from their units.

The Paris Peace Treaties

Only at the end of the War were the Italians able to redeem their self respect, with the victory at Vittorio Veneto just twelve days before Armistice Day.

The Italian army in retreat after their defeat at Caporetto in 1917.

By then well over half a million Italian soldiers had been killed, but with very little military progress to show for their sacrifice. This inability to contribute massively to the Allied war effort, probably told against the Italians at the Paris Peace Conference. The other Allies, particularly the Americans, were not inclined to honour in full the terms of the Treaty of London, which had been agreed before the United States entered the War.

Although Italy was granted the South Tyrol, Trieste and part of the Dalmatian coastline, she could not get agreement about the Adriatic port of Fiume which she coveted. Fiume had previously been a Hungarian port but its population was partly Croatian (Yugoslav) and partly Italian. Italy was not even given one of the former German colonies as a mandate, nor was she able to expand her existing African colonies of Libya, Eritrea and Somaliland – as she had been promised in 1915.

Instead she incurred crippling debts as a result of her war effort and, in the immediate postwar period, suffered a high rate of inflation. Prices of some commodities rose fourfold between 1915 and 1921.

The failure of the Italian Government, to negotiate all the territorial concessions demanded by Italy, led to a general lack of confidence in the Government. It was a principal grievance of Mussolini's Fascist Party. When they seized power in 1922 they announced that the real enemies of Italy and the Italian people were the 'political class of weak and defective men who in four long years knew not how to give a Government to the nation'.

Mussolini's Italy.

Gabriele d'Annunzio

One hothead decided to show his countrymen what could be done if action rather than deliberation was the motivating force. On 12 September 1919 Gabriele d'Annunzio led a group of right-wing adventurers who seized Fiume for Italy, in direct contravention of the wishes of the delegates at the Paris Peace Conference, particularly those of President Wilson. In any case, Fiume had not been promised to Italy at the Treaty of London in 1915.

Eventually Italy and Yugoslavia had to settle the question of Fiume on their own and the Yugoslavs later agreed that it should become a free city, provided the Italians ejected d'Annunzio. But in March 1922 – before Mussolini's 'March on Rome' – a Fascist group seized power in Fiume and the port was then occupied by Italian forces. In 1924 Yugoslavia agreed with Mussolini that it should become a permanent part of Italy, in return for Italian acknowledgment of other Yugoslav rights in the Adriatic. (After the Second World War Fiume went back to Yugoslavia and is now known as Rijeka.)

Left: September 1919 – Gabriele d'Annunzio enters Fiume in triumph.

The Rise of Mussolini and the Fascists

Mussolini leading a Fascist demonstration in Rome in 1922.

The Communists

Italy in the period immediately after the War was beset by many problems. The rapid increase in the cost of living, a high rate of unemployment and discontent at the lack of progress at the Paris Peace Conference stimulated the growth of dissident groups of workers and ex-soldiers.

The Bolshevik Revolution in Russia acted as a model for Communist workers' groups in Italy, particularly in the industrial north around Milan and Turin. Some of these groups formed organizations called Soviets, after the Russian model. A Soviet is basically an elected ruling council; so the growth of these Soviets was a direct challenge to the Italian Government. In August 1920 many workers in heavy industry were locked out by their employers, so they retaliated by occupying their factories and places of work.

The Fasci

These first hesitant moves towards Communism led Mussolini and other nationalists to start the first of the Fascist Party groups in Milan in March 1919. They were called the *Fasci Italiani del Combattimento*, which roughly means 'groups of fighters for Italy'.

In ancient Rome the *fasces* (Latin word) was the symbol of authority. Magistrates carried a bundle of rods grouped around an axe. Mussolini's Italian Fascists used the same symbol as a sign of their authority and power. They chose a symbol from Ancient Rome because they revered the time when Italy had a great empire and Rome ruled the western world. They hoped to see Italy take her rightful place once more, as one of the most powerful countries on Earth.

Democracy had failed Italy (so they believed). What was needed was strong government. They were ashamed, as nationalists, by the humbling of their armed forces during the War and especially by the supposed humiliation of the Italian delegates at the Paris Peace Conference. For all its high ideals **Fascism** (see Explanatory Notes) appealed most to ex-soldiers and thugs who relished the opportunity to wear a black uniform, carry a weapon, and strut around with other Fascists looking for trouble.

The Fascists did not have far to look for their prey. There were numerous opportunities to engage Communists and their sympathizers in street fighting in the industrial towns of northern Italy between 1919 and 1922. Like the Freikorps in Germany these bully-boys sought to avenge the failures of their leaders after the War.

Mussolini in uniform. He took the title *Il Duce,* the leader.

Mussolini

However, unlike the Freikorps, the Fascists were led by a remarkable politician – Benito Mussolini. He wanted real power and sought political recognition for his Fasci. In 1921 they gained 35 seats in the Italian parliament after Fascist gangs had intimidated voters and opponents. Thereafter they took the name *Partito Nazionale Fascista* (National Fascist Party).

Meanwhile farmers, shopkeepers, landowners and factory-owners, understandably afraid of a Communist revolution, gave the anti-Communist Fascists their money and their support. As the movement grew it soon widened its appeal to the Italian people, even among the police, despite the fact that street violence continued. In February 1921 there were serious riots in Florence, when Fascists and Communists fought in the streets. Two months later, at the time of the elections to the Italian parliament, over five hundred people were killed or wounded in clashes between the Fascists and their opponents.

Fascism becomes respectable

Despite the bloodshed, the Fascist Party was gaining respectability where it mattered most, among the rich and powerful. Very soon it had the financial backing of some of the most distinguished financiers and industrialists in Italy. Bankers and industrial magnates provided the necessary financial backing and support.

These events took place at a time when the conventional political system seemed incapable of providing Italy with the strong democratic government it needed to overcome the problems left behind by the War. A succession of eight prime ministers followed one another in quick succession in a period of only six years. Antonio Salandra, who resigned in December 1916, was succeeded by Paolo Boselli, Vittorio Orlando, Francesco Nitti, Giovanni Giolitti, Ivanhoe Bonomi, Luigi Facta and, eventually, Benito Mussolini.

Strong government

It was Mussolini, who at last gave the Italians the strong government they seemed to need. But he did not give them democracy, nor the chance to replace him with another leader. In 1925 only one political party was permitted in Italy and the Fascists continued to rule Italy under Mussolini's leadership – for a total period of just under 21 years from 1922 to 1943.

Fascism

The Italian Fascist Party came into being at the end of the First World War. Fascist later became a worldwide term of abuse – levelled against anyone, or any government, thought to be too right-wing. In reality, all the so-called Fascist governments (for example, Mussolini's Italy, Hitler's Germany, Franco's Spain) differed from one another.

The Nazis were racist (that is, they persecuted people of different race from themselves, such as the Jews). This was not part of the initial policy of Mussolini's Fascists, nor that of Franco's Falangists in Spain.

Everything fell flat before them. They mobilized their armed forces all over North and Central Italy and quietly took over control from the prefects and other local authorities. They occupied post and telegraph offices, railway stations, and other public buildings, set up a control over the Press, and dispatched large bodies who effected a rapid concentration on Rome. . . . The Army and the police offered no resistance.

The Times, London

The March on Rome. Fascists passing through the Porto del Popolo in Rome on 28 October 1922.

The 'March on Rome'

In the spring and summer of 1922 the Fascists got a taste of power, when they took control of Fiume in March, Bologna in May and Milan in August. The Government seemed unable, or unwilling, to stop the spread of Fascist violence and to protect the rights of all citizens, not merely those who voted Fascist.

The Fascists were fiercely anti-Communist and this made them popular with farmers and factory-owners. They were also passionate nationalists, believing fervently in their country, right or wrong. They believed in compulsory military service (conscription) and relished impressive military parades and ceremonies. They knew the value of propaganda (see page 41) and the indoctrination of the young with their militaristic and nationalistic ideals. Above all they believed in a one-party state with one leader (*Fuhrer* in Germany, *Duce* in Italy and *Caudillo* in Spain). The State was all. The interests of the individual had to be subordinated to, and if necessary, sacrificed in the interests of the State.

In fact the majority parties in the Italian parliament were the Liberals and Democrats with well over twice the seats held by the Socialists and eight times as many as those held by the Fascists. But the Prime Minister, Luigi Facta, acted too late to stop the Fascist tide which was threatening to engulf Italian democracy.

In August 1922 the trade unions called a general strike in protest at the way in which the authorities (police, army and government) seemed to be turning a blind eye to violent Fascist strike-breaking methods. In turn, Mussolini – representing 35 seats in parliament – reacted by demanding that Prime Minister Facta resign in favour of the Fascist Party. The Government refused to take him seriously but by now he had the support and approval of the leading figures in industry and government, including many members of the police force and some of the army's officers. More important, he was able to convince King Victor Emmanuel that his Fascist Party could form an effective government.

In October Mussolini assembled about 25,000 of his supporters, the *squadristi*, in strategic locations

19

to the north and east of Rome. Many were armed but no match for the trained professional soldiers of the Italian army – had the Prime Minister, Luigi Facta, been able to convince the King of the need to impose martial law. At first the King seemed inclined to agree but the threat of civil war, and the backing Mussolini got from some of the most powerful people in Italy, were enough to persuade the King to ask Mussolini to form a government. Some of the squadristi did actually march on Rome but Mussolini himself came by train. He arrived on 30 October in time for the victory parade on the following day!

Mussolini

Benito Mussolini was born in 1883, the son of a blacksmith. In his youth he was a pacifist (against war), an atheist (not believing in the existence of a God) and a republican (wanting a president rather than a king). He was also a revolutionary socialist (he wanted a left-wing revolution) and served a prison sentence in 1908. He left the socialists during the First World War because they wanted Italy to stay neutral. Mussolini thought that Italy stood to gain from the War. He served in the army himself, being invalided out in 1917.

After the War he started the Fascist Party and became prime minister in 1922 and dictator and leader ('Il Duce') until the surrender of Italy in 1943.

At the peak of his power he was idolized by the majority of Italians and regarded by many as 'Italy's

How Mussolini Consolidated his Position

As soon as he came to power Mussolini took steps to ensure that his Fascist government would be long-lasting, unlike those of his democratically elected predecessors. He reorganized the voting system for parliament, and his henchmen and thugs used violence and intimidation to ensure that the Fascist Party would dominate in parliament – which it did.

Giacomo Matteotti, a respected Socialist politician, was incensed by this campaign and spoke openly about Fascist methods. He wrote a book entitled *The Fascisti Exposed*. This was a serious challenge to Mussolini's leadership, with its undeniable charge that he had no democratic entitlement to the position of chief of state.

Mussolini's answer was brutally simple. Fascist thugs abducted Matteotti in 1924 and he was found murdered two months later. The shock caused the

Mussolini – stripped to the waist – urging on farmers at harvest time.

greatest son'. In appearance he was stocky, plump and bull-necked.

When he addressed a crowd he liked to pose in front of a classical building or statue to emphasize Fascist links with the ancient Roman Empire. His salute, the upraised arm, was the one which Roman soldiers had used. Like Hitler, he was a brilliant speaker, able to whip up a crowd to a frenzy of excitement. Arrogant and dramatic gestures were used to make his points, stabbing the air with his hands and arms.

'Fascism wants men to be active and to engage in activity with all their energy', he shouted; so he lived up to this ideal himself – in public. Italian newsreel films show him stripped to the waist, harvesting corn, playing sports, acting the part of the model member of a Fascist State. Italian children were taught to repeat the Fascist Creed – 'I believe in the genius of Mussolini'.

His biggest mistake was to enter the Second World War in June 1940 as an ally of Hitler. When the Allies invaded Italy in 1943 he was imprisoned but later rescued by the Germans and made leader of German-occupied Italy. But in 1945, attempting to flee to safety, he was captured and executed by Italian resistance fighters. His body was later strung up like a meat carcase in the streets of Milan.

Although he met an ignominious end at the hands of his fellow Italians, it is nonetheless true to say that for 21 years, they appeared to be well content to have him as their leader.

non-Fascist members to shun parliament (the 'Aventine secession') hoping that their absence would bring down Mussolini and his government. Instead, it had the opposite effect, since it allowed the Fascists to pass the necessary legislation to turn Italy into a one-party state, banning other political parties.

Measures were introduced to set up machinery to deal with enemies of the State. A secret police force was organized and gangs of Fascist thugs incorporated into a State militia. A special judicial tribunal was established to try crimes against the State. Concentration camps were built for enemies of the State. The State was everything.

The Fascist-dominated parliament gave Mussolini the power to govern by decree. This meant that if Il Duce said it was the law, then it was the law. It did not have to be approved by parliament. Power and authority came from the leader, instead of deriving from the votes of the people, as in a democracy.

Mussolini's Reforms

Foreign visitors, like Winston Churchill, were impressed by the material progress made by the Italians under Fascist rule. These included the following reforms.

* In 1932–33 a large team of engineers drained the Pontine Marshes, an area of malarial swamp which lay between Rome and Naples. This was one of a number of projects designed to combat unemployment during the Depression and to modernize Italy. Other schemes included the construction of hydro-electric dams, hospitals, schools, government offices and other public buildings.

* Mussolini transformed the Italian transport system by insisting that the railways be run efficiently. He was much admired for his ability to get the trains to run on time! The building of bridges, canals and fast motor roads, called *autostrada*, were among other public works which improved internal communications in Italy.

Many of Mussolini's reforms provided jobs for the unemployed and gave Italy some imposing buildings.
Above: The new town of Sabaudia in the newly drained Pontine Marshes.

Above: Milan Railway Station, built in the 1930s.

* Mussolini wanted to make Italy self-sufficient, so that she would produce all her own food and manufactured goods. He declared war on low productivity. There was to be a 'battle of the births', to increase the population of Italy and provide the extra hands needed in an expanding industry and a growing army.

The 'battle' for wheat doubled grain production between 1922 and 1939. Effective too was the 'battle' for steel, with a similar doubling of output. Farmers were encouraged to mechanize their farms and to use up-to-date methods. Industrialists were stimulated to expand and modernize.

* Mussolini insisted that industry be organized on corporate lines. This meant that workers and management were to work together for the good of their industry and ultimately for the State – the highest ideal in a Fascist society. The individual worked for the benefit of everyone, the whole of society and not just for self and personal gain.

To this end, trade unions were banned, since they were unnecessary in a system where the aims of management and workers were said to be identical. Both were represented on the councils and syndicates set up to organize the State economy and ease co-operation between all sides of industry. In practice there were many disputes but the tribunals, which assessed these cases, often took the side of the workers rather than that of the employers. However, it has been argued that on the major issues they usually favoured management.

* Mussolini's government improved educational standards in Italy, raising the school-leaving age, making it more difficult for pupils to avoid going to school, building new schools and setting higher standards. Between 1922 and 1939 the number of pupils in secondary schools more than doubled.

There was another reason, however, for this interest in education. The Fascists recognized that education could be used effectively to indoctrinate the young through propaganda and military training. Sports and keeping fit were stressed. Slogans and memorable phrases were used to drive home the message that 'Nothing has ever been won in history without bloodshed!'

Sayings of Mussolini and the Fascists

*The young must know how to obey.
*Credere! Obbedire! Combattere! (Believe! Obey! Fight!)
*If I advance, follow me: if I retreat, kill me; if I die, avenge me.
*I will make Italy great, respected, feared.

Mussolini's Foreign Policy

Mussolini wanted to make Italy great once more. He proposed to do this in international affairs by showing that he brooked no interference in Italy's spheres of influence – in particular, the Mediterranean and Adriatic regions.

Within a year of taking office he took belligerent action over the Corfu Incident (see Chapter 8) and, as you have seen, made Fiume part of Italy in 1924. In 1926 he signed a treaty with Albania, which virtually turned that small Adriatic nation into an Italian protectorate. He eventually annexed it in April 1939, less than six months before the outbreak of the Second World War.

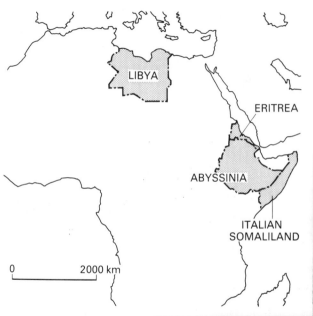

Above: Map of the Italian empire in Africa.

Right: Italian tanks in action in Abyssinia in October 1935.

The Italian empire

The Paris Peace Treaties left Italy without the colonies she coveted. In 1934 the two existing North African territories of Cyrenaica and Tripolitania were combined to form Libya. Then in 1935, Mussolini used a minor incident on the Abyssinian border with Italian Somaliland to provide the justification for a full-scale invasion of Abyssinia (now known as Ethiopia). This was a poor but independent African country ruled by the Emperor Haile Selassie (see Chapter 9). The world was horrified to see a European power, guilty of flagrant aggression, fighting with modern weapons and planes against an army whose soldiers sometimes had to fight with bows and arrows. Abyssinia, together with Eritrea and Italian Somaliland, was later renamed Italian East Africa.

Mussolini liked to couple the role of belligerent soldier with that of statesman. In 1933 he engineered and signed a pact with England, France and Germany. In 1934 he moved troops to the Austrian border to deter Hitler from seizing Austria after the assassination of Dollfuss, the Austrian dictator. In 1938 he played a leading part in negotiating the notorious 'Peace in our time' agreement at Munich (see page 122).

Alliance with Hitler

France, Britain and the League of Nations disapproved of Mussolini's Abyssinian adventure but without doing anything positive to make him pull back. Even so, this disapproval brought him closer to Hitler and he sought an alliance with Germany in 1936. In 1937 he signed the Anti-Comintern Pact (against Communism) with Germany and Japan (see Chapter 9). In 1939 the Pact of Steel – a military alliance – was agreed with Hitler.

The Lateran Treaty and Concordat with the Pope

Ever since the Unification of Italy in the middle of the nineteenth century, the Pope had been a 'prisoner within the Vatican', unwilling to step on to Italian soil, which had formerly been governed by the Papacy. For sixty years the Roman Catholic Church and the Italian Government were in a perpetual state of disagreement. This was why the Pope banned Italian Catholics from voting in elections.

Hitler greets Mussolini in 1938.

1929 – Mussolini signs the Lateran Treaty in the presence of a leading Vatican official.

In February 1929 Mussolini gained one of his greatest achievements when he came to an agreement with the Pope ending the enmity which existed between Church and State in Italy.

This was all the more surprising since Mussolini had originally been an atheist opposed to Church influence in Italy. The Lateran Treaty and Concordat with the Pope provided an amicable settlement of the sixty-year old dispute. The main terms of the Lateran Treaty were as follows:

* The Pope recognized the Italian State. In return the Italian Government acknowledged the Pope's authority as independent sovereign ruler of an enclave of territory in Rome – the Vatican City State.
* The Italian Government agreed to pay 750 million lire in cash and the interest on 1000 million lire worth of Italian government bonds, as compensation for the loss of Papal territories when Italy was unified in 1870.

By the terms of the Concordat with the Pope the Italian Government agreed that in future:
* Catholicism would be the State religion;
* Marriages in the Catholic Church would be recognized by Italian law;
* There would be religious instruction in school;
* The Church would be exempted from the payment of taxes;
* Catholic organizations would be allowed to operate in Italy without hindrance from the Italian State.

Italy in the Years of Depression

The Great Depression of the 1930s hit Italy hard and over a million Italians were thrown out of work, despite the Fascist Government's programme of public works and the Corporate State with its emphasis on harmony between employer and employee.

Mussolini attempted to alleviate the effects of the Depression by shortening working hours, providing welfare benefits and imposing tariffs (taxes) on foreign goods. But he was far less successful in this respect than Hitler in Germany. To make matters worse, the invasion of Abyssinia and the Italian supply of military aid to General Franco in Spain, meant that taxes had to be increased to pay for these foreign adventures.

By 1939 many Italians had second thoughts about the effectiveness of their Fascist State.

Repression in Mussolini's Italy

Although Mussolini's thugs were guilty of violence in the years before he came to power, Fascist Italy was less repressive than many of the other totalitarian regimes of that time, or since. The brutal murder of Matteotti was the most serious blot on the early history of Mussolini's regime; and the persecution of the Jews in Italy from 1938 onwards was probably the gravest crime of the last years of Fascism.

As in most totalitarian systems of government, the press was censored, political opponents could be sent to concentration camps for 're-education'; and the death penalty was introduced for serious crimes against the State. Yet during the 18 years between 1922 and 1940, only ten people were actually executed and five of those were convicted terrorists. At most, something like 4000 people were imprisoned in the concentration camps – an appalling number by democratic standards, but minute compared with the millions who died in Nazi concentration camps or the million Russians who were executed on Stalin's orders in the Purges of 1936–38.

Explanatory Notes

Mussolini wrote his own definition of what was meant by **Fascism**. The main points he made were as follows:
1. Fascism emphasises the supremacy of the State and not the individual. If a choice has to be made then the State must come first.
2. Fascism stands for the liberty of the State – and of the individual in the State.
3. The Fascist idea of the State is all-embracing, encompassing all human and spiritual values.
4. Fascism is totalitarian. The Fascist State stands for authority and power. No other authority can be tolerated; it follows, therefore that there can only be one party.
5. The Fascist State aims to mould man's character and his spiritual beliefs through education, laws and institutions.
6. These aims can only be achieved through the use of undisputed authority. This is why Fascists have chosen the Lictor's rods (fasces) as the symbol of that authority.
[Adapted from a translation of Mussolini's 'The Doctrine of Fascism' quoted in *Documents and Descriptions* edited by Breach: Oxford]

Exercises

1. Why were Italians dissatisfied with the peace agreements made at the end of the First World War?
2. Explain carefully the circumstances in Italy which led to Mussolini's rise to power in 1922.
3. What do you understand by the term Fascism? Why do you think it failed to survive the death of Mussolini?
4. What were the distinguishing characteristics of the Fascist system of government in Italy? Why was it accepted so readily by the Italian people?
5. Write brief notes on three of the following topics:
(a) 'The March on Rome'
(b) Giacomo Matteoti
(c) The Communists in Italy
(d) The Blackshirts
(e) The Concordat with the Vatican
6. What were Mussolini's main reforms at home? Were they successful in changing the face of Italy? What problems were left unsolved?
7. What were the principal characteristics of Mussolini's aggressive foreign policy? Which were his successes and which his failures?
8. What were the terms of the Lateran Treaty and Concordat with the Pope in 1929? What was its significance in Italian history?
9. How did Mussolini attempt to solve the problems which came about as a result of the Great Depression in the 1930s?
10. What, in your opinion, were Mussolini's greatest achievements, and, which his biggest failures?

Further Activities

1. Draw up a chart or table which will allow you to compare the effects of Fascism in Italy with those of National Socialism in Germany.

Write down headings such as (a) system of government, (b) treatment of opponents of the regime, (c) public works, such as roads and dams, (d) the armed forces and police, (f) industry and the trade unions, (g) the treatment of the Jewish people.

Complete the table for the Nazis when you come to study the chapter on Germany on pages 26–43.

CHAPTER 3

Germany and the Rise of Hitler

Above: Hitler addressing a rally in pre-war Germany.
Right: Hitler takes the salute as German workers,
armed with shovels, march past at a Nuremberg
Rally.

On 12 September 1919, a rather nondescript
corporal in the German army attended a meeting
of the newly-founded German Workers' Party in
Munich. It was the beginning of a dramatic and
startling epoch in German history and a fateful step
for Europe and the world.

The man, Adolf Hitler, was then thirty years old
and remarkable neither for his appearance nor his
personality. He had already seen thirty years of his
life go by without achieving any particular distinc-
tion, apart from the Iron Cross awarded for his
bravery during the First World War.

In 1918, recovering from a gas attack in a field
hospital, he learned the news of the Armistice and
the German capitulation. Hitler was horrified. To
make matters worse, Germany now had a Socialist
President, instead of the Kaiser who had abdicated.
Even a Communist Germany seemed a possibility
during the Spartacist uprising in January 1919.
Hitler, like many other Germans, felt that Germany
had been betrayed by its leaders.

Four years after his attendance at the meeting of
the German Workers' Party, ex-Corporal Hitler was
marching, as an equal, next to General Erich Ludendorff, the brilliant Chief of Staff who had jointly led
the German Army during the War. But their
attempt to seize power in the 1923 Munich Putsch
failed.

Yet incredibly, it took only another ten years for
Hitler to become dictator of Germany at the age of
43. By the time he was fifty he had transformed
Germany and was about to launch a war which

would extend his authority from Jersey to Moscow, and from Arctic Norway to the deserts of the Middle East.

The Weimar Republic

Even before the end of the First World War on 11 November 1918, Germany looked as if it might slide into anarchy and chaos. Socialist revolutionaries seized power in Bavaria declaring it a republic; sailors mutinied at Kiel; and members of the Reichstag (the German parliament) called for peace and an end to the War. Bethmann-Hollweg, Michaelis, von Hertling and Prince Max of Baden were all Chancellors (Prime Ministers) of Germany in the short space of 15 months between July 1917 and October 1918 – a crucial period for the German war effort.

The final straw came with the announcement on 9 November, that the Kaiser had abdicated and left Germany for good, for exile in the neighbouring, neutral Netherlands. Germany was proclaimed a republic. Within two months of the Armistice there was an uprising, the Spartacist revolt in Berlin (see page 12). Although this was put down by the Freikorps, it was only a foretaste of things to come, since the Freikorps themselves tried to seize power in the Kapp Putsch of March 1920.

French troops on bicycles occupy Essen on the Ruhr coalfield in 1923.

The new constitution

In the meantime the politicians thrashed out the details of a constitution for the new republic. They did this at the small German town of Weimar, because it was well away from the riots and street fighting now disrupting life in Berlin. It was at Weimar that the new National Assembly met for the first time in February 1919. Soon afterwards its members elected Friedrich Ebert as the first president of the new German republic.

The new constitution laid down rules for the system of government, now that the Emperor had gone. The President was to stay in office for seven years and would appoint the Chancellor (equivalent to a Prime Minister in many countries) from those politicians best able to get the support of the representatives in the Reichstag. The first of these postwar Chancellors was Gustav Bauer. Almost immediately he had the unpleasant task of having to accept the terms of the peace agreement, imposed by the Allies at the Treaty of Versailles.

Problems facing the Weimar Republic

The task facing the new German Chancellor was hardly an enviable one. The problems were many and complex.

1. In the first place, as you have seen, Germany was a hotbed of revolution. Marxist groups, armed ex-soldiers and nationalists made trouble. The humiliation of defeat hit Germany hard. The old way of life had gone. In this vacuum the Germans needed strong and decisive government, to replace the auto-cratic system of government they had been used to under the Kaiser.

2. But the new constitution, which has been described as 'perfect' and 'ideal', provided an electoral system based on **proportional representation** (see Explanatory Notes). This had the virtue of allowing smaller political parties to be represented in the Reichstag. But it also meant that none of the bigger parties in Germany was ever likely to get a majority of the seats in parliament. The most likely result was that coalition governments would have to be formed from two or more of the parties. This could only work if the parties were able to agree on a common policy.

Inflation

The occupation of the Ruhr

The Treaty of Versailles imposed a huge burden of reparations on the German people. Yet in the aftermath of defeat there was little chance that they would ever be able to meet this debt. When Germany fell behind with her payments at the end of 1922 the French and Belgian Governments sent in armed troops (on 11 January 1923) to occupy the Ruhr coalfield, where most of Germany's industry was situated. They hoped to seize coal and steel, and other goods, to make up for the payments promised under the reparations clause of the Treaty.

Passive resistance

There was little the German Government could do to halt this invasion, since the German armed forces had been drastically scaled down under the terms of the same treaty. Equally there was nothing the

French and Belgian armies could do to make German miners actually work down the pits! So the Government called for a campaign of passive resistance. This meant that the Germans did not take up arms against the invaders, neither did they offer them any assistance. Workers were to resist peacefully and to show the foreign troops they were unwelcome.

By the same token, since the German mines and steel works were not producing coal or steel, Germany could not produce the raw materials she needed for her industries. Nor was she earning the wealth which would convince people that her paper money was actually worth the sum of money printed on it. Yet the Government continued to print more paper money, as and when it was needed. Soon the printing presses were working flat out to cope with rising prices.

The worthless mark

Inflation (see Explanatory Notes) was already rampant in Germany. Prices had increased by four times between 1914, at the start of the War, and 1919. By the end of 1921 prices had trebled in two years. But this was nothing compared with the following years. Prices shot up tenfold in 1922 and astronomically in 1923, when French troops occupied the Ruhr. This was the time when postage stamps were overstamped with prices in 'millionen' of marks.

Many tales were told of the effects this rapidly spiralling inflation had on everyday life in Germany. There were stories of workers spending their money in the morning, as soon as they were paid, for fear that their wages would have lost their value by the afternoon. Photographs show Germans wheeling away their pay in wheelbarrows, using boxes instead of tills in shops and using paper money to make kites or to decorate a living room.

The effects of inflation

The effects of this catastrophic inflation were felt by Germans of every class, particularly the small businessmen, farmers and middle classes who found their savings were now worthless. A lifetime's frugal living hardly seemed worthwhile, when their efforts, to save money for a rainy day, could be wiped out overnight by inflation on such a scale. It was not fair; and many of the people who lost their savings looked later to the National Socialist Party for a more effective remedy. There were over 50,000 Nazis in Germany in 1923.

The evils of inflation were not confined to the middle classes, however. Workers, too, found that their wages could not keep pace with the rise in the cost of living. Trade unions lost their funds. Many of the working classes later looked to the Communists to provide a more equitable society. The seeds of doubt about the effectiveness of the Weimar constitution had been sown. Only the industrialists, landowners and property-owners, who had money invested in factories, land and buildings (which kept their value) could survive the collapse of the German mark unscathed.

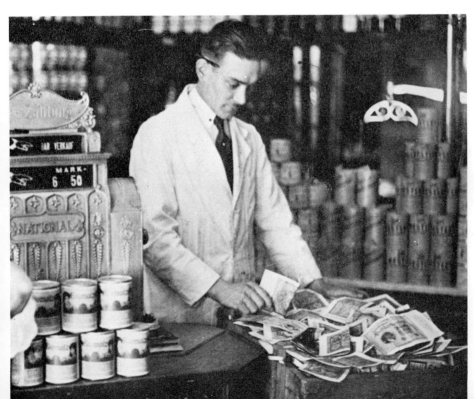

German inflation in 1923. This grocer needed a tea chest to hold the day's takings, not a cash till!

The largest ever denomination of banknote – a one billion mark note issued in 1923. Ten years earlier it would have been worth £50,000 million.

The Rentenmark

By this time (August 1923) a new Chancellor, Gustav Stresemann, had been appointed. He took the commonsense view that the policy of passive resistance in the Ruhr was hurting the Germans as much as the French. The French, for their part, were glad to be let off the hook, since the occupation had produced little material benefit. So the French and Belgian armies eventually withdrew.

The Government replaced the old worthless mark with a new unit of currency called the Rentenmark

Gustav Stresemann.

which was backed by land values, so people had more confidence in it than the old mark. One new Rentenmark was worth 3,000,000,000 old marks!

The Dawes Plan

In the end the Americans came to the rescue. Although they did not ratify the Treaty of Versailles, and retreated instead into a policy of isolationism (America first), they proposed a large loan to Germany which would allow the German Government to pay the reparations which were overdue. This was the Dawes Plan, named after Charles Dawes, the chairman of the committee proposing the loan in April 1924.

The new German Government, led by Wilhelm Marx, readily accept the Dawes Plan and soon American loans were helping German industry to recover. For the next five years (1924–29) Germany prospered. Industry got back on its feet and, as poverty retreated, so the attractions of the minority extremist parties (Communist and Nazi) diminished.

In 1929 the Young plan made further reductions in the reparations to be made by Germany to the Allies.

Foreign Relations

The Treaty of Rapallo

After the War, German statesmen had to rebuild their foreign policy. Germany had been an ally of Italy and the Austro-Hungarian Empire before 1914. By 1920 Europe had changed. The old empires were broken up, new republics formed and parts of Germany itself ceded to neighbouring states. Poland, not Russia, lay immediately to the east.

Right: Walter Rathenau, assassinated in Berlin in 1922, after negotiating the Treaty of Rapallo with Russia.

Russia was now Communist – soon to be known as the Union of Socialist Soviet Republics (from 30 December 1922 onwards).

Friction with the Allies over the terms of the Treaty of Versailles, and the scale of reparations to be paid by Germany, did not promise well for future relations between Germany and the other countries of Europe.

The Allies had tried to intervene, without success, in the civil war in Russia, which raged from 1917 to 1920. Friendly relations between a European nation and Communist Russia were not thought possible. But then, in April 1922, Germany astonished the world by signing the Treaty of Rapallo with Russia – her principal enemy only eight years before at the start of the First World War. Both countries now agreed to establish diplomatic relations (that is, maintain embassies in each other's country), to renounce any financial claims (reparations) arising out of the War, and to co-operate with one another in the future.

The Treaty was negotiated by Germany's Jewish Foreign Minister, Walther Rathenau. But he paid the price for German bitterness against Jews and Communism, when he was assassinated ten weeks later, by two young, anti-Semitic nationalists.

The Treaty of Locarno

Gustav Stresemann was Chancellor of Germany for a short period in the autumn of 1923. Afterwards he became German Foreign Minister until his premature death in 1929. During those six years he worked hard, and with considerable success, to re-establish Germany in Europe.

His greatest triumph was the signing of the Treaty of Locarno with France and Belgium on 1 December 1925. This guaranteed the inviolability of Germany's borders with both countries (the borders were not to be broken). Germany re-affirmed that the Rhineland was to be a demilitarized zone (no German troops were to be stationed there).

This successful coming together of German, French and Belgian diplomats, and those from Britain and Italy as well (they guaranteed the Treaty), led the way to Germany being admitted to the League of Nations in 1926.

Stresemann was awarded the Nobel Peace Prize in 1926 for his work in promoting harmony between Germany and France – no mean achievement after the harsh treatment Germany had received at Versailles only seven years earlier.

The Origins of the Nazi Party

The National Socialist movement came into being in 1919 when the German Workers' Party was founded by Anton Drexler with about forty members. One of its first recruits was Adolf Hitler, who soon made his mark as an able and convincing speaker. The fervour with which he attacked Jews and Communists soon helped him to become head of the new party. His followers called him *Unser Fuhrer* – 'Our Leader'.

Its policy was formally announced in 1920 when the *Twenty-Five Points* were published. You can see some of these listed in the panel below. At about the same time the German Workers' Party changed its name, at Hitler's instigation, to the National Socialist German Workers' Party. In German this was *Nationalsozialistische Deutsche Arbeiter Partei* – abbreviated to NSDAP and later corrupted so that the party became known as the *Nazi* Party.

The National Socialist German Workers' Party
Extracts from the 'Twenty-Five Points'

1. Unite all the German peoples.
2. Overturn the Treaty of Versailles.
3. Obtain territory and colonies for Germany's expanding population.
4. Only Germans to be citizens. Not Jews.
5. Anyone who is not a German citizen to be treated as a foreigner.
10. Each individual must work for the good of the State as a whole.
22. Conscription.
23. Control and censorship of the press.
25. Strong central government.

Adolf Hitler

Adolf Hitler was born in a village in Austria in 1889, the son of a local official who had once been known as Shickelgruber. In his youth he lived in the slums of Vienna, the capital city of Austria and centre of the Austro-Hungarian Empire. It was there that he developed a hatred of the Jews, later blaming them for his poverty, although for a period of his youth he lived comfortably on an inheritance.

In 1913 he left Austria for Germany and settled in the southern city of Munich. When war broke out he joined the German (not the Austrian) army and won the Iron Cross for his bravery in battle. Photographs of Hitler in the army show that he wore a wide drooping moustache at this time, indistinguishable from those of his comrades. At some stage before 1920 he trimmed it back sharply at the sides to take on its unmistakeable and distinctive shape.

Generally speaking, however, Adolf Hitler cut rather an unprepossessing figure in the early 1920s. In photographs he is usually seen wearing a raincoat and a trilby hat. People who knew him in those days recalled a rather moody man, who would suddenly launch into an attack on the Jews and Marxists – if sufficiently moved to anger.

After the War he was disgusted at the treatment meted out to veterans of the fighting, many of whom were now destitute and unemployed. He, and other Germans, contrasted this with the profits made by industrialists from munitions and armaments during the War. This only added fuel to his anti-Semitism. The Spartacist uprising alerted him to the dangers of a Communist revolution. He blamed the Jews for the spread of left-wing ideas in Germany.

It was at this point that he joined the German Workers' Party. The history of Germany from 1920 to 1945 thereafter became inextricably intertwined with the life of Adolf Hitler. He committed suicide in April 1945, after he finally accepted the fact that Germany had lost the Second World War.

The Munich Putsch

The Sturm Abteilung (Storm Troopers)

The National Socialist Party built up its membership quickly in the early 1920s. Hitler wanted a private army, to keep order at his meetings and put fear into his enemies. So in 1921 the para-military organization of Storm Troopers – the *Sturm Abteilung* or SA – was founded.

The NSDAP appealed particuarly to ex-soldiers and nationalists. It even attracted General Ludendorff, who had been Germany's most able military commander during the War. At first it was only a Bavarian political party with little contact with other groups in Berlin and northern Germany but Hitler later began to see his Party as the saviour of Germany as a whole.

Hitler reviews his shock troops in Berlin in 1932, and gives them orders for the coming elections.

The meeting in the Munich beer cellar

When French troops occupied the Ruhr without opposition from the German army, many ex-soldiers were appalled. It was one further humiliation for Germany. The patriots and nationalists had more to complain about when the gross inflation of 1923 made savings and the German mark worthless. Many people blamed the German Government, accusing it of letting the mark decline in value for its own purposes.

When the campaign of passive resistance was called off by Gustav Stresemann, Hitler and his aides decided the time was ripe for a putsch, or coup, in Munich, the capital city of Bavaria.

Hitler knew that the leaders of Bavaria were at odds with the Federal Government in Berlin; so he planned to kidnap the State Commissioner, the Chief of Police and the commander of the German army in Bavaria and persuade them to head the revolution against the central government.

Hitler had information that they were to attend a meeting in the Burgerbrau Keller in Munich on 8 November 1923. The men were seized at gunpoint but refused to co-operate, so Hitler announced that he was taking over the state government in their place.

The march on Berlin

The Nazis and their Storm Troopers then formed up to begin a march on Berlin. They got no farther than the Odeonplatz in Munich when police barred their way. Shots rang out and 14 protesters and

Hitler (extreme left) in Landsberg Prison after the failure of the Munich Putsch. Hess is second from the right.

three policemen were killed and others seriously wounded, including Hermann Goering.

Mein Kampf

Hitler was tried and sentenced to five years imprisonment. But his nine month stay in Landsberg Prison was comfortable enough. He had many visitors and his assistant, Rudolf Hess, wrote down his thoughts and philosophy in the book which later became the bible of the National Socialists – Hitler's autobiography, *Mein Kampf* (My Struggle).

But on his release from prison in December 1924 Hitler found that Germany had changed. The country was now gaining in prosperity, most of the French troops had gone; there was none of the despair and anger which had fuelled the attempted putsch a year earlier. For the next five years the Nazis reorganized their movement and laid the foundations for the years ahead. Men like Josef Goebbels and Heinrich Himmler proved their worth to Hitler.

It was at this time, however, that Hitler first doubted the reliability of the SA under its leader Ernst Rohm. This was why he founded another private army, the *Schutz Staffeln* (the notorious and feared SS), as an elite corps of guards owing allegiance only to the Fuhrer.

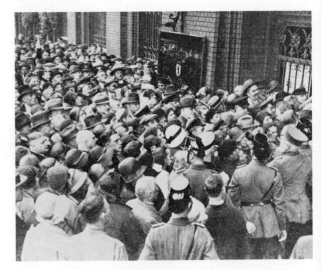

Above: 1931 – a crowd of anxious customers forms outside a German bank which has just gone bust. Left: Unemployed Germans pleading for work in 1931.

National Socialism

Its policies right from the outset were:
* Anti-semitic and racist. The Nazis blamed the Jewish people for Germany's misfortunes. They believed that Germany's peoples could be divided into two classes. Pure-bred Germans, typically tall and blonde, were the Aryans; the *Herrenvolk* or 'Master Race'. Non-Aryans were said to be racially inferior, such as the Jews and Slavs; the enslaved races.
* Anti-Communist.
* Nationalistic. They wanted to unite all the German-speaking peoples of Germany and those living in Austria and the new republics created under the terms of the Paris Peace Treaties.
* Totalitarian. They maintained that the State was more important than the individual and that the interest of the State should come before individual freedoms.
* Expansionistic. They thought that Germany should expand her territories to gain *lebensraum* or 'living room'.
* Militaristic. Germany could only get her own way if she was strong. Conscription was necessary to build up the army and provide a disciplined training for the youth of Germany. Rearmament was vital to give the armed forces the tanks, planes and ships they needed. Goering summed it up when he demanded 'Guns before butter'.

Germany in the Depression

In 1929 Germany had become prosperous, enjoying the same sort of boom in industry and consumer goods as in the United States (see Chapter 6). But it was a false prosperity, founded on American loans and the assumption that people would continue to buy everything the factories and farms produced.

The Wall Street Crash in October 1929 changed all that. Stocks and shares which had been greatly over-valued in the months before, suddenly plunged sharply on the New York Stock Exchange. Many people and many businesses were ruined. The Crash triggered off a slump in industry which had long been overdue.

The outcome for Germany was bleak. American banks and financiers needed the money back, which they had loaned to Germany in the wake of the Dawes Plan in 1924. The Depression was worldwide in its scope, affecting countries as far apart as Japan and Italy. German industries could not sell their goods abroad, so many factories closed down or severely cut back their workforces. Unemployment figures shot up – 2 million out of work in 1929, 3 million in 1930, 4.5 million in 1931, and a peak of about 6 million in 1932.

Newsreel film from this period shows poor people sifting through slag heaps in search of coal. Queues of people lined up for charity. Banks failed. The middle classes were afraid of the consequences of a severe depression and the ever-present possibility of a Communist revolution.

The Growth of the Nazi Party

What was to be done? The German Government was at a loss. But other parties had a simple answer. The Communists pointed to the example set by Lenin and Stalin in the Soviet Union. The National Socialists blamed the Communists and the Jews. Street fights broke out between the rival factions. Both gained support from the workers. Both gained support from the voters as well.

Initially, Hitler despised the electoral system, preferring direct action rather than democracy as the route to the top. But after his imprisonment in Landsberg Prison he decided to try the democratic path. At first the results were disappointing. Only twelve Nazis were elected to the Reichstag in 1928 during the era of prosperity. But in 1930, nearly a year after the Wall Street Crash, the National Socialists gained 107 of the 647 seats. Hitler's newspaper the *Volkischer Beobachter* headlined the news (inaccurately) as '106 National Socialists in the new Reichstag'. Six and a half million people had voted for the Nazis and they were now the second largest party.

Two years later their strength increased dramatically to 230 seats in the Reichstag, with about 14 million Germans voting for the Nazi Party. These numbers dropped to 196 seats in the November elections in the same year (1932) but this was enough to convince some right-wing German politicians that

Police using powerful water cannon and armoured lorries to drive rioting Nazis and Communists from the streets of Berlin in 1932.

Hitler's Nazis could be used to keep the Communists and Socialists at bay.

How Hitler became the Fuhrer

Two of these right-wing leaders, Franz von Papen and General Kurt von Schleicher, persuaded President Hindenberg to offer the post of Vice Chancellor to Hitler. But Hitler refused, insisting instead that he be given the post of Chancellor or nothing at all.

So, on 30 January 1933, Adolf Hitler became Chancellor of Germany. For the nationalists, and for German democracy, it was a fatal mistake. Franz von Papen boasted that he would be able to control Hitler, but in the end he was lucky to escape with his life – after Hitler's men murdered his fellow leader General von Schleicher in 1934.

Hitler was now able to use his power as Chancellor to manipulate public opinion, control the forces of law and order, and set the wheels in motion which would establish the Nazi Party as the only political party to be allowed by law in Germany. He boasted that the Third Reich (Hitler's name for his empire) would last for a thousand years. But, as you will see, it lasted for only twelve.

35

The Reichstag on fire in 1933.

How Hitler held on to Power

The March 1933 election
Hitler's first action was to call a general election, to get public backing for his Nazi policies. Although this sounds as if he was laying himself open to the risk of a defeat at the ballot box, it was nothing of the kind. Hitler controlled the police and the Nazi private armies of Brownshirts (SA) and Blackshirts (SS). As a result Nazi political meetings went unmolested but those of the Communists and Socialists were broken up. People were encouraged to associate chaos and collapse of law and order with the left-wing parties but only disciplined and patriotic behaviour from the uniformed supporters of Chancellor Hitler's Nazi Party.

By a stroke of luck – for Hitler – a Dutch Communist, called van der Lubbe, set fire to the Reichstag building on 27 February 1933, a few days before the election. At the time people suspected that the Nazis engineered the fire themselves but it now seems clear that van der Lubbe was indeed guilty. Nonetheless it gave Hitler the splendid legal opportunity to get President Hindenberg to agree to measures leading to the imprisonment of Communists and banning the Party.

At the election (March 1933) Hitler won a convincing victory with 288 seats but it was not a majority of the total of 647 seats in the Reichstag. Even with the support of von Papen's German Nationalist Party the Nazis still did not have the necessary two-thirds majority which would enable Hitler to make his next move. This was simply to turn Germany from a democracy into a dictatorship.

The Enabling Law
The problem was resolved by:
(a) banning the 81 Communist members from attending the meeting of the Reichstag;
(b) assembling a large number of Blackshirts (SS) to ring the Kroll Opera House, where the Reichstag was to meet after the fire;
(c) packing the interior of the building with row upon row of Brownshirts (SA).

On 23 March 1933, those members of the Reichstag who could force their way into the building were invited to vote for an Enabling Law – giving Hitler the power to suspend the constitution and rule as a dictator for four years. Any decrees announced by Hitler were to have the force of law within 24 hours.

To their eternal shame (although understandable in the presence of Hitler's loud-mouthed brown- and black-shirted thugs), 153 members, of the other political parties in the Reichstag, voted with the Nazis; so Germany ceased to be a democracy. Only the 94 Social Democrats had the courage to ignore the intimidation of the Nazi bully-boys to vote against Hitler.

The Enabling Law gave Hitler all the power he needed but when President Hindenburg died the following year (1934), Hitler took over as Head of State as well, but preferring the title Fuhrer to that of President.

The Night of the Long Knives
Only one potential source of danger remained, apart from that of foreign invasion. This was the German army (the *Reichswehr*), which, even in its depleted state after Versailles, was still strong enough to stage a military coup. In practice many officers were Nazis who welcomed the role that Hitler had assigned the armed forces – to say nothing of the improvements in morale that the introduction of conscription and rearmament would bring.

But there was one stumbling block. Ernst Rohm, leader of the SA, wanted to become a general and to integrate the SA into the regular army. Hitler knew that the aristocratic officers of the Reichswehr despised Rohm as a homosexual and had nothing but contempt for his ill-disciplined private army of Brownshirts.

Hitler's actions provided a foretaste of things to come. The SS, led by Hitler and Himmler, surprised the SA leaders while they were still in bed. Rohm and other leading SA commanders were summarily

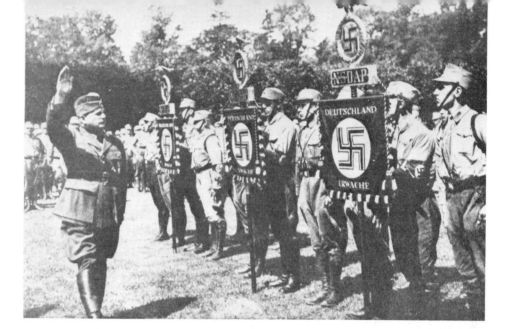

Ernst Rohm, leader of the SA, greets some of his men.

executed on the Night of the Long Knives (29 June 1934). Afterwards Hitler justified his actions. 'I alone during those 24 hours was the supreme court of justice of the German people' he said. 'I ordered the leaders of the guilty shot'.

The news of the massacre appalled the world but it satisfied the Reichswehr, since it seemed to ensure there would only be one army in Hitler's Germany.

Totalitarian Government

A one-party state

Hitler further consolidated his position as Fuhrer when he banned all political parties other than the National Socialists in July 1933. The introduction of a one-party state meant that all democratic opposition was crushed. Socialists and Communists were imprisoned and some executed.

Local government

Even at local government level the Nazis left nothing to chance. The state parliaments (such as in Bavaria) were subordinated to the central government in Berlin. *Gauleiters* were appointed as governors of the different provinces which made up Germany (*Gau* meant 'province' and *leiter* meant 'leader').

Education

Education was strictly controlled. The Nazis recognized the importance of indoctrinating the young to believe implicitly in the essentials of National Socialist policy. Young children were encouraged to despise the Jews and to regard themselves as members of the Master Race. To this end their textbooks were altered in line with Nazi theories of race (biology) and history.

Hitler Youth on parade.

Jesse Owens wins the 100 metres at the Berlin Olympics in 1936.

Boys were made to join the Hitler Youth, membership of which was compulsory at the age of 14. Girls joined the League of German Maidens. The Nazis stressed the virtues of physical fitness; this would prove the superiority of the Master Race. Fit Germans were needed to fulfil Germany's destiny.

The Berlin Olympics

This was why the Nazis took pride in the fact that Berlin was the venue for the 1936 Olympic Games. Nazi Germany was on show, visited by thousands of people from all over the world. Most were impressed, since the Nazis took care to ensure that prosperity and ceremony were on show, rather than repression and terror. Less pleasing to Hitler and the believers in the 'Master Race' theory was the fact that the Black American athlete, Jesse Owens, showed up the fallacies of the Nazi theories of race, by winning four gold medals!

Persecution and Repression

The Gestapo

In April 1933, a month after Hitler became dictator of Germany, Hermann Goering as Minister of the Interior ordered the formation of a secret police force – the GESTAPO (GEheime STAats POlizei). The name Gestapo later became a byword for fear, terror and torture. It was through terror that Hitler and the Nazis ultimately dealt with their known or supposed opponents. Concentration camps were established soon after Hitler came to power.

Trade unions

Trade unions were banned in May 1933, since it was inconceivable to the Nazis that workers could be allowed to strike or otherwise coerce their employers. Leading trade unionists were rounded up and sent to concentration camps for 're-education'.

In place of the unions the Nazis created a German Labour Front which provided workers with benefits, such as subsidized holidays. Welfare benefits were also provided and workers got holidays with pay. Since few were without a job, it was easier for them

Prisoners held at Dachau concentration camp before the War. They were arrested without being charged or tried and held indefinitely. Later millions were killed in such camps.

to remember the good things about National Socialism and to forget the occasional reminders that Germany was now a police state.

The Church

Church leaders who spoke out against the regime, like the Protestant minister Pastor Niemoller, were also sent to concentration camps. Hitler signed a Concordat with the Pope in 1933 agreeing to permit religious freedom for German Catholics but he soon broke the terms of the agreement and later sent nuns and priests to the concentration camps as well. Despite these actions, many Christian churchmen of all denominations supported the Nazis.

The persecution of the Jews

When the final horrors of the persecution of the Jews were known after the War, some Germans were so ashamed of the acts performed in the name of Germany, they committed suicide.

At first the persecution took the familiar form, well-known to the Jewish people from past experiences in Russia and in other countries in Europe. Shop windows were smashed, synagogues were destroyed, people beaten up in the street and Jewish children ridiculed at school. Cartoonists drew grotesque pictures of Jewish moneylenders, to whip up hatred – even in children's story books. '*Achtung Juden*' was painted across shop windows.

Books were burned and the works of Jewish writers and composers banned (such as the music of Mendelssohn). Great men, like Albert Einstein, the physicist, were forced to leave Germany because they were Jewish.

The Nuremberg Laws in 1935 defined the status of a Jew in Germany – no rights as a citizen; marriage between Jews and Germans was forbidden; a Jew was anyone with at least one Jewish grandparent. Inevitably these laws caused great distress, both to Jews and 'Germans'.

But it was as nothing, compared to the horrors to come. On 9 November 1938 the Nazis seized upon an incident in France to launch a government-inspired terrorist campaign against the Jews of Germany. It was called Crystal Night because so many shop windows were smashed.

Some Jews were sent to concentration camps before 1939. But it was the Holocaust – the mass murder of millions of Jews during the Second World War – which provided the most degrading, revolting and appalling evidence of the stark terror and brutal depths to which the Nazi leaders could sink. The Jews of Germany and Occupied Europe were rounded up and herded together in railway trucks, to be transported to the death camps at Belsen, Dachau, Buchenwald and Auschwitz where gas chambers awaited the defenceless victims of the 'Final Solution' (see Explanatory Notes, page 137).

Anti-Jewish posters. Above left: 'If you buy from a Jew, you are a traitor to your country.' Above right: 'German women remember – Boycott the Jews.' Right: All Jewish businesses had to carry this sign warning their fellow Germans that theirs was a 'Jewish business'.

Unemployment

When Hitler accepted office as Chancellor of Germany he faced many problems which previous governments had been unable to solve or alleviate. The most important of these was the problem of unemployment with 6 million people out of work in 1932. It seems probable that the numbers were actually declining before Hitler took office. But there is no denying the fact that his methods, however unscrupulous, were successful in reducing unemployment. By 1934 less than 3 million were out of work, by 1936 less than 2 million, and the numbers fell to under a million in 1937 and were negligible by the end of 1939.

This contrasted strikingly with what little progress was seen in Britain or in Italy – or even in the United States, for all the success of President Roosevelt's 'New Deal' (see Chapter 6). It is doubtful, however, whether Hitler ever tackled the problem of unemployment deliberately. His success came about largely as a result of policies condemned by the rest of the world.

* Conscription was introduced in 1935 and the armed forces greatly enlarged.
* Rearmament provided thousands of jobs in arms factories making guns, tanks, planes, ships. This stimulated the growth of the steel and chemical industries which provided the raw materials, and the coal mining industry which provided the fuel.
* Nazi policy, like that of Fascist Italy, tried to make the country self-sufficient in food, raw materials and manufactures. So farmers and manufacturers received government help to stimulate production – and this, too, created jobs. Efforts were made to make synthetic (artificial) products such as petrol

from coal and synthetic fibres (rayon, for example) from cellulose.
* Public works were inaugurated, such as grandiose public buildings to symbolize the achievements of the Third Reich, fast motorways (*autobahns*) and reclamation of land by drainage and the use of artificial fertilizers.
* Workers were sent to work wherever there was a shortage of labour. Factory-owners were also directed to switch production to essentials, or even to close down plants producing non-essential goods. Wages and prices were firmly controlled, so manufacturers were better able to forecast how much labour they needed.
* It is also true, if sad to relate, that the persecution of the Jewish people, the imprisonment of thousands of Communists and trade unionists in concentration camps, the recruitment of a large secret police force and the establishment of a vast bureaucracy to run the apparatus of the State, all helped to solve the problem of unemployment in pre-war Germany.

Hitler's Germany

The adulation of the German people

Despite the persecution of the Jews, the abolition of the trade unions, the violence of the Brownshirts and Blackshirts and the activities of the Gestapo, the majority of the German people appeared to idolize Hitler. Newsreel films of processions and rallies show enthusiastic crowds ecstatic in their acclamation of the Fuhrer.

Hitler had a remarkable gift as an orator, with a fiery and dramatic way with words which undoubtedly attracted and mesmerized the crowds.

His image as a national leader, sent to save the

A new motorway is opened to link Berlin with Stettin.

German people and lead them to greatness once more, was enhanced by the activities of his brilliant but unscrupulous director of propaganda, Dr Josef Goebbels.

The propaganda machine

Goebbels used all the different types of media – newspapers, pamphlets, books, films, radio – to whip up support for the Nazis and incite hatred against their enemies. The Nuremberg rallies – splendid uniforms, impressive ceremonies, stirring marches and patriotic songs, torchlight processions, and military parades with goose-stepping standard-bearers carrying giant swastikas – were used to impress and thrill the German crowds.

The swastika was everywhere. The crowds were encouraged to shout in unison the slogans of the Nazi Party, such as '*Ein Volk, ein Reich, ein Fuhrer!*' (One People, one Country, one Leader!) Rudolf Hess informed them 'The Party is Hitler. But Hitler is Germany and Germany is Hitler!' Goebbels told the truth about his methods – if nothing else – when he claimed 'If you tell a lie, tell a big lie. If you tell a big lie often enough people will believe it.'

Nuremberg, 4 September 1934

Like a Roman emperor Hitler rode into this mediaeval town at sundown today past solid phalanxes of wildly cheering Nazis who packed the narrow streets . . . . Tens of thousands of swastika flags blot out the gothic beauties of the place, the facades of the old houses, the gabled roofs. The streets, hardly wider than alleys, are a sea of brown and black uniforms. I got my first glimpse of Hitler as he drove by our hotel . . . . He fumbled his cap with his left hand as he stood in his car acknowledging the delirious welcome with somewhat feeble Nazi salutes from his right arm. He was clad in a rather worn gaberdine trench-coat, his face had no particular expression at all – I expected it to be stronger – and for the life of me I could not quite comprehend what hidden springs he undoubtedly unloosed in the hysterical mob which was greeting him so wildly. He does not stand before the crowd with that theatrical imperiousness which I have seen Mussolini use. I was glad to see that he did not poke out his chin and throw his head back as does the Duce nor make his eyes glassy . . .

About ten o'clock tonight I got caught in a mob of ten thousand hysterics who jammed the moat in front of Hitler's hotel, shouting: 'We want our Fuhrer'. I was a little shocked at the faces, especially those of the women, when Hitler finally appeared on the balcony for a moment . . . They looked up at him as if he were a Messiah, their faces transformed into something positively inhuman. If he had remained in sight for more than a few moments, I think many of the women would have swooned from excitement.

William L. Shirer, *Berlin Diary*

Hitler greets the crowds at a Nuremberg rally.

Hitler's Foreign Policy

Hitler was a self-taught politician, who had served in the German army as a corporal. Yet in the six years to the start of the Second World War he displayed a remarkable aptitude in his dealings with foreign powers.

He tore up the Treaty of Versailles, item by item, as you will see in succeeding chapters in this book. He ignored those parts of the Treaty which had been designed to keep Germany weak and prevent her from starting another war. Had the Allies been sufficiently willing they could have insisted that Germany abide by the Treaty. For instance, the Peace Agreement forbade Germany building up her armed forces by conscription, which Hitler introduced in 1935. He ignored the limitations imposed on the number of warships and launched U-boats and built up the *Luftwaffe*, contrary to the ban on Germany possessing either submarines or an air force. In 1936 he marched troops into the Rhineland, although his generals warned that the Allies would be bound to intervene. In 1938 he forced through a union (Anschluss) between Germany and Austria, although this too, was expressly forbidden by the Treaty of Versailles.

Each time, Hitler's advisers and generals were proved wrong when they advocated caution. Not surprisingly, Hitler began to think he was infallible in judging how far he could go without provoking a reaction from the other countries of Europe.

His judgement proved sound again when he threatened to invade Czechoslovakia in September 1938. Neville Chamberlain, the British Prime Minister, claimed to have averted war by signing a document at Munich which promised peace in Europe – at the price of Czech freedom.

These hopes were shattered less than a year later when Hitler's army launched a massive attack on Poland, and belatedly, and reluctantly, Britain and France finally intervened.

Hitler and his Cabinet. Goebbels is second from the left; Goering is on Hitler's right.

Explanatory Notes

Proportional representation is a system of voting for an organization, such as parliament, in which the number of seats won by a political party is decided according to their share (or proportion) of the total votes cast. This is contrary to the practice in many national elections, such as for the British House of Commons, where seats are won by the party which gets more votes than any other single party.

Proportional representation is undoubtedly a fairer method of ensuring that all shades of opinion are represented in a parliament, but it has the disadvantage that only rarely does it produce a government with an overall majority.

Inflation simply means a rise in prices. In practice it is usually accompanied by a rise in wages as well, since workers invariably demand an increase in income to keep pace with the increase in prices.

Inflation is as old as civilization, since many different factors can cause prices to rise, such as a shortage of food due to a poor harvest. But, when inflation rises very rapidly in a short space of time, there is a danger that people will lose confidence in their currency and try to exchange their savings for something (such as gold) which they know will hold its value, whatever the rate of inflation.

Exercises

1. How did the Weimar Republic come into being and why was it replaced by the Third Reich?
2. Write brief notes on three of the following:
(a) Inflation of the German mark in 1922–23
(b) The Munich Putsch in 1923
(c) The Dawes Plan of 1924
(d) *Mein Kampf*
(e) The French occupation of the Ruhr in 1923
(f) Gustav Stresemann

3. Explain carefully the circumstances which enabled Hitler to come to power in 1933.
4. What were the distinctive characteristics of Hitler's system of government?
5. How did Hitler and the Nazis strengthen and consolidate their position once in power?
6. What methods did Hitler and the Nazi Party use to quell opposition to the regime? How did they deal with (a) the Jews, (b) the trade unions, (c) the Church, (d) the Communists, (e) dissatisfied members of their own organization, such as the Sturm Abteilung (SA)?
7. What aspects of Nazi rule in Germany were totalitarian?
8. Write briefly about any three of the following and comment on the significance of the three you have chosen to the history of Germany before 1939:
(a) The Enabling Law of 1933
(b) President Hindenburg
(c) Unemployment in Germany in the 1930s
(d) The Olympic Games in 1936
9. What were Hitler's main achievements in his domestic policy? Before 1939 were the German people worse off, or better off, than they had been under the Weimar Governments before 1933?
10. There is no doubting the fact that Hitler was immensely popular with the German people in the years before the outbreak of the Second World War. How do you account for this phenomenon?

Further Activities

1 Write a biography of Hitler, filling out the skeleton details shown in the panel on page 32. See if you can explain why he was able to rise from the relatively low rank of corporal in the German Army in 1918 to the supreme power of dictator in 1933, less than 15 years later. What talents did he possess and how did he misuse them?

CHAPTER 4

Britain and France between the Wars

London went wild with delight when the great news came through yesterday.

It was the greatest, gladdest, most wonderful day in British history.

Bells burst into joyful chimes, maroons were exploded, bands paraded the streets, and London gave itself up wholeheartedly to rejoicing.

Windows were decorated in all directions and Paris soon presented a holiday aspect.

Displaying great emotion, the Premier exclaimed: 'Vive la France!' The crowd repeated the cry with intense enthusiasm.

In a Nutshell

* Britain and France are exhausted after the War. Both borrowed huge sums of money to pay for the war effort; both lost a large number of young men (Britain about one million, France a million and a half).
* At first there is a short boom in prosperity but this is soon followed by a long period of high unemployment, particularly in Britain. This causes great distress in the industrial regions and becomes a serious problem during the Great Depression from 1929 to about 1934.
* In Britain there are serious labour problems in the 1920s, culminating in the General Strike of 1926. Political problems in France, such as the Stavisky Affair in 1934, lead to riots and demonstrations.
* Poor living conditions and the problems caused by unemployment cause many people to seek a simple solution to these problems in the policies of the extremist parties – the Fascists and the Communists. Sir Oswald Mosley leads the British Union of Fascists; its counterpart in France is the Croix de Feu.
* Although there are two short periods with a Labour Government, the British Government of the inter-war period is predominantly Conservative.
* Political opinion in France tends to be either right- or left-wing. No one party dominates in French politics, so most governments are coalitions which include representatives from a number of different parties.
* In foreign affairs both the British and French Governments follow a policy of *appeasement*, preferring to give in to dictators rather than confront them. So Mussolini gets away with his invasion of Abyssinia in 1935. In 1938 Hitler takes part of Czechoslovakia, with British and French agreement (see Chapter 9).

The extracts above show how a British newspaper, the *Daily Mirror*, reported the end of the First World War in its issue for 12 November 1918. 'HOW JOYFUL LONDONERS KEPT ARMISTICE DAY IN THE STREETS' and 'HOW PARIS RECEIVED THE GREAT NEWS' were the headlines.

The people of France and Britain had high hopes for the future, now that the War was over. 'A new chapter of the world's history is beginning,' said the *Daily Mirror* and on the front page claimed 'There never again will be such news.'

Yet there was – in 1945 – less than 27 years later. And part of the blame lay with the governments of Britain and France between the Wars (as you will see in Chapter 9). Their failure to take concerted action against Nazi Germany was partly due to the pressing problems they had to solve at home, arising from the aftermath of the First World War and the Great Depression (1929–34).

The Postwar Slump

Unemployment in Britain
In 1919 and 1920, after a war in which most people were fully employed, there seemed little immediate danger of there being a serious unemployment problem in Britain. Less than 3 per cent of the workforce was unemployed at the time.

But in 1921 to 1922 the proportion of people out of work increased to 15 per cent. It dropped to about 10 per cent for the rest of the 1920s, but shot up again to 15 per cent in 1930, and to a peak of 22.5 per cent in 1932.

Armistice Day, 11 November 1918. People everywhere celebrated. Buses were free and cars took anyone anywhere. This loaded bus makes its way down Fleet Street in London.

Although the figures later improved, over a million and a half people (12 per cent of the workforce) were out of work in 1939. So for most of the inter-war years, at least one British worker in every ten was out of a job.

Unemployment in France
France, with a similar population, was far better placed to ride out the problems caused by the Depression, since a large percentage of her workers were farmers (over 9 million in 1921, compared with less than a million and a half in Great Britain). Even so, unemployment in France soared from 64,000 in 1931 to over 300,000 in 1932. This was insignificant by British or German standards, but a problem, nonetheless, for the French Government.

Dancing the Charleston in 1926.

A Changing Europe

To many returning soldiers it seemed as if the War had changed nothing. Yet the old Europe had gone. There was a much greater sense of freedom, particularly among young women. Until 1916 women had always covered their legs in garments reaching to the ground. By 1926 many were wearing knee-length skirts and dresses. They wore their hair in boyish styles; favoured straight, shapeless fashions with a lower waistline; smoked cigarettes; drank in public; and danced to jazz and ragtime.

Politics in Britain

David Lloyd George, the British Prime Minister during the latter part of the War, continued in office after 1918, as head of a coalition government dominated by the Conservatives, though he himself was a Liberal. He attended the Paris Peace Conferences (see Chapter 1) and played a leading part in the negotiations. But in 1922 he was removed from office by his Conservative partners in the coalition government.

In 1924 Ramsay MacDonald, leader of the British Labour Party, then a minority party in parliament, formed a government with the support of the Liberals. Although his government lasted only ten months, he and his colleagues proved that the British working movement could produce leaders capable of governing the country.

After the 1924 general election, the Conservatives formed a government led by Stanley Baldwin. It was this government which provoked and dealt with the effects of the 1926 General Strike (see pages 48 and 49).

Ireland

Home Rule

In 1918 many of the people of Ireland wanted Home Rule – the right to govern their own country independently from Great Britain. The desire for independence had a long history. Gladstone tried to resolve the Irish Question in the 1880s. But some of Gladstone's fellow Liberals joined with the Conservatives in rejecting the Irish Home Rule Bill of 1886. They went on to form the Unionist Party, which was devoted to maintaining the union between Great Britain and Ireland.

In 1912 the Liberal Government attempted to bring in a new Home Rule Bill but it was again bitterly contested by the Protestants of northern Ireland.

The Easter Rising 1916

During the War the British Government shelved these plans to resolve the Irish problem, but this did not satisfy the Irish nationalists. Members of the Irish Republican Party – Sinn Fein (which means 'We Alone') – organized the Easter Rising in April 1916. They hoped to gain independence for Ireland immediately, instead of having to wait for the British Government to fulfil its promises after the War. But the Rising, led by Patrick Pearse and James Connolly, failed.

The British authorities did nothing to bring calm to Ireland when they then executed 14 of the rebel leaders, making martyrs of Pearse and Connolly. But they reprieved Eamonn de Valera, one of the rebel leaders. He later became Ireland's Prime Minister, staying in that office for a total term of over 21 years and eventually becoming President of Ireland from 1959 to 1973.

The Irish Free State

After the First World War terrorist attacks by the newly formed Irish Republican Army (IRA) were met by violent reprisals from the Black and Tans, a specially recruited unit of the Royal Irish Constabulary. These 'troubles', as they were known, culminated in the assassination of a leading British general at his home in London and the eventual acceptance, by the IRA leader Michael Collins, of a compromise plan partitioning Ireland. Six of the counties of Ulster (mainly Protestant) became part of the United Kingdom as Northern Ireland whilst the remaining counties (mainly Catholic) were granted dominion status as The Irish Free State. This meant that they were virtually independent, like Canada and Australia, but were still part of the British Commonwealth.

Left: Troops in action firing a field gun from Nelson's Column in Dublin in 1922.
Below: de Valera in 1918.
Bottom: The Easter Rising in Dublin in 1916.

Civil War

This did not satisfy men like de Valera and other militant IRA leaders. Collins was assassinated on his return to Ireland and the country was plunged into civil war. Eventually de Valera abandoned militancy and got his way through the ballot box. He made the Republic of Ireland completely independent of Britain in 1949, but failed to achieve his ultimate goal of a United Ireland.

The General Strike

Revolution?

The General Strike from 3 to 12 May 1926 was the nearest Great Britain has been to a revolution since the Civil War in the middle of the seventeenth century. Over 2 million workers in many of the key industries went on strike, closing down factories and transport services. Moderate trade union leaders, politicians (including some from the Labour Party), and government ministers, feared there might be riots, serious bloodshed, or even a revolution. In fact they had little to fear. In some places policemen even played football against the strikers!

What caused the General Strike?

The strike was called to support the coal miners.

The mining industry had been hard hit after the War. Many pits were badly in need of moderniz-ation, lacking the mechanical coal-cutting machinery which many overseas rivals were using. At that time much of Britain's coal was exported; so a sharp increase in foreign competition meant a fall in demand for Britain's surplus coal. At the same time more and more vehicles, ships and factories were using alternative sources of power instead of coal, such as electricity and oil.

In order to cope with this problem the mine-owners said they would have to cut wages in the industry and lengthen the working day from seven to eight hours. But they got a dusty reply from the miners' leader, A. J. Cook, who retorted, 'Not a penny off the pay! Not a minute on the day!'

At this point the Conservative Government inter-vened and offered to subsidize the coal industry (so that wages need not be cut) whilst a Government Commission, led by Sir Herbert Samuel, tried to come up with a solution.

But the Samuel Report pleased neither the miners nor the mine-owners, since it recommended a cut in wages but told the mine-owners to modernize their pits.

The other trade unions were afraid that similar cuts would be made in their industries as well, if the miners lost their battle with the mine-owners. This is why they eventually joined the strike, even though its outcome did not affect them directly or immediately.

The British Worker, Monday, 10 May 1926

Nothing could be more wonderful than the magnificent response of millions of workers to the call of their leaders.

The General Council . . . are especially desirous of commending the workers on their strict obedience to the instruction to avoid all conflict and to conduct themselves in an orderly manner. Their behaviour during the first week of the stoppage is a great example to the whole world.

The General Council's message at the opening of the second week is 'Stand firm. Be loyal to instructions and Trust Your Leaders.'

Right: A. J. Cook, leader of the Miners' Federation, addressing a large crowd of miners in 1926 after the General Strike had collapsed. He told the crowd, 'Blacklegs are industrial lepers, and as such must be isolated'.

Far left: During the General Strike of 1926, many farmers delivered their own milk to depots in London.
Left: Volunteer bus driver with police escort during the General Strike.

What happened?

Talks between the miners and their employers broke down, the miners called a strike for 1 May but were 'locked out' anyway, when the mine-owners closed the pits. The Government tried to talk the TUC (Trades Union Congress) out of implementing its promise to call a general strike in support of the miners; but these talks also broke down.

The General Strike began on 3 May 1926 but soon proved ineffective. Although trade unionists came out on strike in force in the key industries chosen by the TUC for the protest, the effect was less keenly felt because the Government had had time to make emergency plans during the nine months it took the Samuel Commission to report.

The armed forces and a large force of volunteers helped to keep law and order, move food supplies, provide public transport services and maintain vital power supplies.

The newspapers tried different ways of getting their papers printed and some issued duplicated sheets of news. The TUC published *The British Worker* and the Government had its own newspaper *The British Gazette*, edited by Winston Churchill.

After nine days the moderate union leaders called off the General Strike without consulting the mineworkers and their union. The miners continued their strike for some time afterwards, feeling betrayed by the workers in the other unions.

The aftermath of the General Strike

In 1927 the Government brought in the Trade Disputes and Trade Union Act which banned general strikes, the closed shop (union insistence in a factory that all employees belong to the same union), and strikes by the police force and other public servants. It also laid down that trade unions could not use their members' membership subscriptions and union dues to contribute funds to political parties (for example, the Labour Party) without first giving their members the opportunity to say whether they wanted to contribute or not.

Trade union membership fell sharply in the next few years, partly because of the disillusionment of some workers with the trade union movement after the General Strike, and partly because the sharp rise in unemployment meant there were fewer workers in industry anyway.

ORDER AND QUIET THROUGH THE LAND
Growing Dissatisfaction Among The Strikers
INCREASING NUMBERS OF MEN RETURNING TO WORK
850 Omnibuses In The Streets Of London
MORE AND MORE TRAINS
WORK AS USUAL
The British Gazette, Wednesday, 12 May 1926

49

The National Government

Ramsay MacDonald

In 1929 Ramsay MacDonald led Britain's second Labour Government. But it was not a good moment to introduce radical reforms. The Wall Street Crash (see page 81) in October 1929, and the subsequent worldwide **depression** (see Explanatory Notes) in trade and industry, created severe problems for Britain's Labour Government.

Causes of the Depression

1. Manufacturers and farmers in Britain and Europe had produced more goods and foodstuffs than people could pay for. The Wall Street Crash in October 1929 reflected this sudden lack of confidence in industry when the price of shares on the New York Stock Exchange plunged in value.

2. The British industries worst affected were those which normally exported much of their output abroad. Coal mining, iron and steel, and textiles suffered severely. Since the depression affected most countries in the world (including the USSR, Germany and Japan) there was a general decline in trade. Fewer cargo ships were needed; so Britain's shipyards which produced most of the world's shipping, got fewer orders to build new ships. Some shipbuilding towns, such as Jarrow on Tyneside in north-eastern England, were so badly affected, that only one man in three had a job.

Ramsay MacDonald.

3. Some countries attempted to deal with the falling off in trade by raising duties (tariffs) on imported goods. This made British exports even more expensive than before, particularly since the pound was overvalued compared with other currencies, such as the American dollar.

4. In 1931 foreign investors, always suspicious of left-wing politics, began to withdraw their money from Britain. This only made the economic crisis worse.

The National Government

MacDonald's advisers negotiated foreign loans to support the pound but there were strings attached – the high cost of unemployment benefit had to be reduced. Half of MacDonald's Cabinet colleagues would not agree to the 10 per cent cut in benefit which he proposed. It looked as if he would have to resign.

Then to everyone's astonishment Ramsay MacDonald, a Labour Prime Minister, agreed to lead a National Government consisting mainly of Conservative ministers and backed by the Conservative Party in parliament. Only a handful of Labour Party members supported him in the House of Commons, the remainder going into opposition.

MacDonald continued in office as leader of the National Government until 1935 when he was succeeded by Stanley Baldwin. This split in the Labour Party caused great controversy at the time, and ever since, because many people thought he had betrayed the Labour movement. The more charitable view is that the King persuaded him to stay on as national leader, in order to reassure overseas investors.

Government action

The first task of the National Government was to restore confidence in the pound. Economy measures were introduced. These included the 10 per cent cut in unemployment benefit and the introduction of the means test. This reduced benefits if other members of a household were earning money. As a result many unemployed men and women found themselves having to rely on their children for their keep.

The National Government also cut the wages of various public employees, including teachers, civil servants and members of the armed forces. They abandoned the long-standing principle of free trade in Britain and followed other countries in imposing a tariff on foreign imports, apart from those on goods coming from countries of the Commonwealth or Empire.

MacDonald's efforts to preserve the value of the pound, at the cost of splitting the Labour Party, came to nought, however, when the pound was effectively **devalued** (see Explanatory Notes) in September 1931.

Left: In 1936 a deputation of unemployed men marched from Jarrow to London.

Fascists and Communists

A side effect of the Depression was the stimulus it gave the extremist parties to the left and right of centre. The Communists pointed to Stalin's Five Year Plans and the benefits a planned economy could bring to a nation suffering the effects of a severe slump in trade.

Right-wing organizations pointed instead to the achievements and objectives of Hitler's Nazi Party and Mussolini's Fascists. The most successful of these right-wing extremist groups was Sir Oswald Mosley's British Union of Fascists. Despite its name it had more in common with Hitler's National Socialists than Mussolini's supporters. Unlike the Italians, Mosley's British Fascists were anti-Semitic and organized provocative marches in London's East End in order to goad the Jews and the Communists.

Appeasement

In the 1930s the problems of the Depression lessened in gravity with each succeeding year. Foreign affairs took on a deeper meaning after the coming to power, in 1933, of Adolf Hitler.

British and French statesmen were reluctant to provoke a world war, so they tended to turn a blind eye to the evils they heard about in Germany and to pretend that Hitler did not pose a menace to the free world. When Hitler made demands, based on the restitution to Germany of the rights she had enjoyed before the Versailles Peace Agreement, politicians in both France and Britain tended to see these demands as reasonable, instead of insisting that the terms of the Treaty be kept. This policy was called **appeasement** (see Explanatory Notes and Chapter 9).

Sir Oswald Mosley leading a demonstration of the British Union of Fascists in London in 1936.

Relations between France and Germany

French demands after the War

At the Paris Peace Conference all the delegates wanted to impose terms which would ensure a lasting peace in Europe and the world. But, as you have seen, they found it difficult to agree on how best to achieve this.

It was easy enough to set up a League of Nations (see Chapter 8) or even to redistribute former German colonies as mandates of the League. But there were fundamental conflicts of opinion regarding the role Germany could be expected to play in the future history of Europe. The British Prime Minister, David Lloyd George, had no desire to see France become the strong man of Europe in place of Germany.

However, the French Prime Minister, Georges Clemenceau, pressed hard for a settlement that would weaken Germany, both militarily and economically. The French were sure that this alone would ensure peace in Western Europe.

French gains at Versailles

Accordingly, by the terms of the Treaty of Versailles:
* The long-disputed border region of Alsace–Lorraine was given back to France. It had been French until her defeat by Germany in the disastrous Franco-Prussian War of 1870–71.
* The rich Saar coalfield, which was undeniably German and which lay between Lorraine and the German Rhineland, was put in French hands for a period of 15 years as compensation for the damage that was done to French coal mines in northern France during the war. Its future at the end of that time (1935) was to be determined by the people of the Saar in a plebiscite (vote). If they voted to return to Germany then the coal mines, which were now French property, were to be sold back to the Germans. France was short of coal; and although this was a practical method of ensuring she got compensation, it could also be seen as an attempt to enlarge her frontiers at Germany's expense.
* The French argued strongly that the River Rhine should be made the new boundary between France and Germany. This would have given the French a large part of Germany, on the left bank of the Rhine, but the other Allies refused to agree to these demands. Instead it was to become a demilitarized zone, also for 15 years, under Allied military occupation. In practice, however, British troops left in 1926 and the French in 1930. Its status as a demilitarized zone later disappeared when Hitler sent his army into the Rhineland in 1936.
* Germany was also made to pay a large sum in war reparations (see Chapter 1). When she defaulted on these payments, French troops occupied the Ruhr coalfield, on the right bank of the Rhine (see Chapter 3).

Alliances and frontier guarantees

Later French policy was dominated by the same obsession – that of preventing Germany from becoming strong again. Gustav Stresemann of Germany and Aristide Briand of France shared the

The Maginot Line. It stretched along the eastern frontier of France with Germany, but proved useless, when the Germans attacked through Belgium in 1940.

Nobel Peace Prize in 1926 for their work in promoting Franco-German friendship. But this did not stop the French from erecting a supposedly impregnable line of fortifications on the German frontier between 1927 and 1934 (the Maginot Line).

Nor did it prevent France from concluding friendly alliances with other nations surrounding Germany. In 1921 came an agreement with Poland guaranteeing each other's security. The Locarno Pact of 1925 guaranteed frontiers with Belgium and Germany. The Stresa Front, signed in 1935, was an agreement between France, Italy and Britain on common action to be taken against Hitler. It followed Germany's announcement that she was going to rearm, in contravention of the terms of the Treaty of Versailles. Other treaties were signed with Russia and the Little Entente powers (Romania, Czechoslovakia and Yugoslavia).

France in the 1920s and 1930s

The weaknesses of the French political system

Between 1918 and 1940 France had no less than 44 different governments, led by twenty different prime ministers. During this same period there were just two leaders in Russia (Lenin and Stalin) and five in the United States (Wilson, Harding, Coolidge, Hoover and Roosevelt).

The problem in France was that there were too many political parties. At one stage there were 19 represented in the Chamber of Deputies. As a result all governments had to be coalitions of several different parties. If the dominant parties were right wing they had to get support from the parties in the middle; but so too did the left-wing parties if they tried to form a government. These coalition groups were known by names such as the Union Nationale, which was right wing, and the Cartel des Gauches, which represented the left wing.

Not surprisingly the members of these parties soon fell out, and then a new coalition government was formed, and then another! The tragedy for France was that these successive governments gave no stability to the political system, nor was France ever able to maintain a consistent foreign policy.

Progressively the differences widened between left and right, so that they ranged from the Fascist Croix de Feu organization at one extreme to the Communist Party at the other.

One of the most progressive coalition governments, that of the Front Populaire, was led by a Socialist Prime Minister, Leon Blum, but supported by Communists as well as Socialists. Blum was Jewish and some of the bitterest opposition and racial prejudice he encountered came from groups with Fascist or near-Fascist leanings.

Mass meeting of French Communists in Paris in 1936.

Scandals – the Stavisky Affair

Serge Stavisky was a Russian-born businessman who used French government ministers and officials to promote his shady financial deals, which included the fraudulent issue of bonds.

Before the French police could make an arrest, he committed suicide, in 1934. Subsequent investigations implicated a number of well-known figures in French political circles.

Demonstrations and strikes were held in protest and the Government fell when it seemed to some observers that there was a very real danger the unrest could lead to civil war.

The affair had serious repercussions for France, since it brought the entire political system into disrepute and caused many French people to doubt the merits of a democratic system, which seemed incapable of providing strong, honest government.

The weaknesses of the French economy

France had been seriously weakened by her war effort and the destruction caused by the fighting in northern France. This was particularly serious since most of France's limited industrial resources were in the war-zone areas.

France was still an agricultural country with a large peasant population. Her population of 41 million in 1931 was about the same size as that of England and Wales (40 million). But it had grown very little in the nineteenth and twentieth centuries, whereas those of her rivals in Europe had greatly multiplied.

A jazz band performs for the benefit of fellow-strikers at the Delaye factory in 1936.

One hundred years earlier, in 1831, her population of 33 million had been well over twice that of England and Wales (14 million). Germany, too, had increased in the same period from 27 to 65 million and Italy from 21 to 41 million.

Accordingly, France was less well placed than the other great powers of Europe to build a sound industrial base.

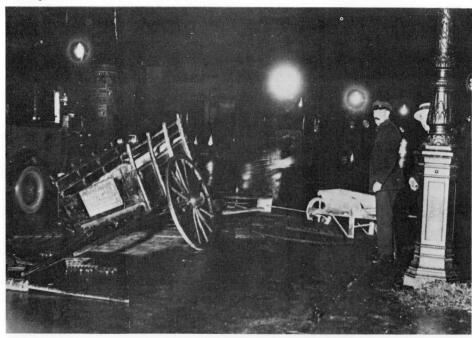

The Stavisky riots of 1934 left many French streets like this – littered with the ruins of barricades.

Explanatory Notes

Appeasement is the term used to describe the policy of giving in to the demands of an aggressive power in the hope that this will preserve peace. To appease someone is to calm them down. French and British statesmen, like the British Prime Minister, Neville Chamberlain, thought that if Hitler could be 'calmed down' there would be peace in Europe.

A **depression** in trade and industry is when a decline or slump in demand for goods leads to falling prices, high rates of unemployment and a decline in the amount of money invested in new factories and machinery. *Slump* is another name used for a low point in trading and business activities. *Downturn* is a more recent expression, usually referring to a temporary setback.

Devaluation is when the value of a nation's main unit of currency drops in relation to the value of the currency of other nations. For example, suppose the normal rate of exchange for one British pound is 12 Hong Kong dollars. If the pound is devalued and the new exchange rate is 10 Hong Kong dollars to the pound, then a British car costing £10,000 in Britain will cost 120,000$ (Hong Kong) *before* devaluation, but only 100,000$ (Hong Kong) *after* devaluation.

Exercises

1. What were the principal weaknesses of France during the inter-war years?
2. What was the French attitude to Germany at the end of the First World War? How, and with what success, did French statesmen attempt to weaken Germany and strengthen the position of France in Europe in the inter-war years?
3. Why did the TUC call a General Strike in Britain in May 1926? How effective was it? What were its effects? Did it advance or retard the cause of the trade union movement in Britain?
4. Why were the effects of the Great Depression of 1929–34 so keenly felt in Britain? What problems lay at the root of the slump in British trade? Why was shipbuilding one of the worst hit industries? How did the Government attempt to deal with this problem?
5. What similarities and what differences were there between the problems facing Britain and those facing France in the inter-war years?
6. Write brief notes explaining the significance of any three of the following in twentieth-century history:
(a) the IRA
(b) the British Union of Fascists
(c) the National Government 1931
(d) the Stavisky Affair 1934
(e) the Easter Rising 1916
(f) coalition government in France 1918–39

Further Activities

1. Draw up a list of reasons which you think help to explain French attitudes to Germany at the end of the First World War.
2. Use your list to help you prepare a brief speech on this subject which you think a French politician could have delivered in the Chamber of Deputies during the inter-war years. Prepare another speech presenting the point of view of a representative of the British Government on the same issues.

CHAPTER 5

Russia under Lenin and Stalin

Saturday, 10 March 1917. Over 250,000 striking workers demonstrate in the streets of Petrograd, then Russia's capital city (now known as Leningrad). Some are shouting for the downfall of the Czar and his government, blaming them for food shortages and for leading Russia into a disastrous war with Germany, which has killed over a million soldiers.

Two days later the situation is out of control. Police and soldiers join in the demonstrations. A provisional government is formed and on 15 March the Czar abdicates.

In April, Lenin, Trotsky and other revolutionary leaders (mainly Bolsheviks) return to Russia from exile abroad. In July their attempt to seize power is thwarted and many are put in prison. Alexander Kerensky becomes Prime Minister but later turns to the Bolsheviks for help when General Kornilov threatens an Army takeover.

The War continues. So do the shortages of food and fuel, and the strikes. Trotsky and Lenin make plans. By the end of October Russia is on the verge of revolution. Some peasants have taken advantage of the collapse of law and order to seize land, many workers are on strike, large numbers of soldiers have deserted from the army. Many support Lenin's **Bolsheviks** (see Explanatory Notes) whose slogan promises 'Peace – Land – Bread – Freedom'.

Wednesday, 7 November 1917. A red letter day. The Bolsheviks seize all the key points in Petrograd and overthrow Kerensky's Government.

Russia, a great power, the world's largest country, has turned Communist. Foreign leaders fear for the future. Indeed, some Bolsheviks make no bones about their hopes and aspirations. They intend to make Russia the centre of a worldwide revolution.

The Bolshevik Revolution

Lenin's immediate task after seizing power, on 7 November 1917, was to fulfil the promises he had made to the Russian people. They expected Peace – Land – Bread – Freedom.

The Constituent Assembly

The Bolsheviks did not immediately dispense with the idea of democratic elections. Indeed, Lenin promised that all the important decisions about land would be made by the Constituent Assembly when it met on 18 January 1918. But when the new Constituent Assembly was actually elected the Bolsheviks found, to their horror, that they were in a minority. The Social Revolutionary Party (which had once supported Kerensky, the previous Russian Prime Minister – a moderate revolutionary) had gained twice as many seats as Lenin's supporters (370 to Lenin's 175 seats).

In a Nutshell

* Food shortages and a pointless war, in which several million Russian soldiers have been killed or wounded, lead to revolution in March 1917. In November, the Bolsheviks turn Russia into a Communist State.
* Foreign governments provide troops and arms to help the anti-Communist forces in the bloody Civil War which follows.
* To help the war effort against forces opposing the Bolshevik Revolution Lenin introduces a policy of War Communism, in which the peasants have to give their surplus food to the Government. This is neither popular with the peasants nor effective as a tax. It is eventually replaced by the New Economic Policy which allows some private enterprise but is not true Communism.
* Lenin uses dictatorial powers to maintain his position. The Cheka (secret police) ruthlessly search out the enemies of Communism. Terror is used to enforce the authority of the State. Later, Stalin also uses secret police (called OGPU and NKVD in the 1930s) to hang on to power.
* Lenin dies in 1924. In the power struggle which follows, Stalin craftily out-manoeuvres his rivals and becomes the Russian dictator.
* Stalin's economic policies bring a new revolution to the countryside when he merges the millions of small peasant farms into large collective farms. Rich peasants (kulaks) who oppose this are sent to labour camps or shot.
* Stalin is afraid anti-Communist nations will one day wage war against the USSR. Russia needs weapons; it is essential that Soviet industry be modernized and expanded. The First Five Year Plan is introduced in 1928 setting targets for increased production of coal, electricity, steel, chemicals and other essential raw materials.
* Stalin, fearful that rivals may overthrow him, orders the start of the Purges. Millions of potential 'enemies of the State' are rounded up, interrogated, tried, imprisoned or shot. When the Purges end in 1938, Stalin is strong but Russia is weak.

A Swedish Socialist who was in Petrograd at the time, described the excitement on the day the Assembly met for the first and only time. There were demonstrations and red flags in the streets, the Bolshevik *commissars* (important officials), who were inside the building, carried revolvers and many of the delegates wore red roses in their buttonholes.

An artist's impression of the storming of the Winter Palace in Petrograd, 7 November 1917. Armed workers, soldiers and sailors seized the headquarters of the Provisional Government.

ПРОЛЕТАРИИ ВСЕХ СТРАН СОЕДИНЯЙТЕСЬ!

ГОД ПРОЛЕТАРСКОЙ ДИКТАТУРЫ.

ОКТЯБРЬ 1917 – ОКТЯБРЬ 1918

Bolshevik poster of 1918. It says 'Proletariat of the world unite. Year of Proletarian dictatorship October 1917 – October 1918.'

All were Socialists of one sort or another, representing several different parties – some well to the right of Lenin's Bolsheviks, some to the left.

The Social Revolutionaries helped to elect a Chairman who 'praised Socialism, peace and the fight against imperialism endlessly'. But he was not a Bolshevik.

Accordingly Lenin found an excuse for closing the Assembly the next day, 19 January 1918. So democracy lasted only 24 hours! The Central Committee said the Assembly had been elected on the basis of lists of voters drawn up 'before the October Revolution' and that the 'Party of Right-Wing Socialist-Revolutionaries' (who were in a majority) refused to co-operate with the 'supreme body of Soviet power, the Central Executive Committee of the Soviets'.

Lenin's promises – Land
On the day after the October Revolution on 7 November 1917 (see the Explanatory Notes on page 75 for an explanation of this paradox), Lenin abolished ownership of land without compensation. The estates of the Csar, the nobility and the Church were

to be put at the disposal of local soviets (councils) until the Constituent Assembly met. In future the right to use the land would belong to those who worked on it but *ownership* was in the hands of the people – in other words, the State. This was not what some peasants thought Lenin meant when he said that the Bolsheviks would give the people land! They wanted their own farms.

On 27 November 1917 workers were given control over the running of their factories. But the Communists did not nationalize industries at first. They did not want to ruin the economy, so there were no drastic changes – yet.

One month later the Bolshevik Government nationalized the banks but promised to protect the savings of people who had deposited money there.

Lenin's promises – Freedom
The Declaration of the Rights of the Peoples of Russia, which was signed on 15 November 1917 by Stalin as People's Commissar for Nationalities and by Lenin, fulfilled the Bolshevik promise that the Russian peoples would be given their freedom.

The peasants were freed from the rule of the landowners and the factory-workers from the 'tyranny of capitalists' (the bosses).

All the peoples of Russia (that is, the different national groups, such as the Kazakhs) were free and equal. They had the right to self-determination, even to the extent of leaving Russia and forming an independent state.

But, as you have seen, Lenin did not abide by the results of the free elections to the Constituent Assembly. Nor did freedom extend to the newspapers. A publication could be suppressed if it called for 'open resistance or insubordination to the Workers' and Peasants' Government'. Yet one of the early calls of the Petrograd Soviet in March 1917 had been for freedom of speech and freedom of the press!

Lenin's promises – Bread
This promise, made in the light of the food shortages before the Revolution, was more difficult to keep. As you will see below, food shortages during the Civil War resulted in a terrible famine. Lenin's policy of War Communism (see page 63) penalized peasants and actually discouraged them from producing the surplus corn needed by the army and the Russian workers who lived in towns.

Lenin's promises – Peace

This was something that Lenin could bring about promptly and on the day after the seizure of Petrograd, the new Russian Government called on all the warring nations to start peace talks. The Bolsheviks wanted a 'just and democratic peace' in which there would be no territorial gains without a free vote by the peoples concerned.

This proved to be the stumbling block to the successful conclusion of the peace talks between Russia and the Central Powers which began a month later in the town of Brest-Litovsk (December 1917). An armistice (stop to the fighting) was agreed on 15 December but the Russians could not agree to the German territorial demands.

Lenin wanted peace at any price and was prepared to accept the German demands immediately. Other Communist leaders, including Trotsky, objected that a humiliating peace agreement with Germany would destroy the prestige and strength of the Bolshevik Revolution. Trotsky proposed that they should announce the end of the fighting but not actually conclude a peace agreement with the Central Powers. 'Neither peace nor war', he said. But when the German armies started to march on Russia once more, resistance to the German peace terms collapsed. One interesting side effect came about as a result of the German advance on Petrograd. The Bolsheviks moved their government to safety in Moscow, making this their capital city.

Above: Lenin in 1917. He was an inspiring orator and a strong leader.
Below: Council of Commissars in Moscow, 1917. Lenin is by the door. Trotsky, holding a sheet of paper in his hands, is second from Lenin's left.

The Treaty of Brest-Litovsk was signed in 1918. The members of the Russian delegation are on the right of the table; the German, Turkish and Austrian delegates are on the left.

The Treaty of Brest-Litovsk

The Treaty of Brest-Litovsk was signed, reluctantly, on 3 March 1918. By its terms Russia agreed that Latvia, Lithuania, Estonia, Finland and Poland should all become independent. Even more reluctantly, Russia had to agree to the creation of an independent state in the Ukraine. She also agreed to pay a large sum of money in reparations for war damage.

As a result Russia lost about a third of her population, a third of her agricultural land (including much of the rich grain-growing region of the Ukraine), and about two thirds of her heavy industry.

The Germans were well satisfied. They had eliminated one of their major enemies and could now send troops from the Russian front to reinforce those fighting on the Western Front and in Italy. They could also send troops into the newly independent nations recognized by the Treaty, to ensure they stayed within Germany's sphere of influence.

The harsh terms imposed by the Germans were counter-productive, however, since they made a mockery of their own claims in 1919, that the terms of the Treaty of Versailles were harsh and unfair.

The Civil War

Opposition groups

The Civil War which followed the October Revolution was a period of great confusion in Russian history, not least because there were so many different opponents of the Bolshevik Revolution.

Broadly speaking these could be divided into:
(a) political opponents in Russia – discontented members of the other parties, such as Kerensky's Social Revolutionaries;
(b) Russians still loyal to the Czar, such as landowners and others of the upper and middle classes, who had been dispossessed in the Communist takeover;
(c) the national minority groups in the frontier lands which had been added to the Russian empire in the past, and now saw their opportunity to be free of Russia for good;
(d) army officers who wanted to continue the war against the Germans and were opposed to the humiliating terms laid down by the Treaty of Brest-Litovsk;
(e) the Western Allies who, in the spring of 1918, wanted Russia to continue the War against Germany, and, after the November 1918 Armistice, hoped that their support for the anti-Communist White Armies would help to bring down the Bolshevik forces threatening to export international Communism to the rest of the world.

The Cheka and the Red Army

Although Lenin and Trotsky had overthrown Kerensky's Government with ease they recognized the ever-present danger of a counter-revolution by forces loyal either to the Czar or to the previous government. The Decrees on Land and Workers' Control made many enemies of the middle classes and the well-to-do peasants, apart from the landowners and patriotic Russians still loyal to the Czar and the old regime.

Lenin and Trotsky lost no time in building up organizations to guarantee the security of the State. These were:

* The Red Army – formed to defend Russia against her external enemies. It developed out of the Red Guards formed by the Bolsheviks before the October Revolution and was later expanded and brilliantly organized into an efficient fighting force by Trotsky as Commissar for War.

* The Cheka or secret police – formed to deal ruthlessly with 'enemies of the State'. The official title of this government terrorist organization was 'All-Russian Extraordinary Commission for the Suppression of Counter-Revolution, Sabotage and Speculation'.

Counter-revolution

Many army officers and government workers welcomed the overthrow of the Czar but had no liking for the extremes of Communism. As you have seen, the elections to the Constituent Assembly demonstrated that Lenin did not have complete popular support. Members of Kerensky's Social Revolutionary Party began to organize active opposition to the Bolsheviks. Boris Savinkov, a former Minister of War, led an unsuccessful uprising in July 1918. An assassination attempt on Lenin's life failed but the Cheka boss in Petrograd was killed. The Cheka took a terrible revenge, eliminating many so-

Alexander Kerensky, left, head of the Provisional Government in 1917.

Czar Nicholas II and his family in exile in Siberia. They were assassinated soon afterwards, in 1918.

called 'enemies of the State' in an orgy of killings which became known as the Red Terror.

Allied intervention

The Treaty of Brest-Litovsk also infuriated Russia's Allies, since the war on the Western Front – Germany against France, Britain and the United States – had only started because France felt obliged to come to the aid of her ally Russia. But now the Russians were pulling out, without prior consultation. What is more, the terms of the Treaty of Brest-Litovsk would give the Germans great influence in eastern Europe.

The most worrying aspect of the Treaty was the fact that it would now allow the Germans to send reinforcements from the Russian Front to fight against the Allies on the Western Front or in support of Austria against Italy. Some Allied statesmen even thought the Bolsheviks were planning to fight with Germany and the Central Powers against the Allies.

Fear of Communism

Many statesmen feared the effect a successful Communist revolution might have on their own nationals. Russia was not alone in having a system of government which was dominated by a relatively small number of rich landowners and factory-owners, much of whose affluence derived from the labour of a large working class.

Left: Russian cartoon in 1919 showing Denikin, Kolchak and Yudenich as dogs under the control of the United States.

Right: 1919 – the Red Army marches into Odessa in the Crimea.

Trotsky and other Bolshevik leaders wanted to export Communism to other countries, to spark off a world revolution with Russia as its centre. They made no secret of the fact that they hoped to inspire workers in other countries to rise up and overthrow their leaders. Rosa Luxembourg, leader of the unsuccessful Spartacist uprising in Berlin in 1919 (see Chapter 1), praised Lenin and Trotsky for being 'the *first*, those who went ahead as an example to the proletariat (working class) of the world; they are still the *only ones* up to now who can cry: "I have dared!" '

The White Armies

Leading Russian generals started to build up armed forces on six fronts, encircling the area of Russia firmly controlled by the Bolsheviks. They were called the White Armies to distinguish them from the Red Army of the Communists.

The first White Army was led by General Kornilov and General Denikin in the Ukraine. In the east an army led by Admiral Kolchak took control over a large part of Siberia.

Czech nationals, who were prisoners of war from the Austrian army, had volunteered to form a legion to fight with the Allies against the Central Powers. They were being taken by rail across the Trans-Siberian Railway when they got news of the peace negotiations at Brest-Litovsk and a rumour spread that they would be returned to Germany. They rebelled and took control of the towns along the railway. Allied forces landed at Vladivostok to support them and Admiral Kolchak took charge of the White Army in the east. It was the advance of these forces which precipitated the execution in July 1918 of the Czar and his family at Ekaterinburg in the Ural Mountains.

Other White Armies were led by General Yudenich in the west. His forces advanced to within striking distance of Petrograd in September 1919. Already British, American and French troops had landed near Murmansk and Archangel in the north and linked up with soldiers from Finland (formerly part of the Russian empire). British and French troops were also involved in the Crimea and Georgia

The Russian Civil War.

in the south. There were Germans, Lithuanians, Poles and Romanians in the west and Czechs and Japanese in the east. In 1919 it looked as if these forces would almost certainly be able to help the White Armies crush the Communist Government in Moscow.

The Bolshevik defence

But Lenin and the Bolsheviks reacted to the emergency by putting the country on a war footing.
* They used propaganda posters to whip up enthusiasm for the war effort – portraying the White Armies as terrorist bands, backed by rich businessmen and capitalists. They appealed to Russian patriotism by showing that the White Armies were armed and supported by the forces of foreign powers, who were interfering in Russia's internal affairs.
* Trotsky was appointed as Commissar of War to build up the Red Army into an efficient fighting force. He toured the country by train, using propaganda and his powers as an orator to get the recruits needed. His efficient organization of the Red Army undoubtedly played a major part in the successful defeat of the White Armies.
* Less successful was Lenin's decision to turn the economy of Russia on to a war footing by introducing 'War Communism'.

War Communism

The growth in size of the Red Army meant that large numbers of soldiers had to be fed by the Government, so too did the large numbers of workers who were producing weapons and other war materials. Insufficient grain and meat were getting through to the troops, or to feed the poor; so Lenin introduced War Communism, which, as its name suggests, was intended as a temporary measure during the emergency created by the Civil War.

The following measures were taken: industries were nationalized at last (June 1918); wages could be paid in kind (such as food); private trading was abolished; the economy was placed under the control of the Government, which was given the power to requisition goods.

War Communism and the peasant farmer

In June 1918 committees were set up to take grain surpluses away from 'kulaks (well-to-do peasants) and rich people'. They were to be paid for at prices which were substantially below the fixed prices agreed by the Government for normal sales of grain. When this did not work special units were set up to seize the grain, headed by a commander and a detachment of at least 75 men, some armed with machine guns.

But still the peasants resisted. Many concealed their grain hoping to sell it on the black market. A report mentioned the case of Irina Ivashkevich, fined for hiding grain in a hole in her backyard. Many peasants decided there was little point in working hard and farming efficiently, if at the end of all that effort their surplus grain could be taken at gunpoint. The results were disastrous. Grain production fell, instead of rising as Lenin had hoped. What is more, the railway system was inadequate to cope with both the movement of troops and the movement of food and essential materials.

The failure of War Communism

Many Russians died of famine in those early years of the Revolution. One estimate puts the number at over 5 million dead. The problem of food production was aggravated by drought and poor harvests. In 1920 output from the land (grain, sheep, cattle) was only half that of 1913 under the Czar. But even when the Civil War came to an end the policy of War Communism continued By this time Russia was desperately short of food, raw materials and manufactured goods.

Defeat for the White Armies

Despite the difficulties faced by the Bolsheviks, the combined might of the White Armies was unable to overthrow Lenin. Trotsky's Red Army, urged on by patriotism and the threat of execution for deserters, repelled the White Armies one by one.

In June 1920 the last of the White Armies, led by Baron Wrangel (a leading general in the First World War), was defeated by the Red Army in the Crimea. Five months later his entire army, together with thousands of other refugees (many of them Russian aristocrats) were evacuated by sea to the Balkans. The Red Army took Sevastopol on 14 November 1920. Two days later the Civil War was over.

The Bolsheviks were successful partly because the White Armies opposing them were spread thinly on the ground. As you can see from the map on page 62 huge distances separated the different armies. Communications were bad, so it was difficult for one army to reinforce another or come to its rescue.

Nor were the anti-Communist forces agreed on what they would do if they won. Apart from foreign troops, they included aristocratic officers from the Russian Imperial Army and Social Revolutionaries, whose politics were much closer to those of Lenin than to the Czar. All they had in common was hatred of Communism.

The only successful opposition to the Red Army was mounted in Poland, where a Polish army defeated the Russians at the battle of the Vistula

near Warsaw in August 1920. They were then able to negotiate a favourable treaty with Russia at Riga in March 1921, giving them the eastern frontier they wanted.

Over a million Russians died in the Civil War, many of them brutally and in cold blood. They were executed as Bolsheviks by the White Armies or as enemies of the State by the Red Army, the Cheka or by special retribution squads.

Violence became an everyday occurrence. So too, did famine. Beggars, homeless children, disease and squalor were everywhere as the Russian people endured great hardship during the months of bitter fighting. The British author, H. G. Wells described Petrograd after the Civil War. There were gaping holes in the streets, collapsed drains and ruined houses. 'Everyone is shabby; everyone seems to be carrying bundles,' he said.

The Mutiny at Kronstadt

The Mutiny at Kronstadt in March 1921 helped to prepare the way for new policies. Lenin called it 'the flash which lit up reality better than anything else'. Kronstadt was a large naval base on the island of Kotlin in the Gulf of Finland, which had long been used by the Russians to protect Petrograd (originally called St Petersburg and later Leningrad). Its importance to the Russians was undeniable.

Kronstadt was ice-bound during the winter months and its importance during the Civil War had been lessened because of a naval blockade which prevented the warships from leaving harbour. Accordingly many of the experienced members of the armed forces normally based there, had been sent to fight in other parts of Russia during the Civil War.

By 1921, many of the sailors, soldiers and industrial workers based at Kronstadt were drawn from

Trotsky's troops attack Kronstadt in March 1921.

State. The 'commanding heights of the economy' (Lenin's words) – heavy industry, power, transport – remained under State control. In 1923 the State owned about 20,000 enterprises employing some 3 million workers. Private individuals or groups controlled 150,000 enterprises – mainly small workshops with only one or two workers apiece.

Lenin

Vladimir Ilyich Ulyanov was born in 1870. When he was 17 his elder brother Alexander was hanged for taking part in a plot to assassinate Czar Alexander III. Lenin himself was exiled to Siberia in 1897 for his work in organizing a revolutionary group dedicated to the 'liberation of the working classes'.

Thereafter he spent most of his time out of Russia as an exile, living for a time in London and also in Switzerland. When Kerensky became leader after the revolution in March 1917, Lenin returned – in a railway train which passed through Germany, then at war with Russia. The Germans hoped that Lenin would take Russia out of the War if he was successful in overthrowing the Kerensky government. This was achieved in the October Revolution and almost immediately Lenin started to negotiate peace terms with the Germans.

Lenin was a much-loved figure, a man who had demonstrated that he could relate to the peasant and to the worker. When he died of overwork in 1924, at an age when most world leaders are in their prime, the tearful Russians began to develop a Lenin personality cult, worshipping his memory but conveniently forgetting the ruthlessness and the terror he brought to Russia. His body was embalmed and preserved for all time in a mausoleum in Moscow's Red Square, as a shrine which visiting pilgrims to Moscow could venerate.

Lenin's mausoleum in Moscow.

---

peasant families. They demanded 'soviets without Communists', meaning that they wanted local decisions to be made by councils (soviets) which were not controlled by the Communist Party. They wanted greater freedom for the peasant and an end to strict government control of agriculture and industry.

Trotsky crushed the rebellion with ruthless efficiency, sending white-uniformed troops over the frozen ice, after the mutineers refused to surrender. But Lenin took the message to heart. He recognized that there was substance in these grievances and that the appalling shortages in Russia desperately needed effective solutions.

The New Economic Policy

Lenin had already decided that a change of policy was needed but the Mutiny at Kronstadt gave added point to the change. He made his proposal at the Tenth Congress of the Communist Party, which met less than a week after the start of the Mutiny.

The basic elements of the New Economic Policy were:

(a) In future the forcible seizure of surplus grain was to be abolished. In its place was a new tax, fixed in the spring as a percentage of the peasant's output from the land in the following twelve months. Any surplus, over and above this levy, could be sold by the peasant on the free market.

So at last the peasant had an incentive to produce as much food as possible from the land. The right to sell food on the open market meant that the Communist Government acknowledged that free enterprise had a part to play in the Soviet Union.

(b) In addition small businesses were permitted – although all the major undertakings were run by the

Above: Trotsky.   Below: Kamenev.

Left: Zinoviev.

The Rise of Stalin

Tensions in the Party

The New Economic Policy enabled Russia to regain her strength. Agricultural output grew, industrial production increased, the new, more liberal measures staved off unrest and gradually the country recovered from the trauma of the Revolution and the Civil War.

But there was tension among the rulers of the Communist Party. Lenin and Trotsky often took opposing views on issues which were central to the development of a Communist State. In 1921 Lenin and Stalin favoured voluntary trade unions but Trotsky (who lost) wanted government control of the unions.

These tensions figured prominently in the power struggle which developed after the death of Lenin in 1924. There was no obvious successor to Lenin capable of commanding the support of all the other Communist leaders.

Trotsky

The brilliant and dynamic Trotsky was easily the most effective of all the men at the top. His involvement with the Communist movement extended back to the days of the 1905 rebellion when he organized the first Soviet in St Petersburg. He had returned from New York in 1917 to play an active role in the Revolution. He was imprisoned by Kerensky and took much of the responsibility for the planning of the October Revolution.

Lenin chose him, against his will, to lead the negotiations with the Germans at Brest-Litovsk and it was Trotsky who had organized the Red Army so effectively during the Civil War.

Trotsky was an intellectual, a dynamic and original thinker and a forceful orator. But he was not liked! He was arrogant, did not suffer fools gladly and was far too wayward in his behaviour to get the support of his comrades. For instance, he did not bother to return from holiday to attend Lenin's funeral!

The struggle for power

The other leaders – Kamenev, Zinoviev, Radek, Voroshilov, Bukharin, Stalin – had none of Trotsky's obvious brilliance. For a time it looked as if control of the Soviet Union (it became the USSR in 1922) would be in the hands of the collective leadership at the top, rather than under the control of a single leader or dictator, as had happened when Lenin was in command.

Stalin

But Joseph Vissarionovitch Dzhugashvili (Stalin – 'man of steel') had other plans and ambitions. In 1917 he had been Commissar for the different national groups in the Soviet Union and had managed to build up support among the representatives of the non-Russian peoples in the USSR. He himself came from Georgia in the south and not from Russia itself. He was also Commissar of the Workers' and Peasants' Inspectorate, which meant inspecting (and exercising some control over) the work of other government departments.

In 1922 he took on the newly created job of General Secretary of the Central Committee of the Communist Party. It was this post which gave Stalin control of the Party organization. He was therefore better placed to manipulate people and organize committees so that they would arrive at decisions he approved of.

He decided to get to the top by out-manoeuvring his rivals, chiefly Kamenev, Zinoviev, Bukharin and Trotsky. They, for their part, did not see Stalin as a rival for the leadership, since he was generally regarded as a rather faceless Party administrator. Trotsky called him 'the Party's most eminent mediocrity' and someone else said he was a 'grey blur'.

Lenin saw through Stalin and recognized his menace. In 1922 he warned that Comrade Stalin had 'concentrated unlimited authority in his hands'. Lenin was not sure that Stalin would use his power wisely. In 1923 he complained that Stalin was 'too rude' and suggested that the other comrades think of ways of getting rid of Stalin from that post. But Kamenev and Zinoviev ignored these warnings, to their eventual peril.

Stalin survived. He first allied himself with Kamenev and Zinoviev against Trotsky, the extreme left-winger who wanted to abandon the New Economic Policy; then he allied himself with Bukharin, a right-winger, against Kamenev and Zinoviev; and eventually with Voroshilov and Molotov against Bukharin.

Had he tried to take all his rivals on at the same time he might well have sunk into obscurity.

As it turned out, however, he emerged as undisputed leader – and dictator – of the Soviet Union. When he celebrated his 50th birthday in 1929 he was acclaimed as 'True Successor of Lenin' and already three cities had been named after him – Stalino, Stalingrad and Stalinabad.

Socialism in one country

In his dispute with Trotsky, Stalin had stressed the need to strengthen the Communist Party at home.

Joseph Stalin in the 1930s.

'Socialism in one country' was his motto, meaning that the first essential was to concentrate on completing the Socialist transformation of the Soviet Union first.

Trotsky thought differently. He wanted the Party to encourage Communists in other countries and give them the support they needed to overthrow their leaders.

Stalin took the view that this might give other countries an excuse to attack the Soviet Union. He wanted to strengthen the Soviet economy first of all and build up the armed forces to make them capable of withstanding such an onslaught. 'We must catch up in ten years or they will attack us', he warned.

Retribution

Stalin's defeated rivals paid dearly in the end. Despite their long-standing membership of the Communist Party and the parts they played in the Bolshevik Revolution, Trotsky, Kamenev and Zinoviev were expelled in 1927 from the Party they had helped to found. Trotsky was even exiled from Russia in 1929, despite the major part he played in defeating the White Armies in the Civil War. During the Purges (see page 73) Kamenev, Zinoviev and Bukharin were all executed as enemies of the State. And in 1940 a Soviet murder squad hunted down the exiled Trotsky and assassinated him in Mexico.

Stalin

Stalin was born in Georgia in 1879, the son of a cobbler. He trained originally to become a priest but was expelled and later exiled to Siberia as a revolutionary. He escaped but was eventually recaptured and sent back to Siberia.

In 1917 he was released after the First Revolution and later helped Lenin and Trotsky to plan the October Revolution. During the dictatorship of Lenin he played a relatively minor role, until becoming General Secretary of the Russian Communist Party in 1922.

Stalin achieved much during the 25 years that he was Soviet dictator. But millions died to gratify his ambitions. Nonetheless, there is no denying the fact that, cost what it did, Stalin created modern Russia and laid sound foundations which enabled the Soviet Union to become one of the two world superpowers after the Second World War.

During his time as Russian dictator a personality cult developed around the figure of Stalin. 'Our great leader' proclaimed the broadcasts, and pictures showed him as a dominant father-figure leading his country to greatness. In reality his assistants often loathed and certainly feared him.

He died in 1953, a great hero at the time; but three years later his successor, Nikita Khruschev, shocked Russia and the world, by publicly denouncing Stalin at the Twentieth Party Congress in 1956. In particular he drew attention to the many evils associated with Stalin's dictatorship and the crimes committed during the period of the Purges in 1936–38.

The Five Year Plans

Aims

One of Stalin's first actions as Russian dictator was to begin a programme of reconstruction to modernize and expand Soviet industry. Stalin recognized that the Soviet Union could only become strong economically and militarily if it had a solid foundation of heavy industry to provide the basic raw materials and sources of power needed by other industries (such as factories making tractors, aeroplanes or locomotives).

He wanted to make rapid progress, not wait for piecemeal development. Russia had recovered from the effects of the Civil War but she lagged behind her rivals in Europe and in the rest of the world. The New Economic Policy had produced a half-hearted form of Communism, in which free enterprise played a large part. Now was the time for change.

New industries

Stalin recognized that the non-Communist world posed a threat to the Soviet Union. The existing industrial heartland of the country lay primarily in the basin of the River Don in the Ukraine region, a territory which had proclaimed its independence at the end of the First World War.

Stalin decided to build new iron and steelworks in central Russia, well away from the frontier zone.

The new steel town of Magnitogorsk in the Ural Mountains, 1930.

The new steel town of Magnitogorsk (now a city of nearly half a million people) was built in the Ural Mountain region between 1929 and 1931, using local iron ore and nearby coking coal as its main sources of raw materials.

Stalin was justified in his policy of developing new heavy industry away from the Ukraine when, during the Second World War, the Germans occupied the industrial regions of the Don Basin.

Many other industrial projects were undertaken. Tractor factories were built at Kharkov and Chelyabinsk to mechanize Soviet agriculture; vast hydroelectric schemes were constructed on the River Dnieper; the Moscow Underground was built as a showpiece for Communism.

Foreign experts were recruited to provide advice and technical skills but the Russians also developed their own system of technical and university education to provide their own experts and technicians. Scientific and engineering research was encouraged.

New canals, roads and railways were built to speed up the delivery of goods and aid communications over the vast land area of the Soviet Union. Electricity pylons criss-crossed the country. Lenin himself had said that 'Communism is Soviet Power Plus Electrification'.

Right: The Dnieper Dam in the Ukraine, 1936.
Below: Ornate station on the Moscow Underground.

Industrial Production

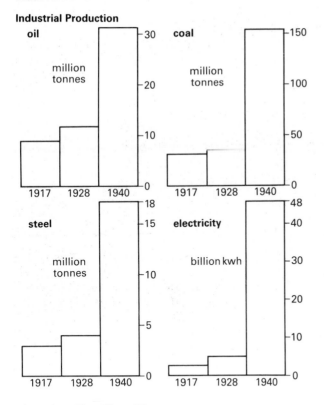

The First Five Year Plan

The new industrial policy was marked by the drawing up of the First Five Year Plan, which was to begin in 1928. It set production targets for the different industries to achieve. Coal and steel production was to be doubled, for example, and that of chemicals trebled.

These production targets were used by planners, in each industry, to set goals for individual mines and factories to meet. Some of these production targets were impossibly high, yet factory managers failing to meet them were punished.

Each manager used the production target to define the norms which had to be achieved by individual workers in the factory. These norms had to be met – or workers, too, could be punished.

Stakhanov

Soviet propaganda made much of the achievements of a coal miner called Stakhanov, who could cut 16 times as much coal in one shift as the ordinary miner. All workers were encouraged to do likewise. Those who exceeded their norm were rewarded. There were subsidized holidays on the Black Sea, free tickets and special privileges.

The Soviet people were deprived of many consumer goods during this time; food was short, discipline strict. Many were worse off than they had

been under the Czars. But there was little unemployment and, taken as a whole, Soviet industry showed a remarkable rate of growth at a time when the United Kingdom, Germany, the United States and Japan were suffering the effects of the great Depression of 1929–34. The graphs show how Soviet industry grew during the period from the start of the First Five Year Plan to the outbreak of the Second World War.

The Second and Third Five Year Plans

The First Five Year Plan 1928–32 was succeeded by the Second Five Year Plan 1933–37 which allowed Russian factories to make more consumer goods than those permitted under the First Five Year Plan. But war loomed ahead when the schedule for the Third Five Year Plan 1938–42 was announced and this placed greater emphasis on the manufacture of guns, planes, tanks and munitions.

By 1940 the Soviet Union was producing well over four times as much coal and steel as in 1928 and ten times as much electricity. When Germany attacked in 1941 the Soviet Union had the industrial might to recover from heavy initial losses. Whatever the cost of the Five Year Plans, there can be little doubt that they saved the Soviet Union from defeat in the War.

The Collectivization of Agriculture

Soviet agriculture and the Five Year Plan

In 1928 Soviet agriculture appeared to have changed little since the days of the Czars. Farming methods were primitive, yields were low and overall output was inadequate to meet the growing needs of the Soviet people.

Stalin needed workers for the new factories and works to be established under the Five Year Plans. The only source for such extra labour was from the land. Now, under the New Economic Policy, peasants produced food for their families and sold the surplus to feed the people in the towns.

Taking people away from agriculture would have two effects:
(a) It would mean fewer peasants to grow corn and tend livestock, so there was likely to be a decline, not a growth, in the output of food from the land.
(b) It would increase the number of people in towns who had to be fed from surplus grain and livestock products from the country.

Unless there was some remarkable transformation in Soviet agriculture, it seemed likely that the successful outcome of the Five Year Plans in industry would be matched by a corresponding decline in Soviet food production.

'Pasha' Angelina driving a tractor in 1937. Workers who were particularly productive were hailed as national heroes.

Change

This is why Stalin went ahead with a radical plan to change Soviet agriculture. In doing so he swept aside traditions which had lasted for centuries and convincingly brought Communism to the countryside, but at an appalling cost in human lives and happiness.

Stalin proposed to adapt mass production methods in industry and use them to increase agricultural production.

Lenin's Land Decree and subsequent legislation had put the land in the common ownership of the people but the peasants had the right to work their individual holdings. There were some 25 million of these holdings in 1928.

The collective farms

Four years later they had been merged to form 250,000 state or collective farms.

The state farms were run by the State and employees received a wage.

The collective farms were co-operative ventures, run by committees of farm-workers. Each worker had a small plot of land on which to keep a cow, grow a few vegetables, keep hens and a pig or two.

In addition he, or she, took a share of the profits from the collective farm in proportion to the amount of work put into the running of the farm.

The State took its share of the profits but it provided facilities and machinery which individual peasants had been unable to provide in the past.

Smashing the kulaks

The Party officials entrusted with the task of implementing the policy of collectivization met bitter opposition. Many peasants had done well under the old system.

These kulaks, as they were called, were reluctant to see the results of their hard work over the years suddenly become common property. The State proposed to take the grain and livestock which the peasant had hitherto been able to sell on the open market. Not surprisingly many preferred to destroy their homes, barns, crops and livestock rather than hand them over to the State.

For its part, the Soviet Government was not prepared to brook any obstacle to its plans. Collectivization and the transformation of agriculture were essential to the success of the First Five Year Plan. Many kulaks were sent to labour camps, many were shot. Stalin urged completion of the collectivization programme. 'We must smash the kulaks!' he said – and meant it.

Advantages of collective farms

In theory the new collective farms meant that farming could be made more efficient, since tractors, combine harvesters, heavy ploughs and many other tools and implements could be used efficiently on the huge fields of the collectives.

It was easier for the Communist Party to control, since there were official committees now. The Government could plan ahead, influencing the extent and nature of crops grown, directing collectives to produce more meat, milk or grain as the demand in the Soviet Union warranted it.

But the workers on the collectives no longer had the profit motive to encourage them to work longer hours than those laid down by the Party. Many devoted more time and energy to their private plots of land than to their official duties on the collectives.

Right: Agricultural production in the Soviet Union during the 1930s.

Below: A Soviet collective farm in 1931.

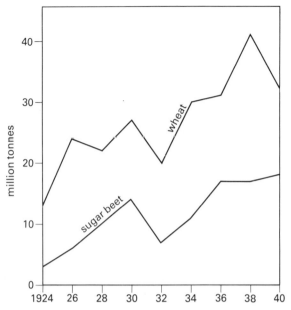

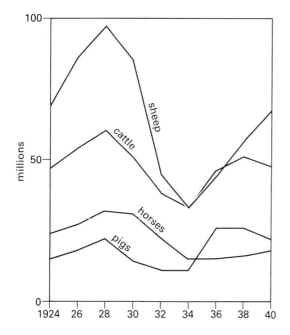

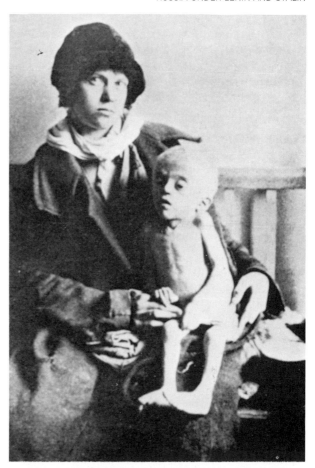

Although officially denied, famine was widespread in Russia in the 1930s. This baby is clearly suffering from malnutrition.

Famine

Collectivization started badly with a fall in agricultural output. The number of cattle fell by nearly a half between 1928 and 1934. The number of pigs fell from 22 million to only 11 million. The number of sheep and goats dropped by a staggering figure – from 146 million to 42 million. Grain production also suffered, from 85 million tonnes in 1930 to 69 million tonnes in 1934. As a result millions of Russians starved in the famine which followed. Yet Stalin was accused of exporting grain at this time, in order to earn foreign currency.

The Purges

Leningrad, 1 December 1934. Sergei Kirov, friend of Stalin and Party Boss in Leningrad, is assassinated by a man called Nikolayev. Immediately Stalin orders the summary trial of all those held responsible and the prompt execution of those found guilty.

This was the beginning of the Purges, although they only began in earnest in 1936. These were a series of show trials at which those accused invariably confessed their crimes, making little attempt to defend themselves against charges of treason. The results of these trials were broadcast to the world.

An English-language broadcast in 1936 began like this:

'The Trotsky-Fascist criminals who have made an attempt against the property of the Soviet State . . . have deserved their merciless punishment. This is the sentence of our great country – Death to the Enemies of the People.'

The Enemies of the People

Those brought to trial in this way included party officials, civil servants, scientists, army officers, police officers, veterans of the Revolution and some of the most outstanding figures in Soviet society. They included all the members of Lenin's Politburo – apart from Stalin and Trotsky (who was in exile abroad – soon to be murdered by Stalin's assassins). Kamenev, Zinoviev and Bukharin were all found guilty and shot. Many of Russia's most senior military commanders were executed in an orgy of senseless killing, including the Red Army Chief, Marshal Tukhachevsky, and the Navy Chief, Admiral Orlov.

In a television broadcast, many years later, a Russian woman recalled the most frightening event of her childhood, when the secret police took her father away in the middle of the night. She never saw him again. When she talked about it later to her friends she discovered that many of them had suffered the same horrifying experience.

A massacre

When the Purges came to an end in 1938 it was estimated that over one million Russians had been put to death and a further eight million sent to labour camps in Siberia and northern Russia.

Innocent or guilty?

Ever since, there has been controversy over the Purges and the extent to which Stalin was justified in his actions. One school of thought even throws suspicion on Stalin himself as instigator of the assassination of Kirov.

Others have defended the show trials. The British author of a book on the history of the USSR wrote in 1950 that Zinoviev, Kamenev and their associates were 'in close contact with the German Gestapo' and that the policy of Yagoda, ex-head of the Soviet Secret Police (OGPU), was 'one of complete subordination to the plans of Hitler'.

But when Russian Premier Nikita Khruschev denounced Stalin in 1956 he was in no doubt that the trials had been engineered by Stalin in order to rid himself of the slightest traces of opposition to his policies.

Results

Whatever the truth behind the story of the Purges there can be little denying the fact that they left Stalin as the undoubted strong man of Russia. At a time when the secret police took away suspects in the middle of the night, and when the most eminent people in the Soviet Union could be arrested on trumped-up charges and shot, it required considerable courage, or foolhardiness, to stand up to Stalin.

But it also reduced the effectiveness of the Soviet armed forces, as Stalin found out to his cost in 1941 when Hitler launched his invasion of the Soviet Union. The Red Army had been deprived of most of its best generals.

Show trial in the Soviet Union in the 1930s. In the dock are, hand on head, Konstantin Semenchuk, a scientist in charge of a Soviet Polar station, and, hand to mouth, S. P. Startsev, a dog-team driver. They were accused of maintaining a reign of terror for two years and were condemned to death by the Moscow Supreme Court.

Explanatory Notes

The Bolshevik seizure of power on 7 November 1917 was called the **October Revolution** because at that time the Russians used the Julian calendar and accordingly they dated the revolution as taking place on 26 October 1917.

Russian Communism originated in the political ideas of Karl Marx (see page 11). The All-Russian Soviet Democratic Workers' Party split into two groups in 1903 – Lenin's **Bolsheviks** (meaning the majority group) and the **Mensheviks** (meaning the minority group).

Karl Marx said that it was the workers who would seize control and bring about a Communist society. However, Lenin and Trotsky were intellectuals, not labourers. Indeed, Lenin came from a middle class family and at one time studied law at university. So when he established a dictatorship in Russia it was *not* a **dictatorship of the proletariat**.

Lenin introduced a number of **Communist** measures, such as common ownership of the land and workers' control of factories. The policy of War Communism was a temporary measure to alleviate Russia's problems in the Civil War. It was abandoned in 1921 during a period of acute shortages. The New Economic Policy which took its place, restored some degree of private enterprise to Russia, making it possible for peasants to sell their surplus food at a profit.

This was successful and it restored the Soviet economy; but it was not Communism.

Exercises

1. Do you agree with the judgement that Lenin was one of the greatest and most influential figures in the history of the world?

2. Why did civil war erupt in 1918? Who opposed Lenin and the Communists and why were Allied troops involved? How and why did the Bolshevik Government survive?

3. What was (a) War Communism (b) the New Economic Policy? Why did Lenin change from the one to the other?

4. What problems did Lenin and his Bolshevik Government have to deal with after the October Revolution? How did they tackle these problems? What were their achievements and what were their failures?

5. How far is it true to say that neither Lenin nor Stalin was able to make Russia a genuine Communist State?

6. Write brief notes on three of the following:
(a) The Cheka
(b) The Civil War
(c) The Mutiny at Kronstadt
(d) The Red Army
(e) Stalin's struggle with Trotsky

7. Lenin warned the Communist Party that Stalin was not to be trusted. How, then, did Stalin rise to become supreme leader of the Soviet Union on Lenin's death. Was Lenin's warning justified?

8. Describe and explain what is meant by the Russian Five Year Plans for industry. How important were they to the development of the Soviet Union as a great power?

9. Why did Stalin order the Purges of 1936–38? What was he afraid of? How did they weaken Russia yet strengthen the position of Stalin?

10. What was Stalin's policy towards the peasants? What did he hope to achieve through collectivization? How did he hope to modernize the farms? Do you think his agricultural policy was basically a success or a terrible mistake?

11. Write briefly, explaining what happened to:
(a) Czar Nicholas II and his family
(b) The kulaks
(c) Trotsky

12. Summarize and account for the main changes in economic policy made by Soviet governments in the period between 1917 and 1939.

Further Activities

1. Take part with your friends in a series of imaginary discussions between a group of Russians living in *either* a village in the Ukraine *or* a suburb of Moscow or Leningrad. Each member of the discussion group should take the role of a different Russian citizen. In a village one student could act the role of the village landowner, another could be a well-to-do kulak (rich peasant), others could be peasants. In a city suburb one could be a factory-owner, another a shopkeeper, a factory-worker, etc.

Try to imagine what each member of the group might want to say:
(a) In 1914 before the Revolution;
(b) In 1917 or 1918, soon after Lenin and the Communist Party seized power;
(c) Twenty years later, in 1937 or 1938.

Try to make your contribution to the discussion as realistic as possible. Do not put words into the mouth of your character which could only be made by someone who knows what happens next.

CHAPTER 6

Boom and Bust in the United States

Friday, 3 August 1923, 2.47 am. In the living room of a remote farmhouse in the New England state of Vermont, by the light of a paraffin lamp, John C. Coolidge administers the oath of office to his son Calvin, now (due to the sudden death of Warren Harding) the Thirtieth President of the United States.

It was the beginning of a period of unbelievable prosperity for many Americans – a period called 'the boom years', 'the roaring twenties' and 'the jazz age'. America had fully recovered from the First World War. After registering 6 million unemployed in 1921 most Americans now had a job, industry was booming, people were enjoying luxuries. Most of the signs of unrest at the end of the War – demonstrations, strikes, Communist agitation – had gone.

President Coolidge told his countrymen, 'The business of America is business'. In 1928 his successor, Herbert Hoover, claimed 'The poor man is vanishing from among us.' The ruling Republican Party boasted 'a chicken in every pot' and 'two cars in every garage'.

But by 1930 it all seemed a mirage to the average American. On Thursday, 28 July 1932, soldiers of the United States army had to be called in to break up a demonstration in Washington by desperate out-of-work veterans of that very same army. Four were killed and many wounded. In every American city, unemployed workers lined up at soup kitchens for charity.

The Roaring Twenties

Before Warren Harding was elected President in 1920 he said he wanted a return to 'normalcy'. He meant an America which would lead a normal life and behave in a normal manner. America wanted no part of the revolutions and strikes affecting much of Europe after the War.

By 1929 the United States had become, beyond any shadow of doubt, the richest nation on earth. Several factors helped to create the wealth:
1. Although the American army played a big part in the defeat of Germany, she was only actively involved after April 1917, when President Wilson declared war. For two and a half years, since 1914, American manufacturers had prospered, selling arms to the Allies. Britain and France had borrowed money from the United States Government to pay for these purchases.

Left: Times Square, New York, in the 'boom and bust' years of the 1920s. The plethora of advertisements and cars shows that people had plenty of money to spend.

In a Nutshell

* President Woodrow Wilson plays a leading part in the Paris Peace Conference but the United States Senate refuses to ratify the Treaty; so the United States is not a member of the League of Nations.
* The United States has done well out of the War, selling arms to the Allies in Europe.
* Wages rise, credit (hire purchase) is freely available, sales of consumer goods (cars, radios and washing machines) do well, aided by radio and cinema advertising. Many people speculate on the stock exchange, hoping to make quick profits.
* Farmers do not share in the prosperity. High American customs duties on foreign imports discourage foreigners from buying surplus American crops.
* Blacks, particularly in the American South, are little better off than they were in the days of slavery.
* Fewer immigrants from Europe are allowed into the United States and the Japanese are barred.
* In October 1929 the American stock market slumps. Many shares are worthless. Banks fail; factories shut down; many businesses are bankrupt; the unemployment rate rises to 14 million.
* Millions of out-of-work Americans are destitute and rely on charity.
* Franklin Delano Roosevelt is elected President in 1932 and immediately embarks on his 'New Deal' programme, designed to relieve distress and suffering and restore American prosperity.
* Despite opposition, Roosevelt's New Deal is seen as a success. Americans re-elect him as President in 1936, in 1940 and in 1944!

2. After the War the Americans insisted that these loans be paid back and some of them were, although most were eventually forgotten.
3. In 1922 the Americans introduced the Fordney-McCumber tariff on many foreign imports. The purpose of a tariff is to 'protect' the interests of home producers, whose livelihood might be at risk if foreign products were imported at lower prices than those at home.

The main drawback is that foreign governments usually retaliate by putting high tariffs on goods imported into their countries as well. This happened in the 1920s and especially after 1930 when the Hawley-Smoot Tariff Act raised duties even higher.

American manufacturers did very well as a result of these Fordney-McCumber tariffs. They seemed to be able to sell all the goods they could manufacture.

4. New industries boomed in America. Nearly 6 million cars were sold in 1929 compared with 2 million in 1919. The car manufacturers were good customers for other manufacturers' raw materials. They took four fifths of America's rubber (for tyres), half the sheet glass and about a tenth of the steel.

Other consumer industries also prospered. The American radio industry sold $60 million worth in 1922 and $800 million worth only seven years later in 1929. The same happened with washing machines, electric shavers, vacuum cleaners, gramophones, and gramophone records.

5. Mass production methods, pioneered by car-maker Henry Ford, made the manufacture of many goods much cheaper.

6. Demand for goods was stimulated by advertising. Mail order catalogues, posters, radio and cinema commercials persuaded customers to buy. If you did not have the ready cash you could always borrow the money you needed on hire purchase.

7. Some people even borrowed money from banks to buy shares on the New York Stock Exchange. Shares and stocks were booming. This provided finance for industry and helped big business to expand and prosper. All was well, so long as share prices continued to rise. In 1928 alone, some shares multiplied in value by five times.

8. Workers in industry generally got higher wages at a time when taxes fell; so people had more money in their pockets to spend on cars, domestic appliances, shares, cinema tickets and records.

Poverty in the 1920s

There were many Americans, however, who did not share in the prosperity of the boom years.

The farmers

About a million people left the land in the 1920s. Many were evicted from their farms and smallholdings because they were unable to pay the rent, or keep up with the payments on machinery and buildings they had bought during the War – when the demand for food meant high prices. Prices tumbled after the War when food was plentiful but rents, mortgage repayments, machinery and fertilizer costs rose by an estimated 30 per cent.

Even so, farmers might still have prospered had they been able to sell their surpluses overseas. But the introduction of the Fordney-McCumber tariff penalized foreign manufacturers exporting goods to the United States. When foreign countries earned fewer American dollars from their exports, it meant they had fewer dollars with which to buy American imports such as meat and corn.

Many countries did the same and put tariffs on foreign imports to protect their own farmers and manufacturers. American farmers found it difficult to sell the food they produced. They were too productive. The small or less efficient farmers went bankrupt. Many farm incomes in 1932 were only a third of what they had been some twelve years earlier.

The wife of a Louisiana sharecropper with her daughter, sitting on the steps of a derelict southern mansion, now being used as a doss house for destitute sharecroppers.

A Ku Klux Klan initiation ceremony, 1922.

By the end of the 1920s tempers were rising and there were ugly demonstrations in the Mid-West. Farmers demanded protection. They wanted the Government to buy their surplus grain and livestock in order to keep farm prices high.

The Hawley-Smoot Tariff Act introduced in 1929 made matters worse by imposing even higher tariffs. American trade fell by 50 per cent in the next two years. Wheat prices fell from 233 cents a bushel in 1920 to 32 cents a bushel in 1932.

Black Americans

In the Deep South black people lived in rural slums, worked long hours on the cotton and tobacco plantations for low wages, and suffered the degradation of having to live in a society where they were not treated as equals.

The law failed to protect them from racial discrimination. If they 'didn't know their place' then racial bullies soon reminded them. Lynchings, brandings, tarrings and beatings were common, many of them carried out at night by the nightriders of the Ku Klux Klan.

This was a secret society of white people, usually drawn from the poorest sectors of the community. Many were sharecroppers, poor farmers hit hard by the slump in farm prices after the War. But they had the support, in some southern states, of members of the police force, judges, state senators and congressmen.

The members of the Ku Klux Klan usually met at night beneath a blazing cross. They wore white hoods with slits in them. Their victims also included Jews, Catholics, foreign immigrants and other minority groups.

By 1926 their numbers had grown to several million. But a scandal involving one of the national leaders of the Ku Klux Klan and increasing prosperity helped eventually to lessen their appeal.

The immigrants

Before the First World War the United States had welcomed a million European immigrants each year. After 1918 the United States Government decided to control immigration. Some Americans (eg the trade unions) saw foreign immigrants as a threat to American prosperity and to American jobs.

So despite the welcoming lines by the poet Emma Lazarus on the Statue of Liberty – 'Give me your tired, your poor, your huddled masses yearning to breathe free' – the United States introduced a quota system in 1921 which restricted the number of immigrants each year to 3 per cent of the total of each nationality living in the United States in 1910. A maximum of 357,000 immigrants could be allowed in any one year.

A United States marshal pours bootlegged liquor down the sewers during the days of prohibition.

America in the 1920s

The rise of the automobile

In 1909 the Model T Ford cost $950. Just 15 years later its price had dropped to only $290 and the Ford motor company was producing them at the rate of 7500 cars a day.

The development of cheap motoring for the ordinary worker owed much to the ingenuity of Henry Ford and other motor manufacturers who developed the assembly line. Workers were trained to perform a specific task as a vehicle or engine passed by on the production line. All the cars looked the same but nobody minded.

Soon everyone seemed to have a car, some even putting it ahead of other desirable acquisitions for the home.

Leisure in the 1920s

Motoring became one of the most popular leisure activities in America between the Wars. Americans could now see more of their own country.

Young people found freedom in jazz, ragtime, dancing, smoking, motoring and the cinema. Hollywood film stars influenced the way women dressed, the perfume they used, the manner in which men combed their hair or wore a moustache.

Gangsterism and prohibition

In the Twenties many decent Americans knowingly broke the law when they entered a 'speakeasy' (illegal bar). They were infringing the Volstead Act (named after a Congressman) which had been passed by Congress in 1919 after the 18th Amendment to the American constitution prohibited the sale of liquor (alcohol) in the United States.

Many of the supporters of prohibition came from the small towns of America. They pointed to the evils of drink and the virtues of temperance. They even hoped that by eliminating alcohol they would cut down organized crime!

How wrong they were! Organized crime expanded at a rapid rate when the gangsters moved in and took charge of the illegal supply of alcohol. Law enforcement officers were bribed and city mayors were even put on the payroll of gangsters like Al Capone of Chicago. Capone earned well over $100 million from crime in 1928 alone. When other gangsters tried to muscle in on the racket, they were eliminated. Gangland killings multiplied and cities like Chicago seemed to be lawless.

Capone was eventually sent to prison – for tax evasion! The law seemed unable to bring the ringleaders to heel. Prohibition was eventually repealed in 1933.

The Wall Street Crash

Warning signs

In the summer of 1929 people in the know began to worry whether the boom years could last much longer. After the election of President Hoover, a Republican, people had put even more of their savings and their borrowings into the stock market. Some even mortgaged their houses or their businesses to invest on New York's Wall Street.

As a result many companies were over-valued by the stock market prices. Their factories, resources and profits were not worth as much as the investors seemed to think they were. What was worse American industry was producing more manufactured goods than people could buy. Some experts said as much and forecast that share prices would go down.

So long as the investors had confidence that their money was safely invested and likely to make a profit, there was no call for alarm. It was when some people began to sell their shares – and others started to follow – that the calamity happened.

The Crash

The headlines from the *New York Times* tell their own story. Huge fortunes were lost in a day when the stock market crashed in October 1929. The first crash came on 'Black Thursday', 24 October, when

New York street scene during the Wall Street Crash in 1929. Shareholders wait anxiously for news.

billions of dollars were wiped off the market value of many leading American companies. The papers reported that some investors had committed suicide rather than face financial ruin. But bankers and financiers tried to reassure speculators that their money was safe and that share prices would rise again soon.

But investors panicked. They tried to get out whilst the going was good; so stockbrokers were told to sell shares and get the best price they could. On Tuesday 29th October, the bottom fell out of the market. The shares of some companies became worthless; no one wanted to buy them. Even shares of giant corporations, with enormous assets and millions of dollars worth of property, plunged sharply. All the confidence that had caused the shares to rise in the first place had gone. The New York Stock Exchange was plunged in turmoil; mounted police had to be called in to control the crowds as speculators tried to reach their stockbrokers with orders to sell, sell, sell.

WORST STOCK CRASH STEMMED BY BANKS;
12,894,650–SHARE DAY SWAMPS MARKET;
LEADERS CONFER, FIND CONDITIONS SOUND
FINANCIERS EASE TENSION
LOSSES RECOVERED IN PART
UPWARD TREND START

Wall Street Optimistic After Stormy Day
  New York Times, Friday, 25 October 1929

STOCKS COLLAPSE IN 16,410,030–SHARE DAY,
BUT RALLY AT CLOSE CHEERS BROKERS;
BANKERS OPTIMISTIC, TO CONTINUE AID

240 Issues Lose $15,894,818,894 in Month;
Slump in Full Exchange List Vastly Larger
  New York Times, Wednesday, 30 October 1929

The Great Depression

Collapse

The Wall Street Crash not only proved disastrous for the American economy it precipitated a crisis in almost every country in the world. It did not actually cause the Great Depression because this would almost certainly have happened anyway. But what it did do was to trigger it off – just as the assassination at Sarajevo triggered off the First World War.

As you have seen, most industries were over-valued. Factories (and farms) were producing more goods and foodstuffs than could be sold. People had borrowed huge sums to buy shares, cars and businesses. America had been living on credit.

More speculators committed suicide. Thousands of small businesses collapsed and many banks closed their doors. So even the people who had put their savings into banks rather than into the stock market lost their money. Factories shut their gates. People tightened their belts, fewer luxuries were needed, many more factories closed their gates.

Unemployment

Soon, as you can see from the graph, the numbers of the unemployed rose to record levels. In 1932, 14 million Americans were out of work. Their plight was appalling, since there were no welfare benefits, no unemployment pay. They had to queue in line for handouts from private charities.

A Chicago soup kitchen for the unemployed in 1930. This one was opened by Al Capone, the notorious gangster.

Unemployed workers could be seen in the streets carrying billboards asking for a job. Some towns even put up large signs telling the jobless to move on to another town, since there was no work to be had there. Inevitably there were evictions and families were thrown on to the street.

Around the large cities the new, homeless, poor slept under bridges, in ditches, or in empty railway waggons.

Hoover and the Hoovervilles

Shanty towns sprang up on the outskirts of the major cities, with crude huts built out of waste materials. The unemployed workers who built them, called their settlements *Hoovervilles* as a sarcastic reminder that President Hoover had done nothing, and was doing nothing, to remedy matters or to alleviate distress.

Hoover believed in 'rugged individualism'; in the capacity of any worker to get out of a rut and get rich. This was the 'American dream'. Self-help was all the working man needed.

But to many Americans this was not enough. The boom and the prosperity had been promoted under Republican presidents. 'They got us into this mess, they should get us out again' was how many people saw the Depression.

Hoover did in fact spend government money on projects designed to put the unemployed to work. In December 1930 he got Congress to agree to spend

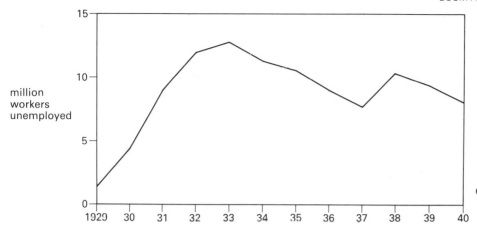

million workers unemployed

The number of unemployed people rose sharply in the United States in the early 1930s, then fell off as Roosevelt's policies took effect.

$116 million for the construction of various public works such as new roads and public buildings.

But still unemployment continued to rise whilst more and more businesses failed. By 1932 the average income was less than two thirds the 1929 figure, and American industry was operating at half its capacity.

A songwriter summed up the effects of the Depression:

'Once I built a railroad, I made it run.
Made it race against time.
Once I built a railroad, now it's done.
Brother can you spare a dime?'

In June 1932 President Hoover belatedly introduced a much bigger relief scheme. A Reconstruction Finance Corporation was founded with the vast sum of $2 billion (ie $2000 million) to be used to provide loans to railways, insurance companies, banks and other organizations in danger of going to the wall for want of capital. But it was too late. By then the American people had had their fill of the Republicans and false promises, such as Hoover's 'Prosperity is just around the corner' (March 1931).

In 1932 these shacks were home to many unemployed families in Hoovertown, on the outskirts of Los Angeles.

President Roosevelt and the New Deal

Ex-President Hoover (left) congratulates President Roosevelt as he becomes leader of the United States in 1933.

Instead, America turned to the Democrats for their salvation. In 1932 Franklin Delano Roosevelt struck a chord when he called for a 'new deal'.

At the Democratic Party Convention in 1932 he talked of 'prophets of a new order of confidence and courage'. He issued a 'call to arms' which would enable the Democrats 'to win in this crusade to restore America to its own people'.

His bounding confidence, despite a severe disability, and cheerful optimism hit home and he was elected President by a convincing majority.

But Roosevelt had many pressing problems to solve when he took office in January 1933. If he had any doubts he did not show them. He told the crowd who listened to his inauguration:

'The only thing we have to fear is fear itself. Nameless, unreasoning, unjustified terror.'

Roosevelt told them he was going to demand from Congress powers as great as those needed in wartime to 'wage war against the emergency'. And he did. His first action was to close all the banks for a few days whilst his advisers decided how to deal with the financial problems facing America. He followed this by putting forward 15 major new laws in the next hundred days. At last, Americans thought, the country is on the move again.

Aims

Roosevelt had three main aims. First he would alleviate distress. Second he would create new jobs. Third he would try to ensure that nothing like this ever happened again. This is why the stock market was reformed. In future shares could not be bought on credit without payment of a substantial deposit.

The Alphabet Agencies

Apart from the Social Security Act of 1935 (see below) which provided welfare benefits, the most lasting and most memorable achievements of the New Deal were the imaginative and far-reaching projects instigated by the Federal Government under the so-called Alphabet Laws. The reason for the title is fairly obvious, as you can see in the panel opposite.

These government agencies and organizations were specifically designed to create new jobs. In this they succeeded. Millions of Americans got jobs under the schemes and millions more regained their confidence in America and 'the American dream'.

Roosevelt faced opposition from many quarters – particularly from American big business. Some said he was a Fascist, and others thought he was a Communist.

Roosevelt faced both criticisms with equanimity. This is what he said in one of his regular broadcasts to the American people.

'It is true that the toes of some people are being stepped on and are going to be stepped on. But these toes belong to the comparative few. A few timid people who fear progress will try to give new and strange names for what we are doing. Sometimes they will call it Fascism and sometimes Communism and sometimes Regimentation and sometimes Socialism. But in so doing they are trying to make very complex and theoretical something that is really very simple and very practical. I believe in practical explanations and in practical policies.'

THE ALPHABET AGENCIES

AAA Agricultural Adjustment Act 1933

The aim was to lower farm production and so cause prices to rise, since it was the food surplus which was keeping them well below the pre-war level. Farmers agreed to plough up growing crops and to kill off young livestock in return for cash; 6 million piglets were killed in 1933 alone.

As a result the average farmer's income rose two and a half times between 1932 and 1935. Critics who hated government interference in industry or agriculture, denounced the Act. In 1936 the Supreme Court ruled that it was unconstitutional.

Roosevelt replaced it with other Acts which paid farmers to grow different crops.

CCC Civilian Conservation Corps 1933

This was one of the most popular schemes and Roosevelt's favourite. Unemployed youths volunteered to join the Conservation Corps, where they were sent away to temporary camps to care for the American countryside. There they were paid a wage and given accommodation and meals. In return they laid forest trails, built forest roads, sprayed pests, and planted 200 million trees.

Over 2 million boys took part in the scheme, wearing the green CCC uniform. Most enjoyed the experience and were fitter and healthier as a result. But trade union leaders disapproved, some claiming it was Fascism – and similar to the activities of the Hitler Youth.

CWA Civil Works Administration 1933

Like the Works Progress Administration which took over much of its work, the CWA put the unemployed to work on projects such as dams, roads, schools and other public buildings.

FERA Federal Emergency Relief Administration 1933

This was a temporary measure providing unemployment benefit or dole money. It was not much but it helped to alleviate dire poverty.

FHA Federal Housing Administration 1934

This provided government loans to help householders buy, repair or improve their homes.

FSA Farm Security Administration 1937

This provided government loans to help farm-workers and tenant farmers.

NLRB National Labor Relations Board 1935

This Board was established to deal with strikes and disputes between the workers (labor) and the employers. In its first two years it successfully resolved 75 per cent of the disputes it reviewed.

Young men on their way to a New Deal work camp in California where they will work in factories or on public works projects, such as building roads.

NRA National Recovery Administration 1933

This was another popular scheme, since it aimed to improve working conditions in factories, encouraging employers to set minimum wages, to eliminate sweated (ie cheap) labour and to recognize trade unions.

Firms were encouraged to agree to codes of behaviour. In return they could display the NRA Blue Eagle badge with its slogan 'We Do Our Part'. But some of the major companies refused to take part or comply with the codes. So in the end NRA had only a limited success.

Many employers were opposed to the growing strength of the American Labor Movement and refused to recognize the unions. During the 1930s many factory sit-ins and strikes were organized. These demonstrations were sometimes broken up by private armies of strike-breakers organized by the employers.

PWA Public Works Administration 1933

This scheme undertook various public works, such as slum clearance, until most of its work was incorporated in the WPA.

REA Rural Electrification Administration 1935

As its name suggests, it was set up to help build power lines to cover parts of rural America not already served by the private electricity companies.

TVA Tennessee Valley Authority 1933

This is probably the best known of all the New Deal schemes. It was set up to solve the problems caused by the Tennessee River and its tributaries. In this area of the American South the rivers frequently flooded. Soil had been eroded from the valleys because trees no longer protected the river banks. There was little industry and the people were very poor. Few homes had electricity.

TVA was set up to:
(a) control flooding;
(b) provide cheap hydro-electricity;
(c) improve navigation on the rivers;
(d) control soil erosion;
(e) plant trees;
(f) improve living conditions.

It achieved all of these aims. Large areas were saved from soil erosion; 33 dams were built; forests were planted; lakes created; hydro-electric power stations constructed; new roads and factories built. The living standards of the people of the area rose dramatically and tourists have been attracted to the lakes and forests. The Tennessee has been brought under control and it is possible to send goods by barge along the valley.

An interesting result of TVA was the fact that its plentiful supply of cheap electricity made it possible for the United States to manufacture the atom bomb.

WPA Works Progress Administration 1935

This took over much of the work of the CWA and PWA (see above). It was responsible for the construction of hydro-electric dams (such as Boulder Dam, which the

Above: Tennessee Valley dam in the United States.

Republicans later renamed Hoover Dam), bridges, airports, power stations, sewers, waterworks and many public buildings (including 70 per cent of all new schools built in this period).

These public works improved America, and at the same time employed 8 million workers, who would otherwise have been unemployed. But again the critics denounced them, particularly employers who now found the unemployed reluctant to accept low rates of pay to get a job.

Below: Putting unemployed Americans to work – planting trees in Arkansas.

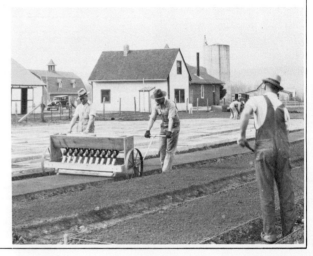

Roosevelt's Other Achievements and Failures

Roosevelt persuaded Congress to pass many other laws designed to improve living conditions, to eliminate injustices and to come to the aid of those unable to help themselves. For instance, the Social Security Act of 1935 set up an unemployment insurance scheme for workers. It provided social welfare benefits for the handicapped, and it introduced a compulsory retirement pension scheme. All of these were long overdue in the United States.

Roosevelt did not get everything his own way. In 1936, as you have seen, the Supreme Court ruled that the Agricultural Adjustment Act was unconstitutional. Although he got round this Roosevelt was disturbed that the law courts should be able to over-rule the laws, which he, as the elected President, and Congress had enacted. He attributed this to the fact that they were old men who still lived in 'the horse and buggy days'.

After his re-election in 1936 he proposed a law which would compel Supreme Court judges to retire at 70 and in the meantime proposed to increase their number (ie with judges sympathetic to the New Deal). But Congress turned the bill down, with popular approval, since for all its faults the Supreme Court was able to curb the power of the President if he tried to go above the law or the constitution.

Roosevelt's Foreign Policy

Relations with Japan in the Pacific
The United States and Japan were at loggerheads for most of the time President Roosevelt was in office. The United States Government protested in 1931 when Japan invaded Manchuria (see Chapter 7) but did nothing concrete to back up its warning. In 1937 the Japanese invaded China again and relations between Japan and the United States deteriorated once more, particularly when an American naval vessel was sunk by Japanese planes. In 1939 the sale of arms to Japan was stopped.

Relations with Europe
Isolationism in America (see Explanatory Notes) did not mean that Americans approved of the aggressive moves made by Hitler to overturn the Treaty of Versailles (see Chapter 9). But they did not want to get involved in another war in Europe. Roosevelt intervened by sending telegrams to Hitler and Mussolini during the Czech crises of 1938 and 1939 but since they were not backed by anything stronger than American disapproval, they were ignored.

President Roosevelt taking office in 1945.

Roosevelt

Franklin Delano Roosevelt was born in 1883, the son of wealthy and prominent parents. He trained as a lawyer and became a member of President Wilson's administration during the First World War.

In 1921 he was struck down with poliomyelitis and spent the rest of his life as a cripple. But this did not deter him from standing and winning the election for the Presidency in 1932. Subsequently the American people elected Roosevelt to the Presidency for a record four terms of office; so he was President from 1933 to 1945.

Although he was crippled he did not let that stand in his way. In particular he was determined to act with vigour and decisiveness and do something positive about the problems caused by the Great Depression.

His first hundred days in office (1933) produced a rich array of measures designed to put American industry and agriculture back on its feet and to help cure the problem of unemployment.

In foreign policy he was less successful, since Americans were fearful that they too might be drawn unwillingly into the war which now seemed inevitable in Europe. After the Japanese attack on the American naval base at Pearl Harbor in 1941, however, Hitler declared war on the United States.

Roosevelt threw himself into his new role as a war leader and prosecuted the American war effort with determination and confidence. He spared no effort to reach an agreement with the other Allies and attended the wartime conferences with Churchill and Stalin (see Chapter 11).

But his health deteriorated and he died in April 1945 only weeks away from victory in Europe.

On 1 May 1937 Roosevelt signed the Neutrality Act which prevented the sale of American arms and munitions to countries which were deemed to be at war. In addition, the Act had a 'cash and carry' clause which stated that any warring nations buying goods which were permitted must (a) pay *cash* for them immediately (b) *carry* them in their own merchant ships.

After Hitler's aggressive acts of 1938 and March 1939, Roosevelt tried to get Congress to amend the Neutrality Law but was rebuffed. It was only when Hitler invaded Poland in September 1939 that Congress agreed to repeal the ban on arms sales to countries at war – much to the relief of the British and French Governments.

The War divided American opinion between those who wanted the United States to intervene and those who still favoured isolationism (like Colonel Lindbergh the famous aviator). Although the time was not yet ripe for American participation in the War, Roosevelt gave Britain invaluable material support by supplying arms on credit and by stepping up the production of armaments.

The Good Neighbour policy

The United States has always been conscious of its role as the most powerful nation in the New World. In 1823 President Monroe told Congress that European powers were no longer free to interfere in American affairs (whether North or South America). These issues were the exclusive concern of Americans. The Monroe Doctrine, as it is called, has been upheld by the United States ever since.

President Roosevelt extended the idea even further by proposing the 'Good Neighbour' policy. He recognized that all the countries of North and South America were equal and that they should therefore respect each other's rights without attempting to interfere. This policy was also called Pan-Americanism (*pan* meaning 'all the members of'). At a conference in Lima (in Peru) in 1938 the 21 countries meeting there agreed that common action was to be taken if any member state was threatened.

This pen and ink cartoon about the United States' policy of isolationism was drawn by Clifford Berryman and was published in September 1938.

Explanatory Notes

Isolationism is the term that was used to describe the foreign policy which most Americans wanted their Government to follow between the Wars.

In 1918 Americans had good reason to wonder what had been achieved in Europe during the First World War and why a large number of American soldiers had had to die to help resolve a dispute over 5000 kilometres away.

After the War Americans seemed to want to isolate themselves from the problems of Europe. They could see no good reason why the United States should have any political role to play in Europe. America should get on with her everyday business, not worry about revolutions, Fascism, general strikes and the other problems which seemed to bedevil the Europeans.

President Wilson had played a leading part in founding the League of Nations but his fellow Americans preferred to see themselves in isolation away from Europe. The newly elected Republican President Warren Harding came to power with the campaign promise 'America First'.

Although the United States refused to join the League of Nations, and for much of the next twenty years tried to ignore the growing war clouds over Europe, she could not entirely ignore the problems of the world (as you have already seen in this book). She played a major part in resolving Germany's financial problems with the Dawes Plan and she helped to antagonize the Japanese military with the plans which were made for limiting the navies of Britain, America and Japan at the Washington Conference (see page 92).

But isolationism helped to delay America's entry into the Second World War, until over two years after Hitler's attack on Poland.

Exercises

1. Explain what is meant by isolationism? Why did the United States adopt this policy at the end of the First World War? Did she cut herself off completely from Europe?
2. What were the boom years of the 1920s? How did they lay the foundations for the Wall Street Crash in 1929?
3. What did President Hoover mean when he talked about (a) 'a chicken in every pot', (b) 'rugged individualism', (c) 'prosperity is just around the corner'?
4. What caused the Great Depression in America? What were its effects on the American people?
5. Write brief notes about the following:
(a) Prohibition
(b) Al Capone and organized crime
(c) Henry Ford and mass production
(d) The Ku Klux Klan
(e) Hoovervilles
6. Answer each part of this question separately. What action did each of the following take, and with what success, to solve the problems created by the Depression: (a) President Hoover (b) President Roosevelt?
7. Explain carefully what was meant by the New Deal. What were the Alphabet Agencies and how successful were they in creating new jobs and bringing new prosperity to the United States?
8. Explain the significance of each of these themes in American history in the inter-war period:
(a) The Tennessee Valley Authority;
(b) The 'Good Neighbour' policy.
9. Write a brief biography of Franklin Delano Roosevelt and say whether you approve of the things he did as President of the United States before 1939. What were his main achievements? What were his failures?
10. Why did America not join with Britain and France in declaring war on Germany in September 1939? What action did she take instead?

Further Activities

1. Start a project on the boom and bust years in the United States between 1919 and 1929. Write notes on each of the following topics and see if you can find pictures to illustrate your work:
(a) Isolationism
(b) The boom years
(c) Jazz
(d) Mass production
(e) Advertisements
(f) Crime
(g) Prohibition
(h) The Ku Klux Klan

CHAPTER 7

The Far East in Turmoil

On 16 October 1934 Mao Zedong and a large army of Red Chinese soldiers, in grave danger of their lives, began a gruelling Long March across the mountains of western China. They were evading the Guomindang, the government forces of Chiang Kaishek, who had threatened to exterminate them.

Just over a year later, with much depleted forces, Mao's Red Army reached comparative safety at Yanan in the north.

Part of the Red Army on the Long March after its safe arrival in Yanan.

This epic journey took place at a time when part of their homeland (Manchuria) had been invaded by Japan – China's aggressive, but much smaller, neighbour to the east. Instead of joining forces to expel the invader, the Red Army Chinese fought the Guomindang Chinese.

Yet eight years earlier they had been allies on the Northern Expedition to unify China. About two years later (1937) they buried their differences again and did their best to stop the Japanese conquering the whole of China.

The war with Japan eventually became part of the Second World War, after the Japanese launched a sudden, unforeseen attack on the American naval base of Pearl Harbor in December 1941. By this time millions of people had already suffered and hundreds of thousands had died in the Far East.

Japan in the 1920s

In 1914 Japan joined her British ally in declaring war on Germany and took over German claims in mainland China – the naval base at Jiaozhou and the German concessions in Shandong Province. In 1915 she presented the Chinese Government with the 'Twenty One Demands', to confirm these rights and to make new demands for privileges and concessions in Manchuria in particular, and in the rest of China in general. The Shandong concessions were

The Shandong concessions.

MANCHURIA

Jiaozhou

Shandong

JAPAN

0   500 km

In a Nutshell

* At the Paris Peace Conference in 1919 Japan is given concessions in Shandong Province in China, formerly held by the Germans. The news outrages many Chinese and leads to the growth of the revolutionary May the Fourth Movement.
* Japan has profited from the First World War. Western ideas gain ground in the 1920s – to the fury of the army. But the Depression causes much distress in Japan after 1929.
* In China the Guomindang Party becomes strong under Sun Yixian's leadership. Communists join as Sun Yixian prepares to unify China by defeating the warlords in the north. But Sun dies in 1925.
* His successor Chiang Kaishek leads the successful Northern Expedition in 1926 and captures Nanjing and Shanghai in 1927 and Beijing in 1928.
* Chiang Kaishek tries to eliminate the Chinese Communists. Mao Zedong and other leaders escape. They start the Jiangxi Soviet in southern China in 1928, from where they harass the Guomindang forces.
* Militarism gains ground in Japan – especially after the shooting of Prime Minister Hamaguchi in 1930.
* The Japanese army invades Manchuria in 1931. The League of Nations protests but no positive action is taken.
* Chiang Kaishek offers little resistance to the Japanese invasion of Manchuria but tries to exterminate the Jiangxi Communists instead. In 1934 Mao Zedong leads the Communists to safety on the Long March.
* The Communists and Guomindang unite against Japan a few months before the Japanese invasion of China in July 1937. This Sino-Japanese war is still being fought when the Japanese attack Pearl Harbor in 1941.

granted to Japan under the terms of the Treaty of Versailles, much to the annoyance of China. Japan also wanted the Covenant, setting up the League of Nations, to include a statement guaranteeing racial equality. This the other nations refused to do, some (Australia and the United States) because their policy on immigration discriminated against non-whites. Whatever the reason, it provided Japan with a genuine grievance and one which most of the Japanese people rightly resented.

But Japan had made money out of the War. She had increased her overseas trade at the expense of the Allies, her merchant fleet and navy had been enlarged, her shipbuilding industry had expanded rapidly, and she had gained lucrative contracts manufacturing arms for the Allies.

Some ships of the Japanese navy in Tokyo Bay in the 1920s.

The Washington Conference

By 1918 it was obvious that the British navy was no longer the undisputed mistress of the seas. The United States navy was nearly as big and that of the Japanese ranked third in the world. The United States wanted to ensure that the Open Door policy – guaranteeing equal trading rights in China and the Far East – would be generally accepted. At the same time she wanted to protect existing interests.

A conference, called by the United States, met in Washington in November 1921 with delegates from the United States, Japan, Britain, Italy, France, Portugal, the Netherlands, Belgium and China.

It decided to limit the navies of Britain, the United States and Japan according to the ratio five to five to three. This meant that for every five warships in the Royal Navy, the Americans could also have five and the Japanese three. In addition, the Conference agreed that no new naval bases were to be built in the Far East.

These agreements especially favoured the Japanese because:
(a) her navy was deployed exclusively in the Pacific whilst those of the United States and Britain operated throughout the world;
(b) existing naval bases on the Japanese mainland ensured continued Japanese superiority in southeast Asia.

In return Japan agreed under pressure to renounce her claims to Shandong Province in China and all agreed that China's independence and territory should be guaranteed (the Nine Power Treaty of 1922). Under the terms of the Four Power Treaty, the United States, Japan, Britain and France agreed to consult with one another in the event of any act of aggression in the area, or if their interests came under threat, from another power.

The Rise of Militarism in Japan

Democracy and Western ideas

After 1918 Japan seemed to be strengthening her democratic system. In 1925 every male adult was given the right to vote and political parties flourished, including those of the left. But there were limits to political freedom and the enactment of the Peace Preservation Law effectively suppressed the budding Japanese Communist Party.

People in the West were much encouraged that Japanese politicians now seemed committed to seeking peace rather than war. This was one reason why the Washington Conference reached agreement on limiting naval power and why Japan gave up her claims to Shandong Province.

Western ideas continued to influence the Japanese people. Classical music became popular, more people began to wear Western clothes, golf courses were built, jazz came to Japan. When an appalling earthquake destroyed Yokohama and much of Tokyo in 1923, the old wooden buildings were replaced with fine new buildings of steel and concrete.

The old traditions of Japan seemed to be fading. In the 1920s the last stronghold of the *samurai* warrior tradition was in the Japanese army. Yet the armed forces were contracting in size, not expanding, as most army officers would have liked.

In 1926 the old emperor died and was succeeded by the *Showa* Emperor Hirohito. *Showa* meant 'Enlightened Peace'. But it was not to be. Distrust of liberal-minded politicians grew – particularly in the years of the Great Depression after 1929.

Reasons why Japan turned to militarism

1. The politicians brought little credit to the Diet, the Japanese parliament. There were fights between rival groups and bribery and corruption among officials and politicians was commonplace. As a result ordinary Japanese had little reason to respect their elected assembly. In any case many of the older Japanese disliked the idea of democracy, preferring action rather than debate.

2. Japan was badly hit by the Great Depression after 1929, since her industrial strength depended on exports, which were halved between 1929 and 1931. The decline in trade hit most workers in Japan, particularly the peasant farmers who cultivated silk and the factory workers who turned it into yarn or cloth. Silk was a luxury; so it was inevitable that demand would fall sharply in a depression. Many peasants suffered a two-thirds cut in income. Without exports Japan could not buy the imported goods she needed. Desperate times called for desperate measures. Workers tried strike action, riots and demonstrations.

3. Militant army officers had other plans to resolve the crisis. Many of them came from peasant families and resented the circumstances which had impoverished their relatives. Japan was too small and had too few raw materials (for example, coal, oil, and iron ore) to support the growing population. To some Japanese the answer was obvious – she needed 'living space', just what Hitler thought Germany needed. But:

(a) Unlike Europeans from overcrowded Europe,

Japanese women holding a protest meeting against the low wages received by women factory-workers.

Japanese nationals could not emigrate to California or to Australia.

(b) The agreements signed by Japan's postwar politicians had stopped the development of an Asiatic empire, which would have allowed Japanese emigration to China.

What is more, many Japanese resented European and US influence in the Far East, an area which they believed was Japan's sphere of influence.

Street scene in Tokyo in 1932. The theatre on the right is built in traditional Japanese style, but the new buildings show much Western influence.

Military dictatorship

In 1930 the Japanese Prime Minister, Osachi Hamaguchi, signed the London Naval Treaty. This extended the terms agreed at the Washington Conference and limited the tonnage of other warships.

Extremists in the Japanese army and navy saw this as treason. They regarded Hamaguchi as unfit to advise the Emperor and an assassin gunned him down at Tokyo Railway Station and Hamaguchi died a few months later. Two years later Prime Minister Tsuyoshi Inukai was also assassinated.

In 1936 a group of young officers attempted to stage a coup. Several cabinet ministers were assassinated but the Tokyo Revolt was crushed by senior army officers and the ringleaders were executed. Yet it demonstrated clearly that the military controlled Japan, despite the fact that civilians usually headed the Government. The army derived its authority from the Emperor and could bypass the politicians. Ultimate power lay in their hands and civilians were powerless to go against their wishes. Those who did seemed to die at the assassin's hand.

Military influence

In the 1930s the influence of the army and navy began to penetrate every corner of Japanese life. Children and young people were brainwashed into accepting war as normal and military strength as right. Army officers taught in schools. Children were given training in the martial arts and taught the supposed virtues of war. Even young children were shown how to march and to salute. To die for the Emperor, and for Japan, was portrayed as noble and heroic.

Military parades, martial music, flags and propaganda put the country in a militaristic mood. The military leadership controlled the press, the cinema and the radio. The successful invasions of Manchuria (1931) and central China (1937), and the seeming inability, or unwillingness, of the Western powers to intervene, stirred national pride and added further fuel to the arguments of those who planned a Japanese empire in Asia. Japan's military strength grew as the country spent more and more of its budget (over two thirds) on rearmament and defence.

China before 1923

The 1911 Revolution

China had also seen considerable changes since the early years of the twentieth century. In 1911 a revolution, guided by Sun Yixian, helped to end the old Manchu Dynasty. But the effective leader was Yuan Shikai, the strong man of China, who became President in 1912, backed by a powerful army.

He established his capital at Beijing in the north. The leaders of the revolution had intended that China would have a democratic system of government but Yuan Shikai soon dispensed with elections and tried to assume the title of emperor.

Sun Yixian in 1923.

The Fourth May Protest
Movement in Beijing,
1919.

The warlords

During Yuan Shikai's lifetime he exercised loose control over the other military commanders in China, but his death in 1916 left China without effective government. Military leaders ruled different parts of China as warlords and their private armies controlled most of China.

It was almost as if this vast country had been divided into a number of separate kingdoms. The warlords fought among themselves. Some were little more than bandits, administering rough justice. One was a Christian who claimed to have baptized a troop of his men with a hosepipe! Their followers often lived off the land. Peasants were heavily taxed, property and food were sometimes stolen, young men press-ganged into the private armies.

Sun Yixian

Sun Yixian opposed this betrayal of the revolution. The Guomindang Party which he helped to found in 1912 was banned by Yuan Shikai in 1913 but later re-established in Guangzhou in southern China. It was here, in 1917, that Sun Yixian formed a rival government to the official government in Beijing, but with no greater success in curbing the power of the warlords. In fact he had to have the protection of a warlord himself.

The May the Fourth Movement

Despite its inability to govern China properly, the Beijing Government declared war on Germany and Austria in 1917, hoping to counter Japanese claims to Shandong after the War. But in 1918 the Chinese prime minister negotiated a large loan from Japan and was in no position to argue when Japan got most of Germany's territorial rights in China at Versailles in 1919.

This infuriated the Chinese people and on 4 May 1919 outraged students in Beijing led an angry demonstration against the Government. The demonstrations spread to other parts of China, encouraged by political opponents of the regime. The strength of these protests forced the Government to refuse to sign the Versailles Treaty.

The May the Fourth Movement reawakened the revolutionary spirit in the Chinese, dormant or suppressed during the rule of the warlords. It made ordinary Chinese more receptive to the new Communist ideas which were spreading from Bolshevik Russia.

The influence of the Bolshevik Revolution

Lenin proved that Communists could provide a government of the people. Trotsky and other Bolsheviks were keen to export Communism to other lands; so the Russians offered the Chinese help. They helped to form the Chinese Communist Party in 1921 and two of its founder members – Mao Zedong and Zhou Enlai – later became the outstanding leaders of Communist China when they came to power in 1949.

Sun Yixian was not a Communist. His own policy was expressed in the Three Principles:
(1) Democracy – free elections
(2) Nationalism – China for the Chinese
(3) Socialism – the peasants should own the land

95

The Guomindang

Russian assistance

Sun Yixian accepted Russian offers of assistance in building up the strength of the Guomindang. In particular, he needed military help to organize an army capable of defeating the warlords in northern China and of bringing unity to the country. Only then would the country be strong enough to rid itself of foreign influence and eject the Japanese.

Accordingly, picked members of the Guomindang were dispatched to Russia to receive training from the Red Army's experts. Chiang Kaishek was one of these officers and on his return took charge of a military academy for Guomindang officers near Guangzhou.

A Russian expert, called Michael Borodin, helped Sun Yixian re-organize the Guomindang into an effective Party by creating small groups of activists, called cells. In 1924 members of China's Communist Party were allowed to join the Guomindang.

But preparations for a push against the northern warlords received a setback with the premature death of Sun Yixian in 1925.

The Northern Expedition

Chiang Kaishek was the obvious choice as leader of the expedition against the warlords. But he was a right-wing member of the Guomindang and distrusted the Communists. However, he needed their help; so Mao Zedong and other Communist leaders joined the expedition and formed the first United Front. They organized peasant and worker revolts in advance of the Guomindang armies.

By September 1926 Chiang Kaishek's troops had occupied Hankou and Wuhan. In the spring of 1927 they took Shanghai and Nanjing.

The break with the Communists

It was at this juncture that Chiang Kaishek decided to deal a mortal blow to the Communists in the Guomindang. He felt strong enough to assert his authority now and had every reason to believe there might be a Russian-backed plot to overthrow him once he completed the conquest of China. In any case his right-wing views, and the support he got from wealthy landowners and businessmen, made him suspect the motives of Mao Zedong and other Communists in stirring up peasant and worker revolts.

The Shanghai massacre began when some of the Guomindang soldiers, aided by members of Shanghai's secret societies (old friends of Chiang Kaishek), rounded up Communists, trade union leaders and Communist sympathizers on 12 April 1927. Hundreds, possibly thousands, were executed and only a few, including Zhou Enlai, escaped the death squads.

Street clash in April 1927 in Shanghai. The soldiers are shooting at gunmen in the windows opposite.

The Communists in retreat

The Chinese Communists were in a dilemma. Lenin's successful Bolshevik Revolution seemed to suggest that the Chinese Revolution, when it came, would start in industrial cities like Shanghai.

But Mao Zedong argued that China was a land of peasants rather than industrial cities. He urged his comrades to concentrate their strength and build up support among the peasants.

In 1928 he joined Chu De and other Communist leaders in seeking refuge on a plateau in the Jinggang Mountains of southern China. Here they established the Chinese Soviet Republic in Jiangxi Province in 1929; and in 1931 Mao was elected Chairman of the Jiangxi Soviet Government and Chu De became Commander in Chief of the Red Army.

Chiang Kaishek's Government

Meanwhile Chiang Kaishek had turned his attention to the conquest of the remaining parts of China and entered Beijing in 1928. He defeated other warlords and made contact with men like Zhang Xueliang, the warlord of Manchuria – often known as the Young Marshal, to distinguish him from his father, who had been killed by assassins working for the Japanese.

Chiang Kaishek made Nanjing the new capital city of China. His Guomindang Government was recognized by major world powers as the genuine government of China and it looked as if Chiang Kaishek might achieve Sun Yixian's ambition of a united China under Guomindang leadership.

Map of the Northern Expedition.

Chiang Kaishek

General Chiang Kaishek was born in 1887 the son of a wealthy farmer. He joined the army, trained to become an officer in Japan, and later played an active part in the successful Chinese Revolution of 1911 which overthrew the Manchu Emperor. He joined the Guomindang Party soon after it was formed and became one of Sun Yixian's most trusted officers.

In 1922 he saved Sun Yixian's life and was rewarded with the post of commander of the Guomindang military academy. When Sun Yixian died in 1925, Chiang Kaishek took command of the Guomindang forces and led the Northern Expedition to subdue the warlords of northern China.

During the Second World War he was treated as one of the Big Five Allied leaders, even though his control of China was far from complete. At the end of the War, America helped him to dominate China after the Japanese surrender.

But the long-standing feud with the Communists erupted into civil war once more in 1946. Mao Zedong controlled the countryside and Chiang Kaishek was eventually forced to flee with his supporters to the island of Taiwan off the Chinese mainland, where he died in 1975.

But although he introduced a number of reforms, built roads and railways, and helped to modernize that part of China near the mouths of the Chang Jiang and Huang He, he failed to realize the hopes of Guomindang supporters who expected him to fulfil Sun Yixian's Three Principles.

He did not unify China, he established a one-party system with himself as military dictator, and he did not improve the lot of the industrial workers or of the peasants who remained landless and oppressed by the landlords.

97

Guomindang campaign against Mao Zedong's Communists in about 1930.

The Jiangxi Chinese Soviet Republic

Soviets

Mao's policy was to establish soviets throughout China, which would later be the foundation stones of the Communist Revolution. The most renowned of these soviets was Mao's own headquarters amid the Jinggang Mountains in Jiangxi Province. Mao thought it an ideal base from which to expand and build up the strength of the Red Army and develop friendly relations with the peasants. Mao always believed that great things could have small beginnings. In 1930 he wrote an article entitled 'A Single Spark Can Start A Prairie Fire'.

Mao's methods paid off. In 1929 the Communists had only the support of about 20,000 people (half of them soldiers). By 1934 there were 200,000 soldiers in the Red Army and the Communists could point to the support they got from about 10 million of the Chinese people, although this was only a tiny proportion of China's total population of 500 million. By the early 1930s the Communists had founded about 15 soviets throughout China, besides the Jiangxi Soviet.

Te extermination campaigns

The existence of these soviets was obviously something that Chiang Kaishek could never tolerate. His Northern Expedition had aimed to destroy the power of the warlords. It would have been illogical to stand by and see the Communists establish soviets in their place.

Accordingly he set out to eliminate the Communist threat in a series of extermination campaigns. But although his forces heavily outnumbered the Red Army, his Guomindang soldiers had little initial success. This was because Mao Zedong's Red Army used **guerilla** tactics to overcome the enemy forces sent against them (see the Explanatory Notes below).

Mao's soldiers made friends with the peasants and encouraged them to hate and oppose the Guomindang forces. Chiang Kaishek's troops fell into Communist ambushes and booby traps, assisted by peasants, keen to revenge themselves on the Guomindang forces who stole their food and destroyed their homes. Large numbers of Chiang Kaishek's soldiers were captured and many volunteered to join the Red Army. Thousands of rifles and other weapons were also seized.

When the Japanese invaded Manchuria in 1931 there was a lull in the fighting (see opposite) but in 1932 Chiang Kaishek launched a new campaign with a vast army of 500,000 men.

His German advisers recommended a change of tactics. So this time his soldiers were grouped in much larger units and the Red Army found it difficult to use the tactics of guerilla warfare against them. When they tried conventional warfare (against Mao's advice) the results were disastrous.

The area controlled by Mao's Jiangxi Soviet got smaller and smaller as the Guomindang troops started to surround the area. Chiang Kaishek intended to starve them out or beat them on the battlefield.

At a historic meeting in October 1934 the ruling Communist Party leadership decided to evacuate the Jiangxi Soviet. On 16 October they left, after first loading weapons and valuables on to mules, ponies and donkeys. Over 100,000 people departed on what proved to be one of the greatest journeys of survival in world history.

Japanese soldier-settlers
in Manchuria, marching
to the fields.

The Japanese Invasion of Manchuria in 1931

Manchuria in northern China had rich reserves of the raw materials needed by Japan, including grain, coal and iron ore. Ever since the 1900s, Japanese business interests had worked hard to develop these resources as a result of rights and concessions granted to Japan under the terms of various treaties. Dalian had been developed as a modern port and the Japanese had built the South Manchurian Railway, which they controlled with the aid of a Japanese army stationed in southern Manchuria.

The Japanese hoped to make Manchuria part of the Japanese empire. But their plans were thwarted when it became obvious that Zhang Xueliang – the Young Marshal, the warlord who controlled Manchuria – was about to acknowledge the authority of Chiang Kaishek as leader of China. What would happen to Japan's legitimate business interests if the Guomindang Government controlled Manchuria?

Sun Yixian had promised to rid China of all foreign influences and by 1931 Chiang Kaishek had already been successful in persuading European powers to relinquish many of the concessions they held. The Japanese felt they had too much to lose if the Guomindang cancelled Japan's business interests in Manchuria or if China used its coal and iron ore for her own industries.

Japanese army officers in Manchuria decided to strike first. They plotted to take over the country but the Japanese Government, hearing of the plan, sent an officer to order the army *not* to attack. He deliberately delayed handing over his orders until *after* a bomb explosion blew up part of the railway line on 18 September 1931.

The Japanese army immediately used this as an excuse to march on Shenyang and occupy the whole of Manchuria. The speed and efficiency of their takeover left no doubt that the operation had been planned in advance, and the bomb attack staged to provide a 'legitimate' excuse. They even installed the former Chinese Emperor as the puppet (figure-head) ruler of their newly independent state of Manchukuo. But this attempt to make it look as if the Manchurians were merely seeking independence fooled no one.

Chiang Kaishek's Government in Nanjing could do very little to help the Manchurians, apart from making a complaint to the League of Nations. The Guomindang army could have been used to confront the Japanese in Manchuria but this risked all-out war with Japan. Chiang Kaishek preferred to concentrate his forces against the Communists instead, so the Japanese went unpunished. The Chinese did boycott Japanese goods, however, as a sign of their anger.

The League of Nations sent a team to investigate the Chinese complaint about Japanese aggression. Japan was condemned and ordered to leave Manchuria forthwith, although none of the member nations was prepared to back its condemnation of Japanese aggression with force.

The Japanese Government might well have complied with the order – had they been able to control the army. Their failure to do so paved the way for the Japanese invasion of China in 1937 and the development of a military regime in Tokyo.

In any event Japan left the League of Nations in the spring of 1933 and provided Hitler and Mussolini with concrete evidence of the inability of the League to combat aggression.

Above: China 1936 – a political speaker addresses a meeting to commemorate The Long March.

The Long March

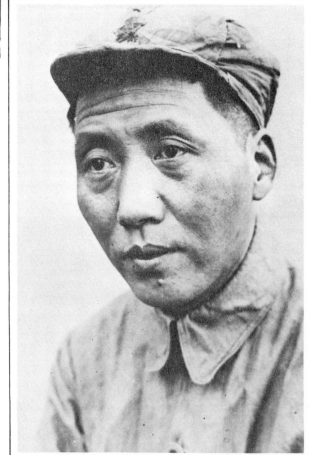

'The Red Army does not fear the difficulties of the Long March.
The thousand rivers and hundred mountains are but routine.'

These lines from a poem by Mao Zedong were translated by Andres D. Onate. The poem describes the ordeal which Mao Zedong's Red Army went through in 1934–35 to avoid extermination by a much larger army led by Chiang Kaishek. Only 30,000 of Mao's original army of 100,000 Chinese Communist soldiers, who left Jiangxi in October 1934, managed to reach journey's end at Yanan in northern China a year later.

The marchers took 368 days to cover the 10,000-kilometre journey. For most of that time they fought running battles with Chiang Kaishek's Nationalist army, the Guomindang. They rested on only 44 days, covering a distance which averaged well over 30 kilometres each day, not counting delays caused by major battles en route.

It has been estimated that they climbed and crossed five snow-capped mountain ranges, to say

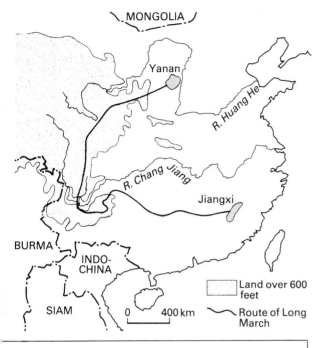

Left: The route of the Communists' Long March through China, 1934–35.

nothing of thirteen other ranges of hills or mountains. They crossed twenty-four major rivers, including the turbulent Chang Jiang – one of the world's greatest rivers.

On one occasion the only possible route across the surging torrent of the Chang Jiang was over a rusty old chain bridge guarded by an enemy machine gun unit. To make matters worse many of the planks in the bridge had been removed by the Guomindang.

Scores of Red Army soldiers crossed over, swinging from hand to hand, whilst their comrades returned the machine gun fire. Several fell into the river deep below but eventually one of the soldiers managed to silence the enemy with a hand grenade.

At last the Red Army reached safety in Yanan, a Communist stronghold in the north-west of China. Here Mao Zedong trained agents (called the cadres) to spread Communism to the people. He wrote training manuals which they could use and bided his time waiting for Chiang Kaishek's next move.

The War with Japan 1937–41

The Xian incident
Chiang Kaishek patched up his differences with Mao Zedong and the Communists in 1937. The circumstances surrounding this change of heart are shrouded in mystery.

In November 1936 he planned yet another extermination campaign to wipe out Mao's Communists. He therefore ordered Zhang Xueliang – the Young Marshal who had been driven out of Manchuria by the Japanese – to attack the Communists at Yanan. Zhang refused, so Chiang Kaishek flew to Xian to reason with him.

But Zhang wanted his revenge on the Japanese. Mao's forces could unite with the Guomindang to force the Japanese out of his native Manchuria. He sent his troops to kidnap Chiang Kaishek and then persuaded the Communists to send Zhou Enlai from Yanan to negotiate peace terms between the two sides.

Chiang Kaishek had no choice but to agree that Mao's Communists would be allowed to stay at Yanan and that in return the Red Army would fight under his orders. This was the Second United Front. Leaders from both sides would draw up plans to combat Japanese aggression. This posed an immediate threat to the Japanese, since it promised a united China once more. The Japanese army made plans and troops were mobilized in Manchuria.

Mao Zedong

Mao Zedong was one of the greatest, if not the greatest, leaders of the twentieth century.

He was born in 1893 and started his career as a teacher. He was influenced at an early stage by the thinking of Karl Marx and became one of the first members of the Chinese Communist Party, when it was founded in 1921.

Mao Zedong was extremely astute and recognized early on that the secret to the eventual control of China lay in the hands of the peasants, since they were by far the largest group in the country. In 1928 he founded the Jiangxi Chinese Soviet Republic in the mountains to the south of Chiang Kaishek's stronghold near Nanjing. When this was besieged and attacked by the Guomindang forces, Mao organized the legendary Long March, leading the Communist soldiers to safety across the mountains and valleys of western China.

After the war against Japan he used his power over the peasants to overthrow Chiang Kaishek and became the leader of Communist China in 1949.

Mao Zedong was a remarkable leader. He inspired adulation among the Chinese people, not merely because he was their leader, but also because he inspired them with his poetry. In the 1960s millions of young people carried with them a little red book containing the thoughts of Chairman Mao.

He died in 1976, having helped to create modern China and to establish beyond doubt his claim to be regarded as one of the most influential leaders the world has ever known.

Japanese troops march into China in 1937.

The Rape of Nanjing

After making Manchuria part of their empire in 1931, the Japanese annexed other Chinese territory between Manchuria and Beijing in 1933.

Now, on 7 July 1937, fighting broke out again after an incident on the Marco Polo bridge near Beijing, on the border between the Japanese-occupied territory and China. The Japanese used it as an excuse to invade China.

This time Chiang Kaishek took action. He said, 'If we allow any more of our land to be taken. We shall be guilty of an unforgivable crime against China.' But words did not stop the Japanese advance. They captured Beijing, Nanjing and Shanghai and invaded Guangzhou from the sea. By the end of 1938 they had captured a large part of north-eastern China, which, with Manchuria, was several times larger than Japan itself.

When the victorious Japanese troops seized Nanjing they were allowed to go on the rampage and, in an orgy of looting and killing, the Chinese capital suffered one of the worst atrocities ever committed by an army on a civilian population.

World war

Chiang Kaishek retreated into the mountains of western China, establishing his base at Chongging on the River Chang Jiang. The Japanese made no serious attempt to destroy his army, since they had obtained most of what they wanted in the area of China now under Japanese occupation.

The Red Army played a more active role, harassing the Japanese with the same guerilla tactics they had used successfully against Chiang Kaishek before the Long March.

After Pearl Harbor the Chinese were joined by other Allies in the war against the Japanese – notably the United States and the countries of the British Commonwealth. The Second World War had begun.

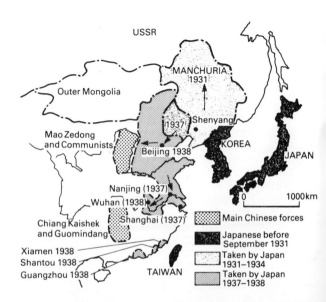

Explanatory Notes

Militarism , as the name implies, glories in war, stressing its effect on the young (who make the sacrifices) and placing emphasis on war as the way to solve problems.

Mao was confident because he was an expert in **guerilla warfare**. He ordered the Red Army to remember four golden rules:
(1) When the enemy advances, we retreat!
(2) When the enemy stops, we harass them!
(3) When the enemy avoids battle, we attack!
(4) When the enemy retreats, we pursue!

He also gave his soldiers strict instructions to behave correctly in the field. They were to be polite to anyone who helped them. They had to pay for all the things they got and there was to be no looting. In this way Mao's Red Army earned the respect, and often the affection of the peasants, unlike the Guomindang armies, who followed the traditional way of life of a Chinese soldier, living off the countryside and brutally treating anyone suspected of sympathizing with their enemy.

Exercises

1. Why was Sun Yixian unable to unify China in the period before 1925? What measures did he take to overcome his difficulties?
2. What was decided at the Washington Conference in 1922? How did this affect Japan?
3. What were the major problems faced by Chiang Kaishek as leader of the Guomindang? How did he attempt to control China? Why did he fail?
4. Why did democracy fail in Japan in the inter-war period? What were the effects of the Great Depression on Japan? How and why did militarism succeed in gaining the support of the Japanese people?
5. Write notes explaining carefully the significance of the following in the history of China before the Second World War:
(a) The power of the warlords in China
(b) The May Fourth Movement 1919
(c) The Northern Expedition
(d) The break between the Guomindang and the Communists in 1927
(e) The Jiangxi Chinese Soviet Republic
(f) The Xian incident 1936
6. Explain carefully the circumstances which led to the Japanese invasion of Manchuria in 1931. What arguments could the Japanese have used to justify the invasion? What was the reaction of the rest of the world to the Japanese invasion of Manchuria?
7. Compare and contrast the careers of Chiang Kaishek and Mao Zedong in the years before 1941.
8. Describe carefully the events leading up to the Long March in 1934–35. How did Mao Zedong manage to lead his soldiers to safety? Draw a map to illustrate your answer. Was it a victory for the Guomindang or for the Communists?

Further Activities

1. Draw a large map of China and mark on it the route taken by Mao Zedong and the Communist forces during the Long March 1934–35. Colour in the areas of China which were occupied by the Japanese (a) after 1931 (b) after 1937.
2. Imagine you are a Chinese worker, soldier or peasant in 1925. You are a member of the Guomindang and Sun Yixian has died. Choose whether you want to be a supporter of Chiang Kaishek or of Mao Zedong and the Communist Party. Take part in class discussions to debate the course of action you think your group should take:
(a) during the Northern Expedition
(b) after the break between the Guomindang and the Communists in 1927
(c) after the Japanese invasion of Manchuria in 1931
(d) immediately before the Long March in 1934
(e) after the Xian incident in 1936

103

CHAPTER 8

International Co-operation between the Wars

On 8 January 1918, President Woodrow Wilson of the United States listed the Fourteen Points which he thought could make up a peace programme for the world. The fourteenth point advocated:

'An Association of Nations affording guarantees of political and territorial independence for all States.'

Ironically, when the Paris Peace Treaties were ratified in 1920, setting up the League of Nations, President Wilson was unable to ratify it on behalf of the United States. The American Senate had effectively voted against joining the League.

Wilson was not the only statesman or politician to desire a world parliament, which could meet to resolve difficult problems affecting relations between member countries. General Smuts of South Africa, Leon Bourgeois of France and many other statesmen urged the formation of such a body.

Prior to 1920 there was no international forum which could be used by national delegates to argue problems and resolve disputes. But the appalling waste of life, and the scale of the conflict during the First World War, persuaded many belligerent countries and neutrals that an international peace-keeping organization was needed in future.

The first meeting of the Assembly of the League of Nations, November 1920.

In a Nutshell

* President Wilson of the United States convinces delegates at the Paris Peace Conference that a Covenant, setting up a League of Nations, should be made an integral part of the Peace Treaties.
* The League of Nations comes into being in 1920 and is run by a *Secretariat*, with every member state being represented in the *Assembly*.
* Four permanent and four elected representatives meet more regularly in the *Council*, which takes decisions on behalf of the League as a whole.
* The League undertakes much useful work – solving the refugee problem, resolving minor frontier disputes, supervising plebiscites, administering the mandated territories created by the Treaty of Versailles.
* But it is powerless to stop the Japanese seizing Manchuria in 1931 and the Italians occupying Abyssinia in 1936. It is discredited in the eyes of smaller nations and plays little part in the crises which dominate Europe in the years immediately before the outbreak of the Second World War.
* Other diplomatic efforts include the Treaty of Locarno in 1925 and the Kellogg-Briand Pact renouncing war in 1928.
* Disarmament conferences are also held but those called by the League of Nations in 1932–34 are too late – Germany is rearming.

The Covenant of the League of Nations

The High Contracting Parties (ie the member nations) agreed to the Covenant of the League of Nations in order to 'promote international co-operation and to achieve international peace and security' by:
* accepting the obligation not to go to war;
* opening relations between nations;
* upholding international law;
* respecting treaty obligations.

Some of the Articles of the Covenant

VIII Peace requires a reduction in armaments
 X The League guarantees the independence and frontiers of all member countries.
XII All disputes to be submitted to arbitration.
XVI Should any Member resort to war it shall be deemed to have committed an act of war against the League. The penalty to be the severance of trade and financial relations.

The League of Nations

The reception of the Covenant was all that could be desired. . . . Henceforth there will be no neutrals in any wars or punitive measures of economic blockade in which the League takes part. The assumption is that if the League is taking part the struggle will be one for the maintenance of common civilization, and that in such a struggle no one has any right to be neutral. . . . The adoption of the Covenant by the Conference was felt to be a moment of great solemnity in the history of the world.
The Times, 29 April 1919

The Covenant
The Covenant which set up the League of Nations had 26 articles. These described the aims and objectives of the League and provided the machinery of government. Since it formed part of each peace treaty, the Covenant ensured that each nation signing the treaty had also to agree to help set up, and join, the League of Nations.

This was President Wilson's idea but, as luck would have it, the United States Senate refused to ratify the Treaty precisely because it would have meant the United States joining the League. As you have seen (Chapter 6), many Americans favoured isolationism at the time, and wanted no part in any organization which might involve them in another war.

Machinery of government
This consisted of: an **Assembly** or parliament for debates; a **Council** or committee of important states, which made most of the League's decisions; a **Secretariat** which ran the League; and a **Court of International Justice** (see the Explanatory Notes below for a more detailed explanation of their functions).

Initially the Council had four permanent members (the British Empire, Japan, Italy and France) and four members who were elected by the Assembly (Belgium, Spain, Greece and Brazil in 1920). When Germany joined the League in 1926 she immediately became a permanent member of the Council; and when Hitler left, Germany's place was taken by the Soviet Union (1934).

Unfortunately, it was the behaviour of the major powers, when they were Council members, which reduced the credibility of the League of Nations as peace-maker and guarantor of frontiers. Japan left in 1933 after seizing Manchuria, Germany in 1933 after Hitler came to power, Italy in 1937 after seizing Abyssinia, and the Soviet Union in 1939 after invading Finland.

105

The headquarters of the League of Nations in Geneva, Switzerland.

The League of Nations in Action

A forum for discussion

The failure of the League of Nations to deter Hitler, Mussolini or the Japanese military leaders from acts of aggression in the years before 1939 is often held up as evidence that the League of Nations was a total failure.

Yet even though the League had relatively few major successes, it did provide an international forum to debate the actions of member states, or non-member states, who broke the rules of international behaviour.

No such facilities for discussion, or arbitration on matters of dispute, existed like this before 1920. In time the League of Nations Assembly became the parent of the United Nations General Assembly and the Council of the League became the parent of the United Nations Security Council.

Successes

The League did valuable work behind the scenes.

1. It helped to alleviate the problem of what to do with refugees after the War.

2. It administered those German and Turkish colonies which had been allocated to the colonial powers as mandates of the League of Nations. It was the League's responsibility to see that those mandates were carried out in accordance with the Treaty of Versailles. It did this through the work of the Mandates Commission.

3. The League also administered the plebiscites in the various frontier territories to decide whether or not they wanted to stay in Germany. A League Commissioner ran the free city of Danzig and the League also administered the Saar until the 1935 plebiscite.

4. The ILO (International Labour Organization) was founded in 1919 and linked to the work of the League of Nations. Non-League countries, like the United States, could also join. It helped to encourage the formation of trade unions and to improve working conditions, minimum wages and pension schemes throughout the world. The ILO was one of the few organizations set up by the League of Nations to be continued after the Second World War.

5. A Health Organization helped to combat the spread of epidemic diseases and the League was also concerned with many other matters affecting the everyday lives of the peoples of the world – such as women's rights, providing loans to developing nations, the eradication of slavery and the control of drugs.

Successes and failures

The League also attempted to resolve the various disputes which were brought before it. Before 1931 its decisions could be, and were, criticized; but they were usually accepted (see panel right). This encouraged many statesmen to think that the League could resolve major disputes as well.

DECISIONS OF THE LEAGUE OF NATIONS BEFORE 1931

1920 Aaland Islands: Dispute between Finland and Sweden over possession of these islands. The inhabitants were of Swedish origin but the islands had been part of the Russian Empire. The League awarded the islands to Finland but granted the islanders a certain amount of independence.

1921 Upper Silesia: The League decided the problem of how to divide this industrial area between Germany and the newly created state of Poland. Neither side was satisfied with the result, since both coveted Silesia's mineral resources and both were eventually left with substantial numbers of their nationals in the other's country.

1923 Corfu: Italy's General Tellini and his companions were assassinated in Greece, when attempting to resolve a frontier dispute between Greece and Albania (then under Italian protection). Mussolini over-reacted to the news and demanded compensation from the Greek Government. When this was not immediately forthcoming, he shelled and then captured the Greek island of Corfu.

Greece protested to the League of Nations. Italy was one of the four permanent members of the Council, so the League trod carefully. Mussolini refused to accept the League's ruling, so the matter was decided by the Council of Ambassadors, which was linked to the League. Greece paid up and Mussolini was persuaded to withdraw. But the action of Italy was not condemned by the League – unlike Greece in 1925 (see below).

1922–26 Mosul: The League decided this frontier dispute in favour of Iraq rather than Turkey. Both claimed Mosul with its rich oilfield. The area had been part of the Ottoman Empire and its population was mainly Kurdish (one of the Turkish peoples). But it fell into British hands towards the end of the First World War and they wanted to see it become part of Iraq (a British mandate).

1925 Greece v Bulgaria: A Greek army invaded Bulgaria after a border incident. The League ordered the Greeks to withdraw and condemned their action.

But the League of Nations proved powerless when the major powers infringed its Covenant. There were a number of such incidents but the two most important were in the Far East and in Africa (see page 108).

The League of Nations was involved in disputes all over the world. The headquarters of the League at Geneva and the locations of the main peace conferences in the inter-war years are also shown here.

★ Conflicts
✳ Conferences

THE LEAGUE OF NATIONS AFTER 1931

1931 Manchuria: The members of the League failed to take decisive action when Japan invaded Manchuria in 1931 (see Chapter 7). Not surprisingly the Japanese delegate vetoed a motion calling on Japanese forces to withdraw. Lord Lytton led an investigation on behalf of the League but his report was unacceptable to the Japanese. Sanctions were not applied, force was not used or contemplated, and the only result was Japan's resignation from the League in 1933. The lesson was not lost on Mussolini and Hitler.

1935 Abyssinia: With even less cause than the Japanese, Mussolini invaded Abyssinia and overthrew the Emperor Haile Selassie (see pages 114–15). Italy was condemned as the aggressor and the League applied economic sanctions, telling its members to stop trading with Italy. But the League was reluctant to enforce the ban with regard to oil, which would really have hurt the Italians.

In the end the sanctions were removed and the League suffered a blow from which it never recovered. When Hitler threatened Czechoslovakia in 1938 the crisis was resolved outside the League of Nations.

Aristide Briand, Foreign Minister of France, worked hard for peace in the 1920s and 30s. In 1926 he and Gustav Stresemann were awarded the Nobel Peace Prize.

Reasons why the League Failed

1. Trade sanctions could not be made to bite. For one thing the League could not control the trade of non-League nations, such as the United States. Member nations were unwilling to contribute troops to a League of Nations force. So the League had no effective way of compelling other countries to accept its decisions.

Small or weak nations could be pressured into accepting League decisions. But powerful states could choose to obey League decisions – or ignore them. This destroyed the trust many smaller countries had in the League.

2. The founder members of the League of Nations did not include Russia (because of the Bolshevik Revolution), the United States (because the United States Senate refused to ratify the Treaty of Versailles) and Germany (because she was labelled the aggressor in the First World War). Yet these were major world powers.

Germany became a member in 1926 and the Soviet Union in 1934 but the United States, the most powerful nation on Earth, remained outside the League of Nations. As a consequence the League could never speak for the world as a whole.

3. It was set up as a result of a Peace Conference which imposed harsh terms on five countries (including Germany, a permanent member of the Council in 1926) and which disappointed several others (eg China and Italy).

A major part of its work arose out of the terms of the Paris Peace Treaties – conducting plebiscites and administering the mandates. This was hardly the concern of nations which had been neutral during the War.

4. The member nations of the League were rarely united on the great issues which came before them, such as disarmament.

It was only in the late 1920s that the League worked really well – at a time when the permanent members of the Council were supported by three talented foreign ministers – Gustav Stresemann of Germany, Aristide Briand of France and Austen Chamberlain of Britain.

Inter-War Diplomacy

The absence of American, German and Russian participation in, or agreement with, decisions taken by the League of Nations, led diplomats to seek

international agreements outside the League. These conferences were concerned primarily with
(a) guaranteeing international frontiers
(b) renouncing war as a means of settling international disputes
(c) seeking a reduction in armaments

The Treaty of Locarno

This Treaty was signed in Locarno, Switzerland, in December 1925. The principal signatories were Germany, France and Belgium. It was a notable diplomatic breakthrough at a time of international tension, since French and Belgian troops had earlier occupied the German Ruhr (in January 1923). Gustav Stresemann (Germany) and Aristide Briand (France) later won the Nobel Peace Prize (1926) for their work in seeking this agreement.

All three countries agreed to confirm existing frontiers and to abide by arbitration, not war, if any disputes arose between them. Other agreements were signed at Locarno between Germany, Poland and Czechoslovakia, and all were guaranteed by Britain and Italy.

The Kellogg-Briand Pact

In 1927 the French Foreign Minister, Aristide Briand, wishing to involve isolationist America in peaceful diplomacy, suggested to his US counterpart

Below: United States Secretary of State, Frank B. Kellogg, signing the Peace Pact at Versailles on 31 August 1928. Many people thought the Pact a hopeful sign for future peace, as the journalist's description (right) of the signing of the Pact shows.

(Secretary of State, Frank Kellogg) that France and the United States should jointly renounce war as a means of settling international disputes.

Kellogg felt that this might be construed as an alliance between France and America; so he proposed, instead, that other nations should be invited to sign the declaration. On 27 August 1928 the Kellogg-Briand Pact was signed in Paris by nine nations (Germany, United States, Belgium, France, Britain, Italy, Japan, Poland and Czechoslovakia). Over sixty nations eventually signed the Pact, including the Soviet Union.

Its provisions were very simple:
* The 'High Contracting Parties' (ie the respective governments) solemnly declared that they condemned war as the way to solve international disputes and renounced it 'in their relations with one another';
* They agreed to settle all disputes between themselves by peaceful means.

> Short and simple as were the proceedings, the ceremony was most impressive, and those who were present will not easily forget the occasion when the plenipotentiaries of the greatest Powers of the modern world 'solemnly declared', in the names of their respective peoples, that they condemned recourse to war for the solution of international controversies, and renounced it as an instrument of national policy in their relations with one another.
>
> *The Times*, 28 August 1928

But the Kellogg-Briand Pact had two fatal flaws. These were:

1. There was no means of enforcing the Pact.

2. The great powers signed the Pact on the understanding that it did not stop them from using force in self defence. Kellogg himself affirmed that 'any nation has the right to defend its interests anywhere in the world'.

The Pact was therefore meaningless, since most wars begin with an actual or engineered incident, which a belligerent can say is an attack calling for the use of armed force in self defence (eg the Manchurian bomb incident).

All it did was to give other nations the right, which they already had under the Covenant, to condemn acts of aggression.

But many people at the time thought differently, as the extract from a London newspaper's description of the ceremony in Paris on page 109 shows.

Disarmament

One of the fundamental causes of the First World War had been rearmament, the heavy build-up of weapons, warships and conscripted armies in the years to 1914. After the War the great powers made a number of efforts to reduce and limit stocks of weapons and the recruitment of armed forces.

(1) Germany and the other Central Powers had to reduce their armed forces under the terms of the Paris Peace Treaties (see Chapter 1).

(2) The Washington Conference in 1921, and subsequent treaties, limited the size of the British, United States and Japanese navies (see Chapter 7).

(3) The League of Nations had been charged with the duty of securing disarmament under the terms of the Covenant. But it was not until 1932 that a Disarmament Conference met in Geneva. The delegates to the Conference spent many months in debate from 1932 to 1934 but could not agree. The French were stubborn and, even before Hitler came to power, the German Government demanded equality with the other European powers. All hope of such agreement vanished when Germany left the Conference in October 1933 and formally announced, in March 1935, that she was rearming her armed forces.

The Stresa Front

Britain, France and Italy reacted to the news of German rearmament by calling the Stresa Conference (April 1935) at which their leaders – Ramsay MacDonald (Britain), Mussolini (Italy) and Flandin (France) – condemned the German repudiation of the Treaty of Versailles and formed the Stresa Front to co-ordinate their opposition.

But this was before Mussolini invaded Abyssinia.

The Krupp Works in Essen. This was only one of many workshops producing armaments. Despite peace agreements, Germany was rearming fast.

Explanatory Notes

The League of Nations had an **Assembly** which met once a year, where the delegates of all the member nations could speak. Every member country had one vote, whatever its size.

The Assembly decided the policy of the League and controlled its finances, but most of its decisions had to be unanimous. Although, in theory, this gave any nation the right of veto, it did not prove an obstacle to the work of the Assembly.

It had a **Council** which met more frequently than the Assembly. This committee, of four (later five) great powers and four elected nations from the Assembly, decided many of the problems put before the League. Each member had one vote.

Like most governments the business of the League was run by officials who carried out the decisions made in the Assembly and in the Council. This was called the **Secretariat** and the first Secretary General was a British official called Sir Eric Drummond.

The League had its headquarters in Geneva in neutral Switzerland.

The Court of International Justice was presided over by 15 judges, chosen from 15 different countries. It met in The Hague (in the Netherlands) and heard cases brought before it by countries complaining of infringements of international law.

Exercises

1. Explain carefully the events leading to the founding of the League of Nations. When, why and how did it come into being?
2. What were the aims and objectives of the states which founded the League of Nations? How consistent were they in following the rules they helped to set up? Which great powers left the League and why?
3. Describe the structure and organization of the League of Nations. Explain the functions of each of the following: (a) the Secretariat (b) the Assembly (c) the Council (d) the Court of International Justice (e) the International Labour Organization
4. Write brief notes commenting on the effectiveness of the League of Nations in resolving the crises in: (a) Upper Silesia 1921 (b) Corfu 1923 (c) Mosul 1924
5. Why was the failure of the United States to join the League a major setback?
6. Why did the League of Nations fail to resolve the crises in Manchuria (1931) and in Abyssinia (1935)? What effect did these failures have on subsequent events?
7. What do you think were the chief weaknesses of the League? How should its powers have been enlarged?
8. Write brief notes commenting on the significance of each of the following international agreements, or attempts to reach agreement, in the inter-war years:
(a) The Locarno Pact
(b) The Kellogg-Briand Pact
(c) The Disarmament Conferences of the 1930s

Further Activities

1. Join in a mock debate between members of the League of Nations discussing what to do after the Japanese invasion of Manchuria in 1931 and after the Italian invasion of Abyssinia in 1935. You will find further details in Chapter 7 (Manchuria) and Chapter 9 (Abyssinia). The different members of your group can each represent a different country, such as Germany, Japan, Italy, Britain, France, China.
2. Argue the case for or against the League of Nations from the point of view of *either* one of the major powers *or* one of the small countries of the world.

Events Leading to the Second World War

On 3 September 1939 the British Prime Minister declared war on Germany, saying what a blow it had been to him personally to know that his 'long struggle to win peace' had failed.

This chapter is about that 'long struggle to win peace'. Neville Chamberlain's policy, and that of the French Prime Minister Edouard Daladier, is usually described as being one of **appeasement** (see Explanatory Notes), of giving in to Hitler's demands in order to 'win peace'.

Yet in 1918 Britain and France were the victors and Germany, torn by internal dissension and broken by defeat, was at their mercy. As you saw in Chapter 1, the Allies imposed harsh terms under

the terms of the Treaty of Versailles, largely at the instigation of the French, who wanted Germany weak and incapable of going to war again.

Why then was Germany able to rise again and become the dominant power in Europe? Why did France, so keen to weaken Germany in 1919, fail to stand up to Hitler in the 1930s, when it was obvious he was determined to overturn the terms of the Treaty of Versailles?

Part of the answer lies in the fact that many people were ashamed of the Paris Peace Treaties, since they gave the German-speaking peoples many genuine grievances. Germany had been forced to disarm but other countries had not, despite the League of Nations Covenant on disarmament. German-speaking minorities in countries like Czechoslovakia had been unfairly treated and some of the boundary decisions had produced difficulties such as the Polish Corridor separating Germany from East Prussia.

But above all, statesmen in Britain and France could not forget the appalling and horrific slaughter of the war years, when their friends and companions had been mowed down on the battlefields of Flanders. War had to be avoided at all costs. British Foreign Minister, Anthony Eden, told the League of Nations 'There is in our judgement, no dispute between nations that cannot be settled by peaceful means.'

Conflict of Ideologies

In the 1930s many people in Britain and France were more worried about the spread of Soviet Communism than about the growth of Fascism from Italy or Germany. It was no secret that many Communists wanted a world revolution centred on Moscow.

In a Nutshell

* Many people in the 1930s cannot decide whether Communism or Fascism is the greater evil.
* This conflict of opinion is seen in the Spanish Civil War when volunteers from France, America, Britain and other countries fight for either the Soviet-backed Republicans or the Fascist-backed Falangists led by General Franco.
* Italy's invasion of Abyssinia is condemned by the League of Nations but is met by no effective action. Abyssinia's ruler warns of the consequences of bowing to force – the policy of appeasement.
* Mussolini, a former ally of France and Britain (the Stresa Front) turns to Hitler and Japan for support. In 1936 and 1937 they form an *Axis* and sign the Anti-Comintern Pact – against Communism.
* Hitler overturns the main provisions of the Paris Peace Treaties by stages. He starts to rearm the German armed forces in 1935; marches troops into the Rhineland in 1936; unites Germany and Austria (Anschluss) in 1938; demands and gets the Sudetenland from Czechoslovakia at Munich in 1938; takes Bohemia-Moravia and the Memel in 1939; and demands parts of Poland but is rebuffed by the Poles, also in 1939.
* In August 1939, Ribbentrop (Germany) and Molotov (USSR) sign the Nazi-Soviet Non-Aggression Pact. This commits both sides to neutrality if the other is involved in war. A secret agreement clears the way for the German conquest of western Poland in September and the annexation of eastern Poland by the Soviet Union.
* When the German army invades Poland on 1 September 1939, France and Britain stand firm, at last, and war is declared two days later. It is the start of the Second World War.

The Depression put millions of working people on the breadline. It was not hard to imagine the effect a Communist-inspired revolution might have on desperate, unemployed and starving workers, even in democracies such as France and Britain.

Mussolini's Fascists were strongly anti-Communist; so too were Hitler's Nazis. Were they not suitable allies in the struggle against international Communism?

Throughout your study of the 1930s, this conflict of **ideologies** (see Explanatory Notes) should always be borne in mind.

Far left: Hitler reviews a parade by police in Saarbrucken in 1935, after the people of the Saar have voted to rejoin Germany.
Left: Neville Chamberlain, still talking peace, with Mussolini at Munich in 1938.

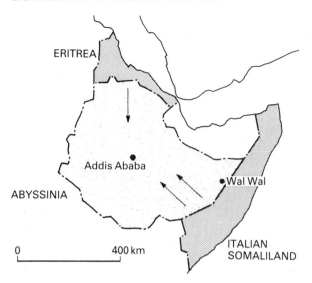

Italy Attacks Abyssinia

Wal Wal

In December 1934 an incident occurred in East Africa at a small desert oasis called Wal Wal inside Abyssinia, but close to the border with Italian Somaliland. Italian troops had camped at Wal Wal for years but Abyssinia wanted the oasis back.

What began as a peaceful confrontation between the two sides suddenly escalated into battle and well over a hundred soldiers were killed. The Italians demanded compensation for the attack and Abyssinia's acknowledgement that Wal Wal was Italian. The dispute was referred to the League of Nations for settlement.

Abyssinia (nowadays known as Ethiopia) was then one of only two independent states in Africa. It had been ruled by Haile Selasse as Emperor since 1930.

Reasons why Mussolini attacked Abyssinia

The Italians had long had an eye on Abyssinia, because it was one of the few undeveloped countries of the world which did not already form part of an existing empire. Several other factors also played a part in shaping the Italian attitude to Abyssinia.

* Italian national pride had been badly hurt in 1896 when an Abyssinian army heavily defeated 12,000 Italian soldiers at the battle of Adowa. After their victory in 1936, the Italians erected a war memorial 'To the Dead of Adowa – Avenged at last.'

* Italy gained no African colonies at the Paris Peace Conference. Italians complained of being 'robbed of a place in the sun'.

* Italy needed to **expand** (see Explanatory Notes). She wanted a colony with resources which she could develop and which could be used to settle emigrants from an overcrowded Italy.

* Mussolini thought that Italy's modern army could easily defeat the Abyssinians. It would be excellent war experience. The glory of a military victory would help to curb criticism of the regime and give renewed vigour to Fascist Italy.

* The League of Nations might intervene but to no effect – as Japan had shown after the invasion of Manchuria in 1931. Germany would not object and the other great European powers, Britain and France were friendly (the Stresa Front).

War

So despite the fact that Italy had signed a Treaty of Friendship with Abyssinia in 1928, Mussolini went ahead with plans to add it to his small overseas empire.

Troops were mobilized in the spring of 1935 and sent to the Italian colonies of Somaliland, to the south of Abyssinia, and Eritrea, to the north. Meanwhile the League of Nations investigated the Wal

Left: Abyssinian troops, armed only with spears, in action against the Italian army in 1935.

Above Left: Map of the war in Abyssinia.

Right: The Emperor Haile Selassie of Abyssinia on his way to the League of Nations in Geneva in June 1936.

Wal incident, but the solution it proposed was unacceptable to Italy. In the face of threatened retaliatory action from other nations, Mussolini went ahead with his invasion.

On 3 October 1935 the Italians launched a pincer movement driving southwards from Eritrea and northwards from Italian Somaliland. Despite the bravery of the Abyssinian soldiers, the result was not in doubt, since they faced a modern army equipped with modern weapons.

The League of Nations

Four days after the invasion, the League of Nations branded Italy the aggressor and agreed to impose economic sanctions, hoping to make Mussolini withdraw his troops. But the sanctions were ineffective since the League failed to include a ban on oil supplies. Mussolini later admitted to Hitler that if oil had been banned he would have had to call off the invasion.

In December the British Foreign Minister, Sir Samuel Hoare, and the French Prime Minister, Pierre Laval, proposed a secret plan which would have given Italy much of the territory she had already conquered but which would have guaranteed Abyssinia's frontiers against further attack. The news was leaked before it became official and the Hoare-Laval Plan was scrapped in the face of scandalized public opinion, which saw it as appeasement in the face of naked aggression.

The Italians completed their conquest in May 1936, with the capture of Addis Ababa, the Abyssinian capital city. Italy could now develop Abyssinia as an Italian colony. To this end she combined all three colonies (Abyssinia, Eritrea and Somaliland) into Italian East Africa.

In June 1936 Haile Selassie addressed the League of Nations and asked whether the League was going to bow before force. He warned that other small states must one day suffer the fate of Abyssinia. 'What reply shall I take back to my people?' he asked. The reply came back a week later – when the Council voted to end sanctions.

Results

Italy resented British and French interference in what was seen as a perfectly legitimate venture, no different from those which had given Britain and France substantial African colonies in the past – and which they still held on to in 1935.

There was resentment too, after the Stresa Pact and Italy's longstanding membership of the Council, that she should be condemned by the League of Nations, which she had helped to found. Italy withdrew from the League in 1937.

Hitler and Mussolini in 1938.

The Axis Pact and the Anti-Comintern Pact

The main effect of Mussolini's invasion of Abyssinia, however, was to draw him closer to Hitler. On 21 October 1936 Italy signed the Axis Pact with Germany. Mussolini claimed:

'This Berlin-Rome link is an axis around which can revolve all the states of Europe with a desire for peace and co-operation.'

On 25 November 1936 the world learned the disturbing news that Germany and Japan had signed a treaty to stop the spread of international Communism. It was called the Anti-Comintern Pact, and, although not strictly an alliance, was viewed with suspicion as such by other countries, notably the Soviet Union, the target of the Pact.

The following year Mussolini added his signature to the Pact on 6 November 1937. A triumphant Ribbentrop claimed that Germany and Italy would keep Communism at bay in Europe, whilst Japan would do the same in the Far East. Both Britain and the United States saw this as a threat to their interests as well – in Europe, the Mediterranean and the Pacific.

The Spanish Civil War

The Republic

In the 1920s Spain was a monarchy, governed by a benevolent dictator called Primo de Rivera. The Depression led to a crisis, which was temporarily resolved when an elected Republican Government came to power in 1931.

In the next five years neither the left- nor the right-wing parties were able to provide stable government. There were strikes, killings, explosions, riots, rebellions and demonstrations.

Communists, Basque and Catalan Separatists (seeking independence for Catalonia and the Basque country in the border region close to France), Socialists, Anarchists (who wanted to abolish the government), Syndicalists (a trade union movement), Nationalists, and Falangists (a would-be Fascist working-class movement) were just some of the different groupings of left- and right-wing activists in Spain before 1936.

The right-wing parties wanted to preserve the privileges of the landed classes, including the dominant roles of the Catholic Church and the army. Yet the liberal and left-wing groups had reason on their side. Over half of Spain was owned by one per cent of the population and the Church had huge estates as well. The army took a quarter of Spain's national budget and was top heavy with officers.

Revolution

On 18 July 1936 General Franco led an army revolt against the Republican Government, which the Spanish people had elected to power only a few months earlier with a majority of nearly five million votes to four million votes. Franco's supporters (the Falangists, Nationalists, Church, landowners, industrialists and middle classes) were afraid that the Government, which was supported by Liberals as well as Socialists and Communists, might create the conditions which would enable the Communists to stage a 'Bolshevik' Revolution in Spain. They decided to strike first. The rebellion began in Spanish Morocco and soon spread to the mainland of Spain.

The resulting civil war lasted just under three years, marked by appalling atrocities on both sides and ending in the deaths (many of them cold-blooded executions) of between half a million and a million Spaniards plus 20,000 of the 60,000 volunteers from Europe and America who joined the International Brigade fighting on the Republican side. Many Communists and Socialists in Britain and France felt it their duty to fight against the 'forces of Fascism'.

Spanish Government forces in action against Franco's Nationalists in 1936.

General Franco

Francisco Franco was born in 1892 and served in the army, reaching the rank of general by the time of the Spanish Civil War in 1936.

His rebellion against the elected Republican Government was supported by both Hitler and Mussolini. This, together with his right-wing, Nationalist policies, the one-party state, and the acknowledgement of a single leader (*El Caudillo*), led to the assumption that he was a Fascist. There were executions after the Civil War but little persecution of the Jews.

Franco kept his distance from the other Fascist leaders and Spain stayed neutral during the Second World War, despite Nazi pressure. As a result Franco's Falangist Government survived after 1945, at a time when democracies were being restored in Germany and Italy. He died in 1975.

General Franco during the Spanish Civil War.

The ruins of Teruel, a Spanish town caught in the bitter fighting between the Nationalists and Spanish Government forces in the Civil War, 1938. Air raids and artillery bombardment have left few buildings intact.

Foreign intervention

Equally, Europe's Fascists offered their support to the Spanish Nationalists. Mussolini sent over 50,000 Italian soldiers ('Fascist volunteers') to fight for Franco, and, together with Hitler, supplied Franco with weapons, munitions and aircraft. This interference in Spain's internal affairs caused a world outcry but there was little the other powers could, or wanted, to do. Stalin's reaction, under pressure, was to supply some arms, weapons and troops to the Republican forces. France already had an agreement to supply the Spanish Government with arms but, not wishing to get involved, helped Britain to form a Non-Intervention Committee to try to prevent arms and munitions reaching either side. This only served to weaken the Republican forces, whilst doing little to curb Hitler and Mussolini.

Guernica

When Nazi bombers attacked the town of Guernica in northern Spain the world was alerted to the peril which air bombardment could bring to a civilian population, as shown by the extracts, right.

End of the Spanish Civil War

The War came to an end in March 1939 with the surrender of Madrid. Many Republicans were executed in the reprisals which took place when Franco became dictator.

He owed his victory partly to the superiority of the professional armed forces (although some supported the Republicans), partly to the fact that his right-wing parties were more united than those of the left-wing, and partly to the foreign aid he received from Germany and Italy.

Despite this, Franco did not repay Hitler and Mussolini by declaring war on Britain and France in 1939 or 1940. Spain was neutral throughout the Second World War.

Newspaper headlines: 28 April 1937

FRANCO WIPES OUT TOWN: 800 VICTIMS OF BARBARIC AIR RAID – Fugitives Fall Under Bullets Of Swooping Rebel Planes

News Chronicle

AIR RAID WIPES OUT BASQUE TOWN – RELAYS OF BOMBERS

Daily Mail

THE TRAGEDY OF GUERNICA – TOWN DESTROYED IN AIR ATTACK

The Times

PRIEST BLESSES CITY AS BOMBS FALL

Daily Express

I have seen many ghastly sights in Spain in the last six months, but none more terrible than the annihilation of the ancient Basque capital of Guernica by Franco's bombing planes.

I walked this evening through the still-burning town. Hundreds of bodies had been found in the debris. Most were charred beyond recognition. At least two hundred others were riddled with machine gun bullets as they fled to the hills.

I stood beside the smouldering Red Cross hospital of Josefinas. The bodies of forty-two wounded soldiers and ten nurses lay buried in the wreckage. They never had a chance. The wounded were killed in their beds, the nurses were killed on duty.

Noel Monks in the *Daily Express*

Hitler's March Towards War

Hitler's foreign policy

Whether Hitler set out in 1933 to achieve world domination is a matter of debate. If every promise he ever made is taken as representing his foreign policy, then there seems little doubt that he intended to enlarge the boundaries of Germany well beyond those of 1914, at the start of the First World War.

But some experts believe he had no master plan and had no real idea of what he intended to do. Instead they think he just exploited opportunities as and when they arose.

Initially, at least, he seemed to know how far he could go without provoking Britain and France into taking action. He took care to overturn the Treaty of Versailles gradually, clause by clause.

His success in putting Germany back on her feet, albeit at the expense of many thousands of imprisoned intellectuals, Jews, trade unionists and other potential opponents, gave him the support and backing of the vast majority of the German people. When he was successful, as he was before 1942, they cheered and applauded. Newsreel film of his reception after the Fall of France in 1940 leaves no doubt that Germany regarded him as a hero.

German rearmament

One of Hitler's first actions was to rearm Germany's armed forces. The Treaty of Versailles had placed severe restrictions on the size and nature of the German army and navy, and it stopped Germany from forming an air force (see Chapter 1). In 1933, the German army, officially limited to 100,000 men, was substantially smaller than that of Czecho-slovakia (140,000) or Poland (270,000). This was intolerable to Hitler, who used to boast to crowds of his front-line experience in the First World War. In October 1933 Germany withdrew from the League of Nation's Disarmament Conference.

Meanwhile Goering was already secretly building up a German air force (the Luftwaffe). Pilots were trained privately and factories had been geared up to produce warplanes. The Allies knew about this in 1934 but made no effective protest.

In 1935 German rearmament became common knowledge. Conscription (compulsory military service) was reintroduced and plans for an army of over half a million men were announced. Goering proudly unveiled the Luftwaffe.

Britain, Italy and France protested and met at Stresa to consider joint action. But the effectiveness of this protest was soon set at nought by the action of Italy in Abyssinia and the naval agreement which Britain signed with Germany in June 1935. This

German troops march into Cologne, in the demilitarized Rhineland, in March 1936.

limited the size of Germany's navy to a fraction of the size of the Royal Navy (for example, less than half the number of submarines). But Germany had been banned from building submarines at Versailles; so to France and other states it looked as if Britain was passively acknowledging Hitler's right to rearm.

Germany marches into the Rhineland

On 7 March 1936 Hitler deliberately sent a small contingent of soldiers into the demilitarized Rhineland to test Allied reaction. This was a blatant breach of the Treaty of Versailles (and of the Locarno Pact). But as Hitler expected, the Allies did nothing, although many German generals had warned him that the reoccupation of the militarized zone would mean certain war. Once again the League of Nations did nothing positive to uphold the Treaty of Versailles. In any case many people could see no good reason why Germany should not be allowed to deploy her own troops wherever she pleased – in her own country.

119

Cheers greeted German troops as they arrived over the frontier and came into Austrian towns. Swastikas hung from windows, crowds gave the Nazi salute; buttonholes, not bullets, greeted the marching men as they penetrated further into the land where Hitler was born.

Report in 1938

Austrian crowds saluting German troops as they march through the city of Innsbruck in 1938.

Anschluss

In February 1938, Austrian Nazis, supported by threats from Hitler, forced the Austrian Chancellor Kurt von Schuschnigg to admit Nazis into his Government. In March Schuschnigg announced a plebiscite which would allow Austrians to vote on whether they wanted to be free and independent or not. Hitler saw this as a threat to his plans for a union of all the German-speaking peoples, so he threatened to invade Austria if Schuschnigg went ahead with the plebiscite.

In the face of these threats Schuschnigg had little choice but to postpone the plebiscite and resign. The Austrian Nazi leader Arthur Seyss-Inquart took over and immediately, at Hitler's instigation, invited in German armed forces 'to help preserve the peace'. At dawn on 12 March the German army crossed over the Austrian border to be greeted by rapturous crowds in Vienna and other Austrian cities.

On 13 March 1938 Seyss-Inquart announced that Austria was now a province of Germany's Third Reich. Three days later Hitler drove through Vienna in his native Austria. Crowds tried to break the police cordons shouting, 'We want to see our Fuhrer! Hitler! Hitler!' A reporter said that the older men and women had 'tears of joy in their eyes'.

A month later Austrians (and Germans) got a chance to vote on whether they wanted the union (Anschluss) to take place or not. They did, by a massive 99 per cent of those who were qualified to vote! By then the persecution of Austria's Jews had already begun.

The Sudetenland

In 1937 Konrad Henlein, leader of the local Nazi Party, asked Hitler for assistance in solving the problems of the large German minority living in the Sudetenland region of Czechoslovakia. This was one of the states which had been created out of the old Austro-Hungarian Empire. There were about 3 million Germans living in a country of 15 million people.

The Germans claimed that the Czechs (about 7 million of them) discriminated against Germans in the civil service and when making promotions in the army. Reforms had been promised but during the Depression there was much unemployment in the industrial areas of Czechoslovakia – most of them in the Sudetenland.

It was then that Konrad Henlein formed the Sudeten German Homeland Party with the eventual support of a large proportion of Germans living in Czechoslovakia. During the spring and summer of 1938, Henlein's Czech Germans began to agitate for self-government, encouraged by Hitler and the German Nazis. Czechoslovakia reacted by calling up some of her reserve troops in May and stationing them in the Sudetenland.

War clouds

The war clouds gathered during the course of the summer. France confirmed she would come to Czechoslovakia's aid in the event of an invasion and Britain told Germany that she too might be forced to take action if France went to war. The Soviet Union proposed collective action to support the Czechs but neither Britain nor France trusted Stalin.

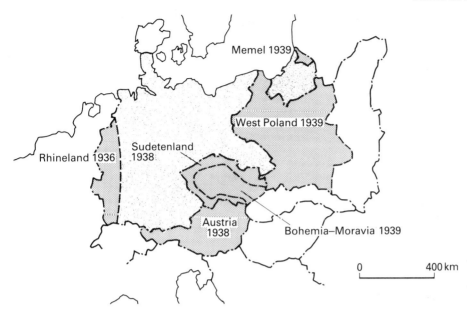

Map showing how Hitler flouted the terms of the Treaty of Versailles.

Memel 1939

West Poland 1939

Sudetenland 1938

Rhineland 1936

Austria 1938

Bohemia–Moravia 1939

0   400 km

The Soviet Union was not a democracy. The main news from Moscow was of Purges not freedom.

In August, Germany started large-scale military exercises near the Czech border; but already voices were being heard in France and Britain advising caution and recommending partition. In early September the Czech Government announced far-reaching concessions to the Sudeten Germans. But these were now too late to mollify the Nazis and the Czech proposals were rejected. On 12 September Hitler whipped up German support for the Sudeten Germans in a vitriolic speech at Nuremberg.

Peace talks

Two days later Chamberlain made his first journey to see Hitler (at Berchtesgaden). Hitler would not budge. So on his return Chamberlain consulted the French and together they drew up a plan conceding the Sudetenland to Germany. The Czech Government reluctantly agreed and Chamberlain made another trip to see Hitler at Godesberg (22 September) but was bitterly disappointed to find that Hitler had new demands to make on Czech territory.

Pressure built up in the next few days. Poland and Hungary both made demands for Czech territory. Poland sent troops to the Czech border to support its claim. Russia prepared to intervene.

Czechoslovakia rejected Hitler's latest demands and on 26 September Hitler made yet another vicious attack on Czechoslovakia, in the Berlin Sports Palace, before a vast crowd of 30,000. He threatened an invasion by the following Monday if his demands were not met:

'Our patience is at an end. Benes (*the Czech Presi-*

dent) will have to surrender this territory to us on October 1st.'

He also made a promise:

'It is the last territorial claim which I have to make in Europe, but it is the claim from which I do not recede and which I shall fulfil, God willing.'

Henlein's supporters armed themselves with rifles and formed Freikorps (Free Corps) to fight a guerilla campaign against the Czech army – if it came to war. By now the Czech Government had declared martial law in the Sudetenland. Troops massed on the borders. The atmosphere in Europe was electric.

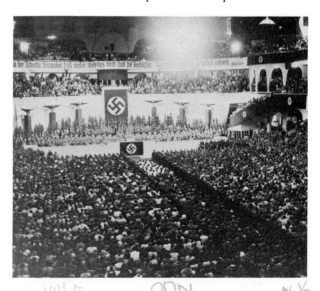

The Berlin Sports Palace, 26 September 1938 – Hitler makes his threat to go to war on 1 October.

Right: Chamberlain and Hitler at Munich in 1938.

Below: Evacuees leaving London.

War preparations

Most people feared the worse and expected war. Trenches were dug in London's parks, air raid shelters were constructed, gas masks issued and children evacuated. On 27 September Neville Chamberlain broadcast to the people of Britain and told them,

> 'How horrible, fantastic, incredible it is that we should be digging trenches and trying on gas masks here because of a quarrel in a far-away country between people of whom we know nothing.'

Although Chamberlain is generally regarded as an appeaser, he did mobilize (make ready for war) the Royal Navy on 27 September and this managed to convince Hitler that he meant business. Hitler is reported to have told a friend afterwards, 'Do you know why I finally yielded at Munich? I thought the Home Fleet might open fire.'

Thanks to the intervention of Mussolini, Hitler was persuaded to call a final conference at Munich.

Chamberlain announced the news to a delighted House of Commons in London: 'Herr Hitler has just agreed to postpone his mobilization for 24 hours and to meet me in conference with Signor Mussolini and Monsieur Daladier (France).'

The Munich Agreement

So the four great powers of Western Europe met in Munich (29–30 September) to decide the fate of Czechoslovakia. Russia, a guarantor of Czech frontiers, was not invited – much to Stalin's fury. As for Czechoslovakia, she, too, was not represented at Munich.

In fact most of the decisions had already been taken, since Czechoslovakia had agreed the proposals for the Sudetenland. Some German historians even think Hitler yielded at Munich, contrary to the view of many British and French historians, who think Daladier and Chamberlain bowed to force once more. The Munich Peace Agreement is forever associated with the idea of appeasement and 'the piece of paper'. When Chamberlain returned to London, he told the crowd at the airport:

> This morning I had another talk with the German Chancellor, Herr Hitler. And here is the paper which bears his name upon it as well as mine.
>
> We regard the agreement signed last night, and the Anglo-German Naval Agreement, as symbolic of the desire of our two peoples never to go to war with one another again.
>
> We are resolved that the method of consultation shall be the method adopted to deal with any other questions that may concern our two countries.

Right: Chamberlain waves the 'piece of paper' signed by Hitler, which, he believed, meant 'peace for our time'.

The fact remains that Hitler got almost everything he demanded through a peace treaty instead of having to use force to get the same concessions directly from Czechoslovakia. The four powers signed away a substantial part of Czechoslovakia, including most of that country's heavy industry, coal mines and fortifications, together with 3 million Sudeten Germans and 700,000 luckless Czechs.

Results of the Munich Agreement

1. It encouraged Hitler to believe that when the crunch came neither Britain nor France would fight. Both had promised military support to Czechoslovakia, and made warlike preparations, but in the end both failed to back up the guarantees they had given Czechoslovakia.

2. It convinced the Russians that neither Britain nor France could be relied upon to form a military alliance to guarantee existing frontiers. This is why the Soviet Union signed the notorious Soviet-German Pact ten months later (see below).

3. It provided Britain and France with a brief respite in which to begin rearmament in earnest. However it has been said that had Germany's enemies combined to take collective action (as Russia wanted), their combined forces would have heavily outnumbered those of the Germans. Czechoslovakia and France combined had over twice as many troops, Russia had four times as many, and the Royal Navy was far more powerful than the German navy.

4. It weakened both the British and the French Governments. Winston Churchill denounced the Munich Agreement as 'a disaster of the first magnitude' and Clement Attlee, Leader of the Labour Party said: 'We have seen a gallant and civilized democratic people betrayed and handed over to ruthless despotism.'

Hitler seizes Bohemia-Moravia and the Memel

The following March Hitler bullied the Czech Government once more and got Czech agreement to make Bohemia and Moravia German Protectorates and later acquired ultimate control of Slovakia as well. Czechoslovakia now ceased to exist as an independent state. Chamberlain argued that this was not an act of aggression which called for a British military response; but within a week Hitler took the Memel (predominantly German) away from Lithuania. People who had cheered Chamberlain the previous September now set their teeth against appeasement.

The Polish Corridor

Hitler's next move was to take steps to link Germany to East Prussia, which as you can see from the map on page 7 was divided from the rest of the country by a strip of territory known as the Polish Corridor. This gave Poland an outlet to the sea and a port she could use – Danzig, which was predominantly German and had a Nazi government. Hitler did not expect any real objection to these proposals, since Germany had helped Poland when she claimed part of Czechoslovakia the previous autumn (in 1938).

But Poland rejected the German demand for Danzig and a routeway across the Corridor. Rumours of German troop movements prompted France and Britain to warn Germany (not Russia) that they guaranteed Poland's independence. This infuriated Hitler and he ordered his army to prepare to invade Poland. At the same time he renounced the agreements he had made with Poland (the 1934 Non-Aggression Treaty) and Britain (the 1935 Naval Agreement). The Soviet Union, alarmed by these moves, suggested collective action to Britain and France, but both countries were reluctant, and delayed making a decision on such an alliance until it was too late.

In May 1939 Mussolini and Hitler agreed the Pact of Steel – a military alliance – which guaranteed immediate aid from the other partner in the event of war.

By August the war clouds had gathered once more. On the 23rd of the month, the world heard the startling and ominous news that the Soviet Union and Germany had signed a non-aggression pact. It was obvious now to anyone, that Hitler could strike at Poland without inviting retaliation from the Red Army, the only armed force in eastern Europe capable of pushing back the German army.

Soviet-German Non-Aggression Pact: 25 August 1939

Guided by the desire to strengthen the cause of peace between the German and Soviet Republics and based on the fundamental stipulations of the neutrality agreement concluded in April 1926, the German Government and Soviet Government have come to the following agreement:
ARTICLE 1 : Both contracting parties pledge themselves to abstain from any acts of violence and any aggressive activities against each other, individually, as well as together with other Powers;
ARTICLE 2 : In case one of the contracting parties becomes the object of aggression by a third Power, the other partner shall not support the aforesaid third Power in any matter whatever.

Daily Telegraph, 26 August 1939

What the world didn't know was that secretly both powers had agreed to partition Poland.

Russia's Stalin (second from right) and Molotov (right) sign the Non-Aggression Treaty with Germany's Ribbentrop (second from left) in August 1939. The treaty is often known as the Nazi-Soviet Pact.

Explanatory Notes

An **ideology** is a set of beliefs and ideas, usually related to the organization of a political system – such as Communism or Fascism or Falangism.

Appeasement is the name given to the policy of trying to buy off dictators by negotiating agreements which concede some of their demands; the alternative being the outright rejection of these demands – with the attendant dangers such a rejection might bring.

At best this policy can only delay temporarily the ambitions of a determined dictator like Stalin or Hitler, at worst it means giving in to brute force, often at the expense of smaller countries, forced to concede territory in the interests of preserving international peace.

Appeasement became an issue in the 1930s, when Germany took progressive measures to overturn the provisions of the Treaty of Versailles. The best example of appeasement occurred in Munich in September 1938 (see page 122).

Expansionism is the name given to the foreign policy of countries like Fascist Italy and Nazi Germany. They aimed to **expand** their territory, by including within their enlarged frontiers: neighbouring peoples of the same race, beliefs or language; lands which had formerly been part of the mother country (for example, those territories which were redistributed as a result of the Paris Peace Treaties); and undeveloped territories abroad (such as Ethiopia) which could form part of an overseas empire.

Exercises

1. What do you understand by the term appeasement? Give two or three examples of events in the inter-war years which can be used as good examples of appeasement at work. What alternatives were there to appeasement?
2. Write brief notes explaining the significance of each of the following:
(a) The German re-occupation of the Rhineland in 1936
(b) The Anti-Comintern Pact
(c) The Polish Corridor
(d) Anschluss (union) between Germany and Austria
3. Explain carefully the events which led to the invasion of Abyssinia in 1935. What was the reaction of the rest of the world? What action did the League of Nations take? How did Britain and France secretly attempt to resolve the dispute? Did Mussolini get away with his act of aggression?
4. What circumstances led to the outbreak of the Spanish Civil War in 1936? How and why did this war involve the Soviet Union, Germany and Italy as well as a large number of volunteers from many parts of Europe? How did other countries attempt to deal with the problems raised by foreign intervention in Spain?
5. Had Hitler a genuine reason for seeking the Sudetenland in 1938 or was the threat of a German invasion of Czechoslovakia yet another example of naked aggression?
6. Explain what happened during the Munich Crisis of September-October 1938? What were the results, both short-term and long-term, of the Munich Peace Agreement?
7. Why was Poland a bone of contention between Germany and the Soviet Union? What was the significance of the Soviet-German Non-Aggression Pact in August 1939?
8. Some experts have claimed that Hitler had a better reason to march into Poland than into the Sudetenland. Yet it was the attack on Poland which precipitated the Second World War. Why was this?

Further Activities

1. Read the extracts which follow and say what each of these statements tells you about the Munich Peace Agreement. Identify the speaker in (a) and the individual referred to in (e):
(a) 'My good friends. This is the second time in our history that a British statesman has come back from Germany with "Peace with honour". I believe it is peace for our time. Now I recommend you to go home, sleep quietly in your beds.'
(b) 'Thousands of people are going to suffer. They must run for their lives or face the rubber truncheons and the concentration camps.'
(c) 'Twice he asserted that if the Sudeten territories were ceded this would be the last territorial demand Germany would make in Europe.'
(d) 'A surrender to blackmail . . . Hitler has won again . . . The settlement is only putting off the evil day . . . . We should have taken a firm line with Hitler from the start.'
(e) 'Posterity will thank God, as we do, that in the time of desperate need, our safety was guarded by such a man.'

Which of these opinions do you think you might have held on 1 October 1938?

The Second World War

> I am speaking to you from the Cabinet Room at 10 Downing Street. This morning the British Ambassador in Berlin handed the German Government a final note stating that, unless we heard from them by eleven o'clock that they were prepared at once to withdraw their troops from Poland, a state of war would exist between us. I have to tell you that no such undertaking has been received, and that consequently this country is at war with Germany.
>
> Neville Chamberlain: British Prime Minister

This BBC radio broadcast, at 11.15 am on Sunday, 3 September 1939, was how many people in Britain heard the news of the outbreak of the Second World War. People who lived through those days can usually remember what they were doing on that day. An hour later an American newspaper reporter heard the same news but in a square in Berlin, capital of Nazi Germany. He describes the experience below.

> I was standing in the Wilhelmplatz about noon when the loud-speakers suddenly announced that England had declared herself at war with Germany. Some 250 people were standing there in the sun. They listened attentively to the announcement. When it was finished, there was not a murmur. They just stood there as they were before. Stunned. The people cannot realize yet that Hitler has led them into a world war.
>
> William L. Shirer, *Berlin Diary*

The war that had just begun was soon to involve people in every continent and to result in the deaths of over fifty million people.

Causes of the Second World War

War had come to Europe for a number of reasons.
1. As you have seen in earlier chapters, the terms of the Treaty of Versailles were so unacceptable to the German people, it was inevitable that sooner or later they would have to be revised, either by negotiation or through the use of force.
2. The failure of the great powers to agree on effective methods of maintaining **collective security** (see Explanatory Notes) meant that they were powerless to face up to the dictators when the latter used force to implement their demands. Their weakness was shown by:
* the failure of the League of Nations to act decisively on Manchuria and Abyssinia;
* the blind faith statesmen put in promises and expressions of goodwill, such as the Locarno Pact and the Kellogg-Briand Pact, instead of backing them up with effective ways of ensuring they could be enforced.
* the reluctance of the great powers to sacrifice any of their own interests to the common good (for example, by putting the Royal Navy at the disposal of the League of Nations);
* the failure of the disarmament conferences.
3. The Depression of the early 1930s created tensions and problems, such as:
* the imposition of high tariffs on foreign imports – which favoured home producers at the expense of consumers, who would have benefited from cheap foreign goods;
* widespread unemployment leading to social unrest – which in turn helped to encourage extreme political parties such as the Fascists and Communists.
4. Determination not to repeat the carnage and horror of the First World War helped to foster pacifism and encourage appeasement – the belief that war must be avoided at all costs, even if it means conceding ground to your opponent. Paradoxically, this honourable and humane policy made war *more* not *less* likely in the years between 1918 and 1939.
5. Hitler's iron determination to get his own way, was a major cause of war, of course, but his actions,

Crowds in Downing Street, London, wait for the declaration of war against Germany on Sunday, 3 September 1939.

In a Nutshell

* The Second World War starts in Europe with the German invasion of Poland on 1 September 1939. But it really began in China over two years earlier, with the Japanese invasion of northern China in July 1937.
* Poland is quickly defeated and the country split between Germany and the Soviet Union.
* In the spring of 1940 the Germans launch attacks on Scandinavia, the Low Countries and France. The British army is evacuated from Dunkirk and France is defeated.
* Britain stands alone in Europe – but with the invaluable support of forces from almost all the Commonwealth countries. An attempted German invasion of Britain in 1940 is thwarted by the Royal Air Force, who defy Goering's Luftwaffe and deny Hitler the mastery of the sky he needs before his invasion forces can attack.
* The conflict becomes a world war in 1941 when the Soviet Union is invaded in June and when the Japanese attack the American naval base at Pearl Harbor in December.
* After bitter fighting the tide turns in favour of the Allies when Montgomery's Eighth Army defeats Rommel's *Afrika Korps* at El Alamein in November 1942; when the Red Army annihilates the German Sixth Army at Stalingrad in January 1943; and when the Americans win significant naval battles in the Coral Sea and at Midway in the summer of 1942.
* In July 1943 the Soviet Union defeats the Germans at the greatest tank battle in history at Kursk. In the same month the Allies invade Italy.
* On 6 June 1944 the Western Allies launch 'Operation Overlord' and establish a bridgehead in Normandy.
* Now Allied forces are attacking Germany from the west (through France and the Low Countries); from the east (through Russia, Poland, Hungary and Romania); from the south (through Yugoslavia and Italy); and from the air.
* American victories in the Far East bring American bombers within range of mainland Japan. Tokyo and other Japanese cities are bombed.
* The War ends in Europe with the death of Hitler and the occupation of Germany by Allied forces.
* Japan surrenders soon after atomic bombs destroy Hiroshima and Nagasaki, and after the Soviet Union declares war on her.

like those of Mussolini and the Japanese, have to be related to the action (and the inaction) taken by other great powers (such as China, the United States, France, the Soviet Union and Britain).

WANTED
FOR MURDER . . FOR KIDNAPPING.
FOR THEFT AND FOR ARSON
ADOLF HITLER
Adolf Schickelgruber
Adolf Hittler or Hidler

Last heard of in Berlin, September 3, 1939. Aged
fifty, height 5 feet 8½ inches, dark hair, frequently
brushes one lock over left forehead. Blue eyes.
Sallow complexion, stout build, weighs about 11
stones 3 pounds. Suffering from acute monomania,
with periodic fits of melancholia. Frequently bursts
into tears when crossed. Harsh, guttural voice, and
has a habit of raising right hand to shoulder level.
DANGEROUS!
THIS RECKLESS CRIMINAL IS WANTED
– DEAD OR ALIVE!
Daily Mirror, 4 September 1939

The Battle of France

The Phoney War
Even though Britain and France were at war with
Germany, their armed forces saw little action for
seven months. This was the *Phoney War*. 'Phoney'
is a slang word, which means fake or not genuine.
Many people throughout the world wondered why
the Allies made no attempt to attack Germany in
this period.

Instead Hitler's army launched a lightning war, or
Blitzkrieg (see Explanatory Notes), on unfortunate
Poland. Five weeks later it was all over. On 17
September Soviet forces invaded Poland from the
east. On 5 October Poland was no more, partitioned
between Germany and the Soviet Union. Hitler
expected Britain and France to agree peace terms,
since they had not fulfilled their promises to the
Polish people and showed little sign of wanting to
fight.

But people were no longer prepared to look on
Hitler as a statesman. Now that war had been
declared he was often portrayed as a criminal. The
war against Germany could be seen as a crusade
against persecution and evil, as shown by the extract
on the left from the *Daily Mirror*.

Norway
The War in Europe began in earnest in 1940, when
German forces attacked Denmark and Norway on
9 April. This was partly to forestall an Allied attack
(which was being planned) which could have imper-
illed Hitler's war plans, since the German iron and
steel industry used Swedish iron ore shipped in
winter through the Norwegian port of Narvik.

An Allied Expeditionary Force was unable to
resist the German invasion and withdrew. Its failure
helped to bring about the downfall of Neville Chamberlain as prime minister – a man of peace. His
successor was Winston Churchill – a man of war.

Winston Churchill – in charge of the Royal Navy
again – October 1939.

Winston Churchill was born in 1874. In 1900 he entered
parliament as a Conservative MP but six years later
became a minister in the Liberal Government at 32. As
First Lord of the Admiralty he was in charge of the
navy at the start of the First World War. After the War
he returned to the Conservative Party.

For much of the inter-war period he was a controversial
figure, arguing forcefully against appeasement.

When war broke out in 1939 he became First Lord of
the Admiralty once again and the news was greeted
by the navy with the signal 'Winston's back!' He
became Prime Minister on 10 May, the day that Hitler
launched his Blitzkrieg on the Low Countries.

Churchill was in his element as a war leader, taking
an active but sometimes ill-informed part, in military
decisions. His greatest value to Britain was as an orator
who raised the morale of troops and general public
alike, when things looked bleak, by insisting that the
War would eventually be won.

He had every reason to expect that he would be re-
elected in 1945. But the people wanted a change and
elected a Labour government instead. When he died in
1965, few begrudged him the title of greatest British
leader of the twentieth century.

Dunkirk

On 10 May 1940 Hitler launched what appeared to be a massive attack on the Low Countries, even though they were neutral. Accordingly, French and British troops rushed to the assistance of the Belgian army. But it was a trap.

The main German attack came instead through the Ardennes, a difficult mountainous area in southern Belgium, which the French had assumed to be unsuitable for modern tank warfare. It was not! German tanks swept through the weakened French armies and raced for the Channel coast.

Ten days later von Kleist's panzers (tanks) reached the sea, cutting off the Allied armies to the north. Luckily, Hitler insisted that his generals keep to the original plan, which was to move towards Paris and not eliminate pockets of resistance trapped by the German attack. They could be dealt with later. Had the Germans continued the attack they were certain to have destroyed the British Expeditionary Force in France, since nearly 400,000 British and French soldiers were trapped.

> We shall not flag or fail. We shall go on to the end; we shall fight in France; we shall fight on the seas and oceans; we shall fight with growing confidence and growing strength in the air; we shall defend our island whatever the cost may be.
>
> We shall fight on the beaches; we shall fight on the landing grounds; we shall fight in the fields and in the streets; we shall fight in the hills. We shall never surrender.
>
> Winston Churchill after Dunkirk

There was only one sensible thing for the British to do – retreat. The Royal Navy organized a rapid evacuation from the port of Dunkirk, gathering together nearly a thousand ships of all shapes and sizes to take a quarter of a million British servicemen and over 100,000 French and Belgian troops back to Britain.

It was a massive, demoralizing defeat and the British Army had to leave most of its vehicles and equipment behind. But there were relatively few casualties and the soldiers lived to fight another day. Churchill had said only three weeks earlier 'I have nothing to offer but blood, toil, tears and sweat.' Now he rose to the occasion with yet another stirring speech, which at the time made Dunkirk seem like a victory.

Fall of France

After Dunkirk there was very little the French army could do to resist the German advance. On 10 June Mussolini declared war on Britain and France. On 14 June German troops goose-stepped into Paris and on 21 June the French Government surrendered at Compiegne – in the same railway carriage which had witnessed Germany's humiliation in 1918.

Germany occupied most of northern France, including the Channel ports and much of the Atlantic coast. Unoccupied France then became neutral, led by Petain and Laval from the small town of Vichy in central France. But Charles de Gaulle a

British soldiers waiting to be evacuated from Dunkirk in 1940. An armada of private boats helped to take the men across the English Channel.

German troops ride down the Champs Elysées in Paris after the Fall of France in June 1940.

French general who escaped to Britain, had other ideas and formed the Free French Government in exile in London.

In July the Vichy Government nearly declared war on her former ally Britain, after British forces destroyed or captured French warships off North Africa – to stop them falling into German hands.

The Battle of Britain

On 18 June 1940 Churchill urged his fellow countrymen:

'Let us therefore brace ourselves to our duty and so bear ourselves that if the British Commonwealth and Empire last for a thousand years men will still say, "This was their finest hour".'

Churchill followed his own advice; and dismissed a German peace offer. So, Hitler and his staff prepared a plan to invade Britain, codenamed 'Operation Sealion'. First they needed command of the air, for without it the Royal Air Force would have been able to destroy the landing craft on the beaches of southern England.

Goering promised that this would be done and sent the Luftwaffe to destroy the RAF in the air and on the ground, bombing airfields and destroying other essential targets, such as radar installations. But the RAF resisted and although hard pressed managed to stave off defeat. They were helped when, towards the end of August, the Germans decided to bomb London rather than RAF airfields.

The London Blitz which followed did a vast amount of damage but it failed to break the spirit of Londoners. On 15 September a massive Luftwaffe raid on London resulted in the shooting down of over fifty German planes. Soon after this Hitler called off 'Operation Sealion' and the danger of an invasion of Britain had passed – for good.

Churchill had already paid his tribute to the Royal Air Force. 'Never in the field of human conflict was so much owed by so many to so few', he said.

Hitler Attacks the Soviet Union

Operation Barbarossa

Hitler turned his attention instead to his archenemy, the Soviet Union. In July 1940 he told his generals, 'The sooner we smash Russia the better.' Stalin did not trust Hitler either and had taken military action against Finland, and annexed Lithuania, Latvia, Estonia and Bessarabia to provide Russia with a buffer zone to her west.

Hitler made plans to attack Russia on 15 May 1941 but this had to be changed in order to allow German troops to attack Greece and Yugoslavia in April. By delaying the attack for five weeks Hitler, unwittingly, helped the Russians to survive the following winter.

The attack began on 22 June 1941 under the codename 'Operation Barbarossa'. It was the biggest invasion the world had ever seen. About 3 million German troops, assisted by soldiers from Finland and Romania, drove forwards into the Soviet Union on a front which was nearly 3000 kilometres wide.

The Russian winter

By the autumn German forces had captured Kiev, capital of the Ukraine, and were laying siege to Leningrad, and threatening Moscow itself. But that fatal delay of five weeks in the summer, prevented the German army from completing the conquest of Russia before the end of 1941. The onset of the Russian winter caught the German army unprepared. Their soldiers had inadequate winter clothing and their tanks and vehicles ran into difficulties, first in the autumn muds and later in the intense cold of the Russian winter.

No such problems hindered the Russians fighting for their native soil, and, in December, white-uniformed Russian soldiers, some on skis, halted the German advance just in front of Moscow. Their leader, Marshall Zhukov, was probably the most successful of all the Soviet commanders.

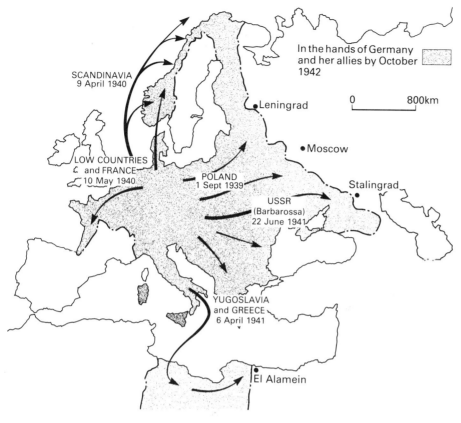

SCANDINAVIA
9 April 1940

In the hands of Germany
and her allies by October
1942

Leningrad

0   800km

Moscow

LOW COUNTRIES
and FRANCE
10 May 1940

POLAND
1 Sept 1939

Stalingrad

USSR
(Barbarossa)
22 June 1941

YUGOSLAVIA
and GREECE
6 April 1941

El Alamein

Axis conquests and
campaigns in Europe and
North Africa; 1939–42.

Stalingrad

The following spring the German army renewed the
offensive but with a change of plan. Hitler ordered
them to take the oilfields of the Caucasus in the
south-east. A large German army laid siege to Stalingrad but once again the Russian winter intervened
to forestall them.

What was worse, Zhukov led them into a trap,
encircling the German Sixth Army under von Paulus
and forcing them to surrender on 31 January 1943
(against Hitler's orders to 'fight to the last man').

That same month other Russian forces relieved
Leningrad, after a devastating siege in which hundreds of thousands of Russians died.

In July the two armies fought a vast tank battle
at Kursk in central Russia and from this time
forward the Russians were on the offensive. The
war in the east had turned.

The ruins of Stalingrad.
The city was besieged
and bombarded from
June 1942 to 31 January
1943. The Russian
victory here was a
turning point in the war
in the east.

Japan Attacks the United States

United States–Japanese relations before 1941

The United States maintained its neutrality throughout the first two years of the War in Europe. The French pleaded for massive American intervention before the Fall of France in 1940 but assistance was not forthcoming. Many influential Americans thought Britain was doomed, including the American Ambassador in London.

But although neutral in the sense of keeping out of the fighting, the United States was not neutral when it came to supplying friends and hampering enemies. The Lend-Lease Act of Congress in March 1941 enabled the President to lend or lease (hire) military equipment to Britain (and the Soviet Union a few months later).

Relations between the United States and Japan had deteriorated by 1941. American aid to China, American volunteers fighting for Chiang Kaishek and the sinking by the Japanese of American gunboats in Chinese waters, led to a crisis which came to a head in July 1941, when defenceless Vichy France was given no option but to allow the Japanese to take over airfields and naval bases in French Indochina (now Vietnam). Japan was anxious that her supplies of vital raw materials should not dry up and told France that these bases were needed to protect her trade.

The United States Government saw it differently, suspecting rightly that the Japanese intended to expand into south-east Asia. So Roosevelt placed an embargo (ban) on the export of oil and petrol to Japan. Japan already coveted the oilfields of the Dutch East Indies (now Indonesia) and the rubber- and tin-producing areas of Malaya (then a British colony).

Whilst talks continued between the United States and Japanese delegations, the Japanese navy made secret preparations for an attack on the US naval base at Pearl Harbor in Hawaii. Other war preparations were made for the eventual seizure of Malaya, the Philippines and the Dutch East Indies and large numbers of Japanese troops were sent to the new bases in Indochina.

On 17 October, General Hideki Tojo, the Japanese Minister of War, replaced Prince Konoye as Prime Minister of Japan. Tojo was a military hardliner and two weeks later he approved Admiral Yamamoto's plan to destroy the American Pacific Fleet at anchor in Pearl Harbor. Talks still continued with the United States Government but the decision to attack was finally made on 1 December 1941 – by this time Admiral Nagumo's task force was already at sea, on course for Pearl Harbor.

Pearl Harbor

> War struck suddenly and without warning from the sky and sea today at the Hawaiian islands, and Japanese bombs took a heavy toll in American lives. Wave after wave of planes streamed over Oahu which the army said started at 8.10 am Honolulu time and which ended at around 9.25, an hour and 15 minutes later.
>
> Associated Press

This was how many people heard the news of the Japanese attack on Pearl Harbor. Six aircraft carriers, supported by battleships, cruisers and destroyers, were somehow able to come within striking distance of the main American naval base in the Pacific *without* being detected. Negotiations with the Japanese were already at a crisis stage yet little heed was paid to the danger signals. The Americans thought the Japanese would attack in the Far East, not nearer home.

When Admiral Nagumo's fleet was about 400 kilometres from Pearl Harbor, some of the 353 planes in his strike force started to take off, at 6 am. When the first wave of planes swept in nearly two hours later, they were picked up on American radar but the report of a massive formation of planes was dismissed out of hand as 'nothing to worry about'. After all it was Sunday morning. Nobody had declared war.

The shock raid completely surprised the American forces on the base. In a brilliantly planned raid, modelled on Hitler's Blitzkrieg, Japanese aircraft destroyed nearly two hundred American warplanes, sank four battleships and damaged four others, together with ten other ships. Luckily the American aircraft carriers *Lexington*, *Saratoga* and *Enterprise* were out at sea. Had they been in port, the war might have ended differently. A total of more than 2300 American servicemen and servicewomen died.

War was declared and President Roosevelt called 7 December 1941 'a date that shall live in infamy'. Four days later, the other Axis powers, Germany and Italy, also declared war on the United States – a fatal mistake.

Meanwhile, the Japanese launched simultaneous attacks on Hong Kong, the Philippines, Malaya, Thailand, Singapore and Guam. The world was truly at war.

On Christmas Day 1941 Japanese forces captured Hong Kong and in January invaded the Dutch East Indies. Singapore fell on 15 February 1942 and the Philippines in May. By the beginning of June the

7 December 1941 – the US fleet burns in Pearl Harbor, after Japan's unexpected and devastating bombing raid.

Japanese had control over a vast empire – which they called the Greater East Asia Co-Prosperity Sphere. It included all or part of Hong Kong, Malaya, Burma, Thailand, Indochina, Java, New Guinea, the Philippines, Borneo and the Dutch East Indies.

The battle of Midway

So far the tide of battle had been in favour of Japan. But now it turned. The Japanese expected the Allies to sue for peace in the face of these lightning conquests and the disabling of the American Pacific Fleet. But although they sank battleships at Pearl Harbor they had not sunk the American aircraft carriers. Their own attack on Pearl Harbor had shown the effectiveness of the carrier in modern

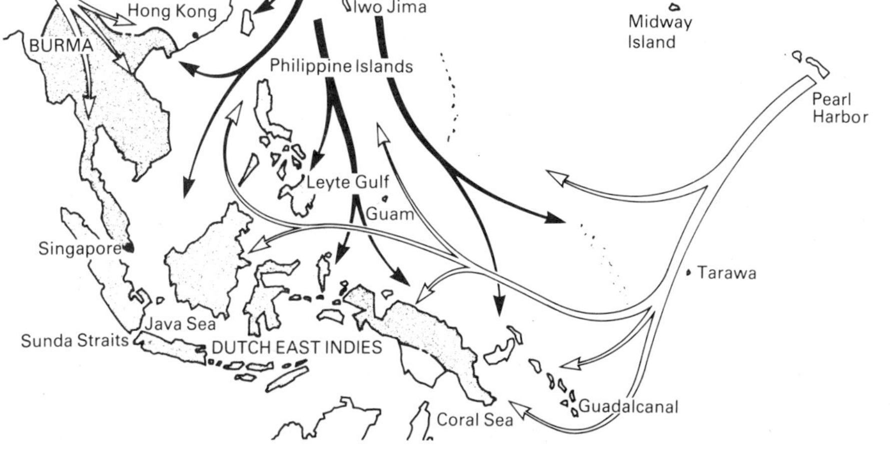

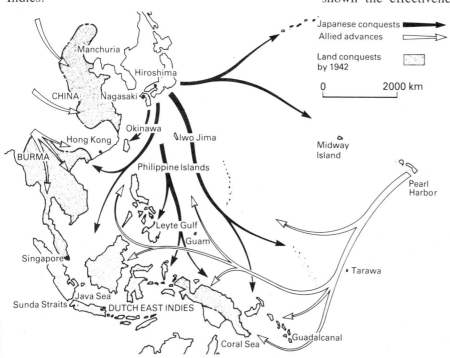

Map of the war in the Far East.

Left: Allied tanks advancing through the desert sand during the battle of El Alamein, November 1942.

Right: D Day. American troops landing in Normandy in June 1944.

warfare as opposed to the battleship. Now it was the turn of the Americans.

In May 1942 American and Japanese aircraft carriers fought the first battle in the history of naval warfare in which the opposing fleets fought a battle without seeing each other. This was the battle of the Coral Sea, near Australia and the Solomon Islands. Although the Americans lost one of their biggest carriers, the *Lexington*, they severely damaged a Japanese carrier, sank another, and prevented the Japanese from taking Port Moresby in Papua, which would have been an effective base from which to invade Australia.

One month later on 4 June 1942 the American navy avenged Pearl Harbour in a battle off Midway Island in the middle of the Pacific. American planes managed to sink four of the aircraft carriers which took part in the raid on Pearl Harbor, together with 332 of their planes. American losses were relatively light by comparison (147 planes and one aircraft carrier). Thereafter American forces were on the offensive against Japan.

In August American forces landed on the island of Guadalcanal, the first of a number of Pacific islands, taken by American marines in the teeth of bitter Japanese opposition. In the next three years the Americans captured many other islands – they called it 'island-hopping'– including the Philippines in 1944, and Okinawa and Iwo Jima, on the fringe of Japan itself, early in 1945.

North Africa and Italy

A third major turning point in the War came in Egypt, where Montgomery's Eighth Army decisively defeated Rommel's crack Afrika Korps at the battle of El Alamein on 4 November 1942. The war in North Africa had originally been fought between Italian and British troops, but a crushing defeat for Italy persuaded Hitler to send troops to aid Mussolini. Now these troops too were on the run.

Four days after El Alamein, American and British forces landed in North Africa ('Operation Torch') and joined up with Montgomery's Eighth Army to invade Sicily in July 1943. Mussolini was deposed by the Italians (25 July), imprisoned, but later freed by German paratroopers in a daring raid. When the Allies invaded the mainland in September, Italy surrendered, to the disgust of the Germans who called it treachery and cowardice. Hitler immediately sent troops into Italy to halt a possible Allied advance into Austria. Slowly the Allies pressed forward but they had to fight for every inch of ground, in the face of stubborn and tenacious German resistance, led by their commander Field Marshal Kesselring.

Invasion of Europe

Stalin had urged Churchill and Roosevelt to open a second front in Europe in order to take the pressure off the Soviet Union. But the Allies knew the risk involved if such an invasion failed. So they made detailed and comprehensive plans.

General Dwight Eisenhower was appointed Supreme Allied Commander of 'Operation Overlord', as it was called. He assembled a team of high-ranking officers from Britain and the United States to train the forces, make preparations and ensure that supplies could be quickly sent to the armies

once they had secured a bridgehead in France. Floating harbours (codenamed Mulberry) and an underwater oil pipeline (PLUTO) were constructed.

On Tuesday 6 June (D-Day), the great armada sailed – the greatest naval invasion in history. Allied troops landed on the Normandy beaches with varying degrees of success. In August they broke through the opposing German forces and launched a rapid advance across northern France and the Low Countries. Paris was liberated on 25 August and Brussels on 3 September. Temporary setbacks included the failure of the Arnhem landings in September 1944 and the battle of the Bulge in December – a major German counter-attack in Belgium.

In March 1945 Eisenhower's armies crossed the Rhine whilst at the same time the Red Army drove towards Berlin from the east. On 25 April American and Russian soldiers shook hands. Four days later Mussolini was killed by partisans in Italy and the next day Hitler committed suicide. Berlin fell to the Russians on 2 May and on 8 May it was all over. Germany had surrendered.

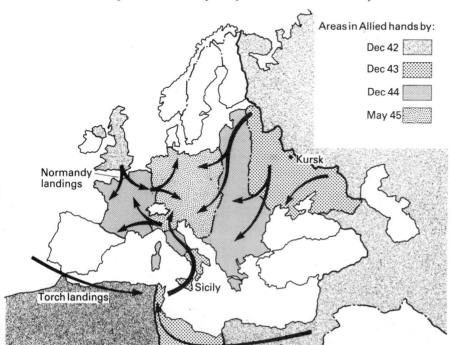

Areas in Allied hands by:

Dec 42

Dec 43

Dec 44

May 45

Allied conquests and campaigns in Europe and North Africa; 1942–45.

Victory over Japan

The Allies could now concentrate on defeating Japan in the Far East. American commanders made plans for the invasion of Japan in 1946. But they knew that these invasions would be costly in both men and materials. The Japanese defenders of Iwo Jima and Okinawa, which had been captured as a result of bitter fighting in March and June 1945, had fought tenaciously to the last man. Over 100,000 Japanese died on Okinawa alone (American dead numbered 12,000). Forecasts of a million casualties were mentioned.

The Japanese Government sent peace feelers to Moscow, hoping to negotiate a settlement (through Stalin) with the United States. But the Soviet Union was itself preparing to fulfil an earlier promise to attack the Japanese in Manchuria. Whether a peace settlement could have been negotiated is a matter of some controversy. It was not in the Japanese nature to surrender, as you can see from their Okinawa casualties. But the threat of an attack from the Soviet Union might well have alarmed them, as it did the Americans, who had no desire to partition

Japan into separate occupation zones as had happened in Germany (See Chapter 11).

But President Truman of the United States (Roosevelt died in April 1945) had a secret weapon – the atom bomb. He told Stalin about this at the Potsdam Conference (see Chapter 11) but Stalin hardly took any notice! On Monday, 6 August 1945, the *Enola Gay* dropped a bomb on Hiroshima, a large Japanese industrial city on the coast. Whilst the Japanese Government considered how to react to the Hiroshima bomb, a second bomb was dropped on Nagasaki. On 14 August the Japanese surrendered. The Second World War was over.

The devastation after the Americans dropped the first atomic bomb on the city of Hiroshima in August 1945. Many of those who survived the bomb itself, died later from the effects of radiation.

The atom bomb literally burned to death all living things, human and animal, in Hiroshima. The dead were burned beyond recognition.

The city became a disastrous ruin. The effect was widespread – those outdoors were burned to death and those indoors were killed by indescribable pressure and heat.

The dead are simply uncountable. It is not possible to distinguish the men from the women among the killed. When buildings were hit by the atrocious bomb, every living being outside simply vanished into air because of the heat. The amount of destruction is simply indescribable.

Tokyo Radio

Explanatory Notes

Blitzkrieg (lightning war) is the name that was given to the rapid attacks made by German armed forces on Poland, the Low Countries, France and Russia in 1939–41. Tanks (panzer units), mechanized infantry, dive bombers, fighter aircraft and other rapidly moving forces were used to surprise and shock the enemy.

The failure of **collective security** stemmed largely from the inability of the great powers to trust each other. This failure in the League of Nations, and elsewhere, to agree on common action to preserve world peace, should have caused no great surprise, since the great powers were often bitter political enemies. Fascism and Communism were opposites.

The democracies, on the other hand, were sometimes represented at international conferences first by left-wing and then by right-wing politicians, each group with different views on disarmament and what was best for their country.

For example, in 1924 Britain's Labour Prime Minister, Ramsay MacDonald, persuaded the League of Nations to accept the Geneva Protocol which would have given the League greater power to make nations settle their disputes peacefully. But this British initiative collapsed, not because Mussolini opposed it, but because the Labour Government was succeeded by a Conservative Government which thought it was against Britain's interests.

If politicians in a peace-loving democracy could not agree on how to maintain world peace, how could the world's statesmen be expected to do so?

Total war is the name given to a war in which the total economy of a country and all of its people are involved, either directly on the battlefield and in factories making weapons, or indirectly when sheltering from air attacks.

Holocaust means 'great loss of life', but in the Second World War usually refers specifically to the mass extermination of people in Nazi concentration camps. Six million Jews are thought to have been killed in this way, one third of them in the gas chambers at Auschwitz in Poland. The Nazis called it the *Final Solution* to disguise what they were doing. Goering instructed Heydrich in July 1941 to submit his proposals for carrying out 'the desired final solution of the Jewish question'.

Exercises

1. What was Blitzkrieg? Explain carefully the sequence of events which enabled Hitler to invade Poland without immediate retaliation by any other army.

2. Describe the events which led to the fall of France in 1940. What happened to France after surrender terms were agreed?

3. To which important events, battles and happenings of the Second World War do the following statements refer? Write brief notes to amplify your answer:

(a) 'Never in the field of human conflict was so much owed by so many to so few' (Churchill). Who were the 'many' and who were the 'few'?

(b) 'OK. Let's go.' (General Eisenhower)

(c) 'MISSILE IS EQUAL TO 20,000 TONS OF TNT; TRUMAN WARNS FOE OF A "RAIN OF RUIN" ' (*New York Times*)

4. What did Japan hope to gain by attacking the American naval base at Pearl Harbor? Examine the steps which led up to the outbreak of war between Japan and the United States and say what its consequences were for both powers.

5. To what extent was each of these battles a major turning point in the War:

(a) Battle of Britain 1940
(b) Pearl Harbor 1941
(c) Midway 1942
(d) El Alamein 1942
(e) Stalingrad 1942–43
(f) D-Day 1944

Further Activities

1. Undoubtedly the most controversial development of the Second World War was the dropping of the atom bomb on Hiroshima in August 1945. Well over 100,000 people were killed or died from the after-effects of the explosion.

Ever since, the arguments have raged – between those who believe that without the atom bomb the war in the Far East would have lasted another year (with an estimated one million Allied casualties), and those who say there are no circumstances whatsoever, which can justify the use of an atom bomb as a weapon of war.

What do you think? Collect information about the dropping of the atom bomb on Hiroshima in August 1945. Draw up a dossier listing the reasons *for* and the reasons *against* dropping an atom bomb on Japan.

CHAPTER 11

The Second World War and its Consequences

The Second World War began in Europe with the German advance into Poland on 1 September 1939 and Hitler's subsequent refusal to withdraw his forces, in response to a British and French ultimatum. So the War began, *because Britain and France had guaranteed Polish independence and with it Poland's existing frontiers.*

But when the War was over, a substantial slice of Polish territory was ceded to the Soviet Union; and the Western Allies found they were no nearer securing for Poland the independence they had guaranteed, and for which half a million British and Commonwealth soldiers had died.

What had happened, as in all great wars, was

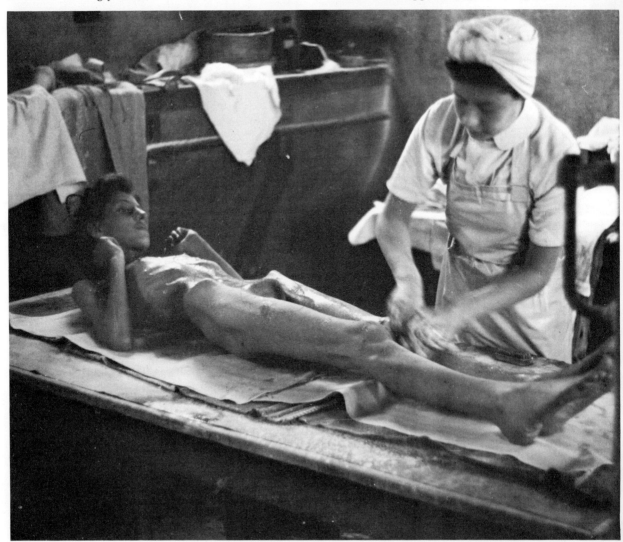

138

simply that circumstances changed during the course of the fighting. The belligerents now had new war aims, new enemies and new allies. The United States and the Soviet Union, which stood by whilst Hitler occupied most of Europe, later bore the brunt of the fighting – although not without complaint. But this gave them the right, which they took, to determine how the War should end.

Throughout the War other powers were invited, or induced, to join the Allies with promises and hints of gains which might follow a successful outcome to the War. Some resisted the temptation and stayed neutral (such as the Irish Free State). Some countries (for example Italy) changed sides, whilst one, France, was forced to become neutral.

Not surprisingly, the war aims of the Allies changed with the course of the War and many promises, whether rash or solemn, were never kept.

It was essential to reach agreement with the other Allies on what would be done with the lands they regained or conquered. For the Western Allies, at least, it was not to be a war of gain. In their deliberations the Allied leaders went back far beyond 1939. It was unthinkable to allow Italy to retain Ethiopia (annexed in 1935), or to let Japan keep Manchuria (1931) or Korea (1910).

Accordingly, diplomatic efforts, such as summit meetings and conferences, continued throughout the War. Allied leaders and diplomats sought agreement on war aims, peace settlements and structures for preserving world peace when the War ended.

Left and above: When Allied troops entered Hitler's concentration camp in Belsen in April 1945, they found 40,000 starving and emaciated people, and 13,000 unburied corpses. These photos were taken several months later, after the Allies had begun to rehabilitate the prisoners.

In a Nutshell

* During the War the Allied leaders meet at intervals to decide the future of Europe after the War. The groundwork for these meetings is often prepared in advance by officials and deputies.
* Churchill and Roosevelt meet in 1941 and proclaim an Atlantic Charter, setting out their hopes and aims for the future. They meet again in 1943 at Casablanca to determine future strategy. Roosevelt demands the unconditional surrender of the Axis powers.
* Churchill, Stalin and Roosevelt have two summit conferences, at Teheran in 1943 and at Yalta in 1945. Among the many points they discuss are the future of Poland after the War, how occupied Germany shall be run, and what form the United Nations should take.
* Earlier agreements are later swept aside in an atmosphere of distrust when Truman, Stalin and Churchill (and later Attlee) meet at Potsdam after the War has ended in Europe in 1945.
* Peace settlements are reached with all the belligerents, with the exception of Germany. Cold War politics prevent German reunification, so there are now two Germanies to settle a war which was begun by only one.
* Japan is exclusively occupied by the United States under the Supreme Allied Commander, General Douglas MacArthur. He rids Japan of its militaristic past and dictatorial institutions.
* American aid and encouragement help the Japanese to transform their country into a vigorous and thriving democracy, with liberal attitudes and Western tastes.

Wartime Diplomacy

In August 1941 Winston Churchill and President Roosevelt had a historic conference on board a warship anchored in Placentia Bay, Newfoundland. Here they drew up a list of eight war aims. These were goals which would serve to show the sort of world they hoped to see after the War. A British newspaper called it the **Atlantic Charter**. (You can see the eight points of this Charter in the Explanatory Notes on page 147.)

At this time (9–12 August 1941) the United States was still neutral, and the war was going badly for Britain. The purpose of the meeting was mainly to strengthen their belief that this was a just war and that a better world would emerge from the wreckage. But, most important (from the British point of view), was the now indisputable fact, that the greatest power on earth, the United States, could be seen to share the same aims as Britain and the Commonwealth, and the same determination to oppose the evils of Fascism. It could only be a matter of time before the United States joined in the conflict.

Five months later, these war aims were endorsed by representatives of 26 nations at war with the Axis powers. In a Joint Declaration, on 1 January 1942, the United Nations (as they were called) looked forward to a world which would involve 'the establishment of a wider and more permanent system of general security' (see clause 8 on page 147 and also Chapter 16 on the United Nations).

The Casablanca Conference

This Conference was held in French Morocco on 14–24 January 1943 between Churchill and Roosevelt. Stalin had been invited but was 'too busy' – this was the month when Leningrad and Stalingrad were both relieved.

Stalin was urging Britain and America to invade the mainland of Europe and start a second front, rather than leave the Soviet Union to do all the fighting. By contrast, some American admirals and generals wanted the United States to concentrate on defeating the Japanese in the Far East if a cross-Channel invasion of northern France was no longer possible in 1943. Churchill felt the Allied forces were not yet ready for such an operation and pressed instead for a Mediterranean invasion.

Roosevelt (left) and Churchill (right) at the Casablanca Conference in 1943.

Eventually, the Allied leaders decided that Sicily, and then Italy, should be invaded as soon as the Axis powers had been defeated in North Africa.

The Conference also decided various other matters concerning the conduct of the War, such as a greater British commitment to the war against Japan after the defeat of Germany.

The biggest bombshell of the Conference was Roosevelt's declaration that the Allies demanded the *unconditional* surrender of their enemies. This had been discussed briefly with Churchill but while his advisers were in London. Loyally he supported Roosevelt but many diplomats were horrified. One of Churchill's chief advisers on foreign affairs later called it 'foolishness'.

The diplomats feared that the use of the word 'unconditional' would frighten off Axis countries, such as Bulgaria, Romania, Hungary or even Italy, who might otherwise be inclined to join the Allies or declare their neutrality.

'Unconditional' meant they would have no negotiating rights and would be completely at the mercy of the Allies. So the argument *against* was that the declaration might unduly prolong the war. Roosevelt, for his part, was not vindictive; but he did not want to end the war discussing terms with his enemies.

The Teheran Conference

This conference was held between 28 November and 1 December 1943 in Teheran, the capital of Iran.

This was the first conference attended by all three leaders. Churchill said that he only realized how small Britain was after sitting between Stalin on one side and Roosevelt on the other. In fact Roosevelt took Stalin's side when the leaders discussed strategy in Europe. Churchill proposed an Anglo-American invasion of the Balkans but Roosevelt supported Stalin in opposing it. Stalin was afraid they might liberate Hungary and Austria before the Red Army.

The main talking points or decisions made at the Conference were:
* That the D-Day landings should take place the following May or June.
* That the Soviet Union should declare war on Japan as soon as the war against Germany was over.
* That there should be a world organization after the War to take the place of the League of Nations. Britain, China, the Soviet Union and the United States were to be the 'Four Policemen' in the Security Council.
* That the Polish frontier with the Soviet Union should be redrawn to give Russia a buffer zone. In return Poland would be given part of Germany as compensation.

The Yalta Conference

This was the second meeting between Stalin, Churchill and Roosevelt. It was held in the Russian Black Sea holiday resort of Yalta between 4 and 11 February 1945. By this time the War was nearly over in Europe and the Allies had to make important decisions about the shape of Europe after the War. Stalin wanted to clear up the question of what to do with Poland. A British diplomat at Yalta thought Stalin . . .

> . . . 'much the most impressive of the three men. He is very quiet and restrained . . . he never used a superfluous word, and spoke very much to the point. He's obviously got a very good sense of humour – and a rather quick temper! . . . I have never known the Russians so easy and accommodating. In particular Joe has been extremely good. He is a great man, and shows up very impressively against the background of the other two ageing statesmen.'
>
> [*The Cadogan Diaries* edited by David Dilkes]

The Conference decided:

1. that the eastern boundary of Poland should follow the approximate line of the partition which Russia had agreed with Hitler in 1939;
2. that in compensation Poland should have part of eastern Germany – on a line approximately following the rivers Oder and Neisse – but no firm decision was reached. This later became a bone of contention between East and West;
3. that representatives of the Polish and Yugoslav Governments in exile – based in London – should be involved in the governments of those countries after the War. The Soviet Union had already helped Polish Communists to form a provisional government based at Lublin in south-eastern Poland, liberated by the Russians in 1944. Since the Russians were already in Poland there was little that Churchill or Roosevelt could do to press the claims of the London-based government any further;
4. that there should be free elections after the War in the countries liberated by the Allies. This was embodied in the *Declaration on Liberated Europe*;
5. that the Soviet Union would definitely declare war on Japan within three months of the end of the war in Europe. In return she would regain territories lost to Japan in the war of 1904–5;
6. that the United Nations Organization should go ahead on the lines already drawn up at the Dumbarton Oaks Conference (see Chapter 16); the three leaders cleared up issues still unresolved, such as the power of veto and difficult questions about entitlement to membership;
7. that there should be four occupation zones in Germany when the War ended (American, British, French, Soviet). Stalin only agreed to the inclusion of France after pressure from the other two leaders;
8. that Germany should pay reparations; and Roosevelt agreed that the sum of $10,000 million to the Soviet Union and another $10,000 million to other victims of Nazi aggression should be regarded as the approximate sum the Allies would have in mind at the end of the War.

Churchill (left), Roosevelt (centre) and Stalin (right) at the Yalta Conference in February 1945. Standing behind them are, from left to right, Lord Leathers, Anthony Eden, Stettinius, Sir Alexander Cadogan, Molotov and Averill Harriman.

141

The Potsdam Conference

This was the last of the wartime conferences between the three great powers. This time it was held in occupied Germany, at a palace in Potsdam on the outskirts of Berlin.

By this time one of the 'ageing statesmen' – Roosevelt – had died. His place was taken by President Truman. The perils of living in a democracy were brought home to Stalin, since Churchill was Prime Minister at the start of the Conference on 16 July 1945; but at the close, on 2 August 1945, his place had been taken by Clement Attlee, leader of the newly elected Labour Government. This was ironic in the circumstances, since the Conference spent much of the time discussing the question of free elections in the countries liberated by the Russians!

At Potsdam the Russians held most of the cards. Eastern Europe was in their hands; so the most the Allied leaders could do was to bring as much pressure to bear as possible. But the atmosphere had changed. Sir Alexander Cadogan said Stalin was being 'very tiresome' about Poland's frontiers. He noted that 'Russia tries to seize all that she can and she uses these meetings to grab as much as she can get'.

The Conference decided:

1. To endorse many of the decisions made at Yalta, such as the boundaries of Poland. But the Oder-Neisse line was to be regarded as temporary – depending upon the formal agreement of the Germans as part of a peace treaty. In fact a peace treaty was never signed. It was only in 1970 that the Federal Government (West Germany) finally accepted the Oder-Neisse line.

2. To form a Council of Foreign Ministers to draw up the peace treaties with the different Axis powers.

3. To prosecute Nazi war criminals.

4. To approve payment of reparations by Germany to Russia and the other countries she had invaded. These reparations were to be paid in kind – whole factories were to be dismantled and the equipment and machinery sent to Russia. But since Germany's leading industrial region, the Ruhr, lay in the occupation zones of the Western Allies it was agreed that in return for machinery and equipment from the West, the Russians would exchange corn and coal from their zone.

Peace in Europe

The Second World War did not end with an impressive conference attended by the world's leaders, as had happened after the First World War, when the Paris Peace Treaties were signed. Perhaps it was as

The Nuremberg Trial of suspected Nazi war criminals began in 1946. All 21 men in the dock have been charged. Goering is bottom left, with Hess on his left, and then Ribbentrop.

well, in view of the tension and aggravation caused by the provisions of the Treaty of Versailles in 1919. This was chiefly because the Western Allies and the Soviet Union increasingly distrusted one another after the end of the War, as the Potsdam Conference in the summer of 1945 showed.

Germany was never reunited. The separation into four occupation zones was not intended as a permanent division. It was just a convenient way of sharing the burden of administering Germany immediately after the War. The Allies wanted to be absolutely certain that the evils of Nazi rule would not return to Germany or to Europe. The War had been fought to eradicate the inhumane policies of National Socialism. So the denazification of Germany was begun – a policy of rooting out all Nazi war criminals and sympathizers. Many were tried and punished.

But long before Germany had recovered sufficiently to contemplate reunification, the Cold War (see Chapter 12) intervened, turning Germany into a pawn to be fought over yet again – this time with words rather than with weapons. The failure to reunite Germany led ultimately to the formation of NATO and the Warsaw Pact (see Chapter 12); and when West Germany joined NATO it was no longer possible to think of a united Germany. As Germany was not one country there could be no peace treaty; since neither East nor West was then prepared to accept the German boundaries as being permanent.

The other Axis powers came out of the War with a more certain future. Italy lost Fiume, Trieste, and her African colonies (under United Nations supervision), paid reparations, and cut back her armed forces. These terms formed part of the Treaty of Paris (1947) which inflicted similar conditions on the other Axis powers of Bulgaria, Finland, Hungary and Romania. Their territorial losses can be seen on the map.

Austria, which had been united with Germany under Hitler, was also divided into occupation zones. In exchange for a guarantee of strict neutrality, the Russians eventually agreed to withdraw their troops and allow Austria to become independent once more. But this was not until 1955 when the Austrian State Treaty was signed.

Peace in the Far East

The Occupation of Japan

It has sometimes been argued that one of the reasons why Truman decided to drop an atom bomb on Hiroshima was his desire to conclude the war against Japan, without first having to call on massive help from the Soviet Union. As you have seen, this assistance had been specifically sought by Roosevelt at

Russian gains

1, 2, 3 from Finland	7 from Germany
4 Estonia	8 from Poland
5 Latvia	9, 10 from Czechoslovakia
6 Lithuania	11 from Romania

Territorial changes at the end of the Second World War.

Teheran and Yalta. But that was before the atom bomb.

Russian intransigence at the conference table, the practical difficulties of co-ordinating the work of the different occupation zones in Germany, and Russian unwillingness to co-operate strengthened American determination to exclude the other Allies, including Britain, from the pacification of Japan.

The Americans argued that their forces had borne the brunt of the fighting in the last three years of the War; it was up to America to finish the job she started the day Pearl Harbor was bombed in December 1941.

To all intents and purposes there was only one army of occupation in Japan after the War. This was almost exclusively American, apart from a small number of British troops. There were no quarrels, no arguments, no vetoes; just one Supreme Commander for the Allied Powers (SCAP) – General Douglas MacArthur.

143

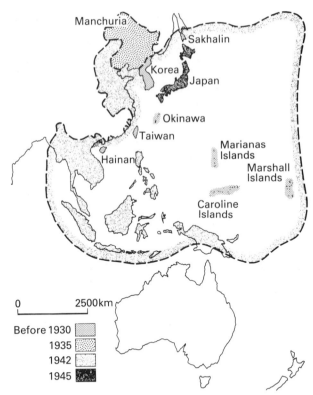

Above: Tokyo in ruins after the War. Over 200,000 Japanese people are believed to have died in the American air raids on the city.
Right: Japanese expansion in the 1930s and 40s. After the War, Japan lost all her overseas territory.

0   2500km

Before 1930
1935
1942
1945

MacArthur had a number of objectives. Some of these had been determined for him at the Cairo Conference during the War, when China, Britain and the United States met in November 1943 and agreed to insist on unconditional surrender and the splitting up of Japan's overseas empire.

The disposal of Japan's overseas empire
* Parts of the empire went to the Soviet Union in the north.
* The Pacific islands which Japan had acquired as League of Nations mandates after the First World War were now to be administered by the United States.
* Taiwan and several other lands, once occupied by Japanese forces, were returned to China.
* Korea, scheduled to be independent, was divided between two occupying armies – Soviet in the north and United States in the south.

These territorial changes were later ratified by the Treaty of San Francisco in 1951.

MacArthur's reforms
MacArthur set himself two main tasks, aside from the breaking up of the Japanese empire. These were:
1. To eradicate the militaristic tradition in Japan, which had helped authoritarian military dictatorships control civilian governments before the War;

2. To turn Japan into a democracy on Western, specifically American, lines. In the process he helped to lay the foundations of Japan's postwar prosperity.

Japan in 1945
The future looked bleak to the Japanese in 1945. Their national pride had suffered a mortal blow when they were forced to surrender. This went against everything the Japanese had been taught to believe during the years of militarism.

In the last years of the War thousands of young men volunteered to become *Kamikaze* (or suicide) pilots, who served their country by aiming explosive-laden planes at Allied warships. Japanese commanders, like Admiral Nagumo, commander of the Japanese fleets at Pearl Harbor and at Midway, committed suicide rather than suffer the disgrace of being taken prisoner. Soldiers were expected to fight to the death – and did so – on Iwo Jima and Okinawa. Japanese who felt contempt for British prisoners surrendering at Singapore, now suffered the same humiliation themselves.

The road to recovery looked insuperable. For one thing, Japan's industrial might had been shattered by Allied bombing. Cities lay in ruins, the transport system was in chaos, the people poor and desperate. Japan's overseas empire had been broken up – even

144

Taiwan (Japanese since 1895) and Korea (Japanese since 1910) were lost – so Japan no longer controlled sources of raw materials on the mainland of Asia, such as Manchurian coal. Many of Japan's traditional markets had been lost and the goodwill dispelled by the actions of her occupying forces during the war years.

Eliminating militarism

MacArthur's first task was to eliminate militarism as a force in Japan. Accordingly war criminals were tried and punished, including General Tojo (ex-Prime Minister) and General Yamashita (conqueror of Singapore) who were both executed.

Government departments and the big business enterprises of Japan were purged of their top officials. The armed forces were disarmed and all traces of authoritarian rule wiped clean (for example, political prisoners were freed).

The Emperor ceased to be a divine ruler and became a symbol of power as head of state; he no longer took an active part in the decisions of the Government.

Creating a democracy

The Japanese constitution was revised so that power now rested with the people of Japan, through their elected representatives, and not in the divinity of the Emperor.

* All adult Japanese citizens over 21, male or female, were given the vote, to elect representatives to the Diet (the Japanese parliament). The government was to be chosen from the majority party in the Diet. Trade unions were permitted and political parties allowed to flourish freely.
* The Japanese were given new liberties, particularly freedom of speech – provided they did not criticize the Occupation Forces!
* The law courts were given powers which made them independent and beyond the control of the government. The whole educational system was overhauled.
* The large organizations (called *zaibatsu*) which used to control Japanese industries, banks and businesses, were broken up.
* Hitherto half of Japan's farmers were tenants, who paid their rent in crops and farm produce. They were now given the opportunity to buy their land cheaply with government loans.

American aid

In addition the Americans increasingly began to realize that a friendly Japan could become a bulwark of freedom, to counter what the Americans viewed as a world-wide Communist conspiracy, responsible for the Communist Revolution in China in 1949 and the Korean War in 1950.

It was in 1951 that 48 nations, including the United States, signed the Japanese peace treaty at San Francisco. But the Americans also signed a security treaty as well, which gave them valuable military bases in the Far East, whilst providing a defence system for Japan.

Japanese recovery

At first Japan made only a slow recovery from the effects of the War and in 1947 the Americans had to provide $400 million worth of aid to stop the people from starving. By 1951 this had escalated to $2000 million and, in the next few years, Japanese businesses were working flat out to supply the American armed forces fighting in Korea.

Trade increased rapidly, particularly with the United States, and Japan's industries thrived as management and workforce adapted skilfully to the changes of the postwar world. Living standards inside Japan rose dramatically and this too stimulated the boom in industry, since Japanese customers also wanted the new consumer goods and electronic products developed by Japan's space age factories.

Modern Tokyo. Japan has not only rebuilt ruined buildings, but her whole economy has thrived since the Second World War. Japan is now one of the leading industrial nations.

The Historical Significance of the Second World War

1. The Second World War was unquestionably the worst war the world has ever known. The death toll is generally placed as high as 50 million, of whom at least half were Russians. They included soldiers killed in action; prisoners of war and Jews exterminated; civilians who were executed, who starved to death, or who died of cold.

2. Barbarism had long been thought extinct among civilized societies. Yet in Germany there were symphony orchestras, great art galleries – and gas chambers where men, women and children were deliberately put to death. When some of the guilty Nazis stood trial for these crimes it shocked observers to see how 'terrifyingly normal' the executioners and torturers seemed to be.

3. The dropping of the atom bomb on Hiroshima heralded a new age of terror. By 1980 the great powers had amassed sufficient nuclear weapons to destroy the world several times over.

4. The Second World War saw the emergence of the two great superpowers – the United States and the Soviet Union. Worse, it saw the origins of the Cold War and the division of much of the world into two armed camps.

But there was a credit side as well.

5. It gave birth to the United Nations, which for all its faults, has proved to be a more effective peace-keeping organization than its predecessor the League of Nations, and an effective tool in the struggle to achieve equality, establish basic human rights and eliminate human suffering.

6. It restored democracies to Japan, Germany, Austria and Italy.

7. It stimulated hopes of independence among the millions of subject peoples in the colonies of the great European powers. Many Africans, West Indians, and Malays fought in the British armies. And for what were they fighting? To guarantee the *independence* of Poland. Yet the triumphant advance of the Japanese armies throughout southeast Asia, showed only too clearly that colonial powers, like France, Britain and the Netherlands were not invincible and could be beaten.

8. By destroying much of Europe it made necessary a new mood of economic, social and political co-operation after the War – leading later to the formation of the European Economic Community as a union of like-minded nations bound by a common purpose.

Indian troops fighting the Japanese in 1944. Such action stimulated the demand for Indian independence.

Explanatory Notes

The **Atlantic Charter** which was signed by Churchill
and Roosevelt in 1941 provided an excellent
summary of Allied **war aims**. Elements of this
statement derive from the Fourteen Points, which
President Wilson issued in 1918 before the end of
the First World War. The Atlantic Charter later
helped to formulate the aims and objectives of the
United Nations Organization when it was founded
in 1945.
1. Their countries (the United States and the United
Kingdom) have no territorial ambitions.
2. They desire no territorial changes without the
consent of the people living in those territories.
3. They respect the right of all peoples to choose
the type of government under which they will live.
4. They will try to ensure that all countries have
free access to raw materials needed for their
economic prosperity.
5. They want international co-operation in
improving labour standards, welfare measures and
economic growth.
6. After the defeat of the Nazi tyranny they want
to establish a lasting peace.
7. They seek freedom for all peoples to cross the
seas without hindrance.
8. They want all nations to abandon the use of
force. They believe that, *pending the establishment
of a wider and more permanent system of general
security*, that the disarmament of such nations is
essential.

Exercises

1. Why did Churchill and Roosevelt sign the
Atlantic Charter? What did they hope to achieve?
What *did* they achieve?
2. For each of the conferences listed below, say (a)
who attended, (b) what issues were discussed and
with what results.
(a) Casablanca 1943
(b) Teheran 1943
(c) Yalta 1945
(d) Potsdam 1945
3. Why was the effective conduct of diplomacy
essential in wartime? Why did the Allies have to
make clear what they were fighting for and what
they intended to do once the War was over?

4. What signs of the Cold War could be detected
during the wartime conferences?
5. Why were Poland's frontiers redrawn after the
War? Why did the Western Allies agree to this, even
though the initial cause of the War had been the
British and French guarantee to Poland?
6. How and why did the Allied treatment of
Germany after 1945 differ from the treatment she
received after the First World War?
7. What were the circumstances which led to the
introduction of a democratic system of government
in Japan.
8. Draw a large scale map of Europe and colour in
the changes that were made to the frontiers of the
Soviet Union and neighbouring states at the end of
the War. What other international boundaries were
altered in 1945?

Further Activities

1. The Potsdam Conference decided that war criminals should be brought to justice. Goering, Ribbentrop, Hess, and other leading Nazis, were tried at
Nuremberg in 1946, and many of those found guilty
were hanged. These trials have excited controversy
ever since.

In wartime it is sometimes difficult to say whether
an act which results in death or destruction is a crime
or not. The extermination of millions of Jews and
Russian prisoners of war and the mass execution of
innocent civilians in reprisals (such as at Lidice in
Czechoslovakia, where all the men were shot) were
obviously inhuman, barbaric, unspeakable and
unforgivable criminal acts. But was the dropping
of the atom bomb a war crime?

How would you distinguish between war crimes
and legitimate acts of war? And who would you say
is responsible for those war crimes – the people who
carried them out (sometimes under pain of death if
they disobeyed), or the people who gave the orders,
or both?

What do you think? Discuss this with your friends.
2. Interview older relatives and friends who lived
through the Second World War. What were the most
important effects of the Second World War on their
lives and those of their families?

CHAPTER 12

The Cold War Begins

'From Stettin in the Baltic to Trieste in the Adriatic, an iron curtain has descended across the Continent.'

This was one of the first public occasions on which a Western leader used the term 'iron curtain' to describe the frontier between Eastern and Western Europe after the Second World War. Winston Churchill was speaking at Westminster College, in the small American town of Fulton, Missouri. He made his speech on 5 March 1946, but had already used the same phrase in a telegram to President Truman on 12 May 1945:

'An iron curtain is drawn down upon their front. We do not know what is going on behind . . . Surely it is vital now to come to an understanding with Russia, or see where we are with her, before we weaken our armies.'

Yet only three months earlier Churchill told the

House of Commons that his impression after the Yalta Conference in February was:

'. . . that Marshal Stalin and the Soviet leaders wish to live in honourable friendship and equality with the Western democracies.'

What had gone wrong? Had relations really deteriorated between the Soviet bloc and the West in only three months?

One year after Churchill's Fulton speech, an American friend of his, called Bernard M. Baruch, told politicians in South Carolina:

'Let us not be deceived – we are today in the midst of a cold war.'

By this he meant a war of words between the Soviet Union and the West. It was not a 'hot' war, nor a 'shooting' war; but a war, nonetheless, in which there would be enemies and friends, losers and winners, defeats and conquests. Coupled with Churchill's idea of an iron curtain, separating and isolating the Communist world, these two ideas helped to shape postwar relations between East and West.

The Cold War Begins

People throughout the world were dismayed when their statesmen started talking about, and acting as if there was a cold war between the Soviet Union and its allies in the East, and the United States, Britain and their allies in the West.

But the Cold War should have come as no surprise in the light of past attitudes and the previous records of both sides. It was a false hope to think that the Second World War, though a massive turning point in history, would change long-held attitudes and government policies.

The Allies had been united in their desire to defeat the Axis powers but this did not mean they saw eye to eye. It was simply that all Hitler's friends were their enemies and all Hitler's enemies were their friends. Churchill said 'If Hitler invaded Hell I would make at least a favourable reference to the Devil.' Immediately after the start of the German invasion of Russia in June 1941 he told radio listeners:

'No one has been a more consistent opponent of Communism than I have . . . I will unsay no word that I have spoken about it. But . . . any man or state who fights on against Nazidom will have our aid.'

Left: The Berlin Crisis in 1948. A US military policeman standing alert on the US sector dividing line. In the background is a Russian jeep.

In a Nutshell

* Mutual suspicion and hatred between the capitalist or Communist worlds start the Cold War between the Soviet Union and the Western Allies.
* Stalin turns the 'liberated' countries of Eastern Europe into satellite states of the Soviet Union. The boundary between the Eastern bloc and the West is called the 'Iron Curtain' because it is difficult for people in the West to make contact with, or to know what is happening in Eastern Europe.
* American intervention in the Greek Civil War helps to thwart a threatened Communist takeover.
* This is why Truman announces that in future the United States will support all free peoples in their fight against repression (the Truman Doctrine).
* An Allied airlift supplies Berlin during the 1948–49 blockade imposed by the Soviet authorities. Stalin had hoped to stop fuel and food supplies reaching the city.
* The Berlin Blockade is the main reason why the Western Allies form NATO and create the Federal Republic out of their occupation zones in Germany.
* American intervention in the Korean War again shows the determination of President Truman to withstand actual or supposed threats of Communist aggression.
* In 1955 the Soviet Union and its allies form the Warsaw Pact in self-defence when Germany joins NATO.

Reasons why the Cold War began

1. In 1939 Stalin and Hitler agreed a non-aggression pact, which dismayed the rest of the world, and which allowed Nazi Germany and Communist Russia to carve Poland in two. In 1939–40 Stalin annexed Bessarabia (then Romanian), the Baltic States (Lithuania, Latvia, Estonia) and invaded Finland. What reason had the Western Allies for supposing that Stalin could now be trusted only five or six years later?

2. **Communism** and **capitalism** were opposites (see Explanatory Notes). Churchill and others had pressed for Western intervention in the Bolshevik Revolution just 25 years earlier. Churchill and Truman were known opponents of Communism. What reason had Stalin for supposing that they could be trusted, now that they had got what they wanted – the destruction of the Nazis?

3. From 1920 to 1941 popular support in the United States had been for a policy of non-intervention in Europe. Why should she change her long-term policy less than three and a half years later? Had she not stood by and watched Hitler overrun the

democratic governments of Western Europe in 1940 at a time when leading Americans forecast that Britain would be defeated – the reason they gave for not involving America in the War?

This worried Churchill, particularly since Truman, understandably, started to move his armed forces out of Europe and into the Pacific soon after the end of the War with Germany. If America pulled out and returned to her pre-war policy of isolationism, who in Europe could withstand the armed might of Stalin's Red Army?

4. Allies invariably quarrel at the successful conclusion of a war over (a) how to treat the defeated enemy, (b) how to share out the spoils of war.

Stalin thought there was no need to try the Nazi war criminals at all, and, according to one distinguished eyewitness, proposed instead that the 50,000 top Nazis should just be taken out and shot.

Germany was in chaos after the War, with her economy in ruins. German civilians were close to starvation; millions of refugees, returning soldiers and prisoners of war, blocked the streets of derelict ruined cities. Humanity called for massive aid to restore minimum living standards there – but the Soviet Union, too, had suffered terribly as a result of the war. Her leaders, understandably, gave priority to Russia not Germany in any reallocation of resources after the War.

5. The Western Allies had proclaimed in the Atlantic Charter in 1941 that 'their countries have no territorial ambitions' (see Chapter 11). But this was obviously not the Russian aim, even though they endorsed the Charter by signing the Joint Declaration on 1 January 1942. This was incompatible with the moves they made in 1939–40 in Eastern Europe and also with their demands at Yalta and Potsdam to have the Polish frontiers redrawn.

6. Both sides had substantial grounds for distrust in 1945. After all, the United States now had the atom bomb – a secret she did not propose to share with any other power. Truman only told Stalin about it after it had been tested and shortly before it was to be used on Hiroshima. Stalin, for his part, failed to keep the promises he made; that people in the liberated territories would be free to choose their own governments. It soon became obvious that, in the countries they now controlled, the Russians would only be prepared to contemplate the formation of pro-Communist governments.

7. Stalin's seizure of the Baltic States Bessarabia and eastern Poland was a reversion to Russia's pre-1914 frontiers.

But Soviet domination of the countries of Eastern Europe, newly liberated by the Red Army, frustrated the Western Allies, because they could not prevent them becoming Communist without going to war with the Soviet Union.

The charitable view was that Russia still feared a Western crusade against Soviet Communism. According to this theory, Stalin wanted a buffer zone of satellites between Russia and the West, which would act as 'a strong defensive perimeter'.

The other view, favoured by most Americans, was that the Communist takeover of Eastern Europe was simply a subtle form of Soviet aggression, enlarging the frontiers of world Communism by peaceful means rather than by force.

The Communist Takeover in Eastern Europe

At first Stalin moved slowly in Eastern Europe. There was no sudden imposition of Soviet Communism. Opposition parties were allowed and at the first elections the voters were given a relatively free choice, *provided* the governments they chose were at least sympathetic to Communist aims and ideals. But gradually the East European Communists took over the running of their countries.

* Georgi Dimitrov became Communist leader of Bulgaria in 1946.
* A coalition government dominated by Communists controlled Poland until all opposition parties were banned in 1947.
* A left-wing coalition government in Hungary, dominated by the non-Communist Smallholders' Party after free elections, made sweeping reforms until it was replaced by a hardline Communist government led by Matyas Rakosi.
* A Communist-dominated coalition government controlled Romania, which, remarkably, remained a monarchy until December 1947 when King Michael was forced to abdicate.
* In Czechoslovakia the 1946 elections gave the Communist Party abour 40 per cent of the votes and a coalition government led by Klement Gottwald, a Communist, came to power. But in a coup, in February 1948, Gottwald managed to get rid of the non-Communists in his government and left President Benes with no option but to resign.

The Cominform
This was the abbreviated name for the COMmunist INFORMation Bureau, an organization which Stalin set up in October 1947 after a conference of Communist Party leaders from Eastern Europe and also from the West (France and Italy).

Apart from actually providing information, its main purpose was said to be one of co-ordinating the work of the Communist Party in Europe. It soon

Klement Gottwald, the Communist President of Czechoslovakia.

Matyas Rakosi, the hardline Communist dictator of Hungary in the early 1950s.

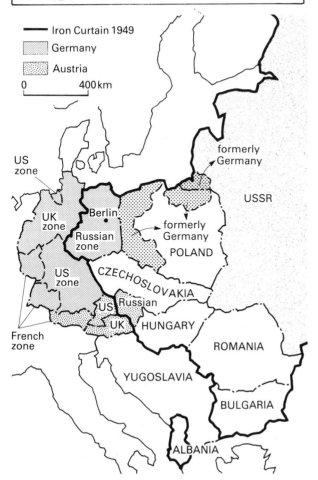

Iron Curtain 1949
Germany
Austria
0   400 km

US zone
UK zone
Berlin
Russian zone
US zone
French zone
US
Russian
UK
formerly Germany
USSR
formerly Germany
POLAND
CZECHOSLOVAKIA
HUNGARY
ROMANIA
YUGOSLAVIA
BULGARIA
ALBANIA

Left: Map of Eastern Europe in 1949 showing the countries of Eastern Europe, the Iron Curtain and the occupation zones in Germany and Austria.

Ex-king Michael of Romania in London in 1948, having been forced to abdicate by the Communists.

Above: Yugoslavia's Communist dictator – President Tito – speaking at a gathering of workers in 1949.

became apparent that its chief function was rather different – to ensure that the other leaders toed the Party line in Moscow. In 1948 it condemned and ordered the expulsion of Yugoslavia from the Cominform, because President Tito refused to follow the Party directives.

Tito, a guerilla leader during the War, remained a thorn in Stalin's side – as a Communist who took an independent, not a Stalinist, line. He was able to keep Yugoslavia independent of the Iron Curtain countries because it had not been 'liberated' by the Red Army at the end of the War.

The Truman Doctrine

The Greek Civil War

Greece had been involved in a civil war since the last years of the War. Communist guerillas, in a group calling themselves the National People's Liberation Army (or ELAS as it is usually known) fought the Germans with considerable success. When Hitler's occupation forces withdrew, ELAS tried to take over the legitimate government of

Below: Civil War in Greece in 1948. Greek Government forces dig trenches for protection against an attack from Communist rebels based in the surrounding hills.

Greece. At this stage they controlled over two thirds of the country.

But when the Germans left, their place was taken by British forces, committed to the restoration of the Greek monarchy. ELAS fought against Greek Government and British troops until a truce was agreed in January 1945.

The establishment of Communist regimes in other parts of Eastern Europe encouraged ELAS to lead another uprising in northern Greece in 1946. By this time British forces were overstretched and unable to provide the Greek Royalist Government with the support and material aid it needed to counter the Communist rebellion.

But President Truman was determined to withstand Communist aggression and it was then, on 12 March 1947, that he made his famous statement to Congress – the Truman doctrine.

'I believe that it must be the policy of the United States to support free peoples who are resisting attempted subjugation by armed minorities or by outside pressures.' (12 March 1947)

Truman put his doctrine into practice by supplying the Greeks with advisers and arms. As a result the attempted Communist takeover was put down, partly because President Tito, who had broken with the Cominform, withdrew his support from the guerillas.

General George Marshall.

The Marshall Plan

The Truman doctrine signalled a change in American foreign policy, from one of co-operation with Soviet Communism to one of confrontation. Truman was not going to stand idly by and watch while Stalin took, by stealth, other territories in Europe.

But what if freely elected Communist governments came to power? What could America do then? This was a distinct possibility, since Europe was still suffering the after-effects and ravages of the War. There were severe food shortages, and lack of money prevented European governments rebuilding their shattered cities. The Americans recalled what had happened after the First World War. They knew that Communism thrived wherever there was poverty and despair.

Accordingly, the Americans prepared a plan which would provide massive financial aid to help the governments of Europe recover from the damage which the war effort had done to their economies. This plan was first outlined, in June 1947, by a former American wartime commander – General Marshall – who was now the American Secretary of State (foreign minister).

The Marshall Plan was yet another way in which the Americans could carry out the Truman doctrine, of helping democratic governments counter the spread of Communism. In Greece the Americans used the 'stick'; now Marshall Aid was to be the 'carrot'.

Any country accepting aid was assumed to be friendly to the United States. This was why the Americans offered help to the countries of the Eastern bloc. Czechoslovakia, governed by a pro-Communist coalition government, originally accepted an offer of Marshall Aid but eventually turned it down on instructions from Moscow. But Yugoslavia accepted, demonstrating Tito's independence from Stalin.

The Russians later provided their own substitute for Marshall Aid when they founded COMECON in January 1949 (COuncil for Mutual ECONomic Assistance).

Marshall Aid was administered by the Organization for European Economic Co-operation (OEEC) and eventually distributed grants totalling $13,000 million as the European Recovery Programme. Countries receiving Marshall Aid included Britain, France, Belgium and Norway of the countries which had been at war with Germany, and Austria, Italy and West Germany of the former Axis powers.

The Berlin Blockade. Food is unloaded straight on to lorries from an American cargo plane, June 1948.

The Berlin Blockade

When the War ended, Germany was divided into four occupation zones – British, American, French and Russian. Because of the importance of Berlin as the capital of Germany, it too was divided into four occupation zones, even though it was over 150 kilometres inside the Russian sector.

It was originally intended that both the Berlin and the German occupation zones should be jointly governed by the four occupying powers. But the Soviet authorities did not allow free access to their zone and the other three occupying powers decided to take steps to merge their sectors into one.

In June 1948 the crisis reached a head when the Allies announced a new system of currency which they intended to use in the Allied zones in Berlin as well as in West Germany. This was to facilitate trade between the two areas; but to the Russians it seemed as if the Allies were thinking of West Berlin as part of West Germany and making both independent of the Russian-dominated Eastern zone.

The Soviet authorities decided to act, thinking they had the whip hand. Rail links between West Berlin and the Allied occupation zones had already been restricted (since 1 April). Now all road and rail links were cut (24 June). Not to be outdone the Allies organized a massive airlift along the air corridors which had been assigned to them across the Soviet zone. The Russians could have interfered with these air traffic routes as well, but they knew that such an action would probably mean war. Equally the Allies knew they could only force a route across land if they used tanks and armoured vehicles. The Russians, and many of the Allies, expected the Berlin Blockade would bring Berlin to its knees and force the Western Allies to abandon their plans. Instead the airlift was a success.

Allied cargo planes, flying night and day, supplied Berliners with everything, including coal. Eventually the Russians had to admit that the Blockade was not having the effect they hoped and normal road and rail routes were re-opened on 12 May 1949.

By then the future course of Europe had changed irrevocably:

(a) The Western Allies had formed a defensive alliance – NATO.

(b) Plans for the creation of the German Federal Republic were finalized and came into being only eleven days after the lifting of the Blockade.

Both these results had an important 'knock-on' effect, since the Russians and their allies regarded the formation of NATO as a hostile act, as an endorsement of the Cold War and a threat to their own security. This led eventually to the formation of the Warsaw Pact alliance in 1955.

The founding of the Federal Republic made it possible for Germans in the three Western occupation zones to start rebuilding their country. But it also ensured that Germany would now be split permanently in two. The German Democratic Republic (East Germany) came into being on 7 October 1949 – little more than four months after the foundation of its rival the Federal Republic on 23 May 1949. When the Federal Republic joined NATO on 9 May 1955 it was followed only five days later by the signing of the Warsaw Pact.

NATO

The North Atlantic Treaty Organization came into being on 4 April 1949. You can see the principal terms of the Treaty in the panel below and the names of the countries who signed it.

The most significant feature of the Treaty was not so much the fact that it was an alliance of twelve powers – ten in Europe and two in North America – but the fact that it committed the United States, bigger than all the other countries put together, to the defence of Europe. This was a convincing answer, at last, to Churchill's worries, in May 1945 at the end of the War, about the future defence of Europe.

Since 1949 NATO has remained strong, despite one or two upsets. In 1952 Greece and Turkey joined the organization, followed three years later by West Germany. France later withdrew her forces from NATO command (1966); so the NATO headquarters were moved from Paris to Brussels.

NATO

The Parties agree that an armed attack against one or more of them in Europe or North America shall be considered an attack against them all; and consequently they agree that, if such an armed attack occurs, each of them, in the exercise of the right of individual or collective self-defence recognised by Article 51 of the Charter of the United Nations, will assist the Party or Parties so attacked by taking forthwith, individually and in concert with the other Parties, such action as it deems necessary, including the use of armed force, to restore and maintain the security of the North Atlantic area.

Signed BELGIUM, CANADA, DENMARK, FRANCE, ICELAND, ITALY, LUXEMBOURG, NETHERLANDS, NORWAY, PORTUGAL, UNITED KINGDOM, UNITED STATES. Washington. 4 April 1949. (GREECE and TURKEY joined in 1952)

The Korean War

When Japan was defeated in 1945 the Allies were faced with the problem of deciding the future of the different parts of the old Japanese empire. The Korean peninsula had been Japanese since 1910. The Allies (but not Stalin) had promised it would become independent after the War. But in 1945 it was partitioned along the 38th parallel – 38° North – with the Japanese forces surrendering to the Red Army in the north and to the Americans in the south.

Plans to unite the two halves failed, so in 1948 both occupation zones were granted their independence – The Republic of Korea on 15 August (formerly the American zone in the *south*) and The Korean People's Democratic Republic (formerly the Soviet zone in the *north*) on 9 September. Neither government was happy with the partition of their country and both claimed to be the rightful government. Nonetheless the Soviet and American garrisons returned home.

Then in June 1950 the armies of North Korea suddenly poured across the frontier, captured the South Korean capital Seoul, and drove the South Korean forces into a small corner of the peninsula near the port of Pusan.

The issue was raised in the United Nations and, after demanding that the North Koreans withdraw, the UN Security Council passed a motion calling on member states to come to the military aid of the

The Korean War, September 1950. Landing craft, manned by troops of the United Nations task force, approach the Korean port of Inchon, near Seoul.

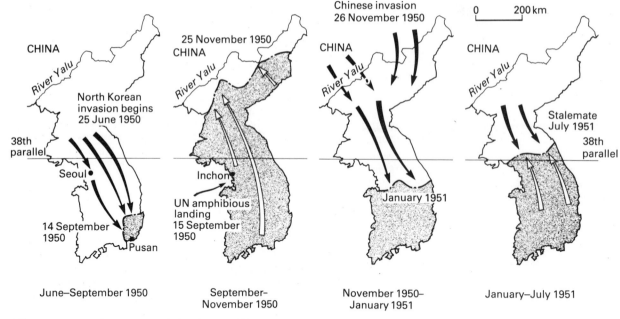

Maps showing the course of the Korean War.

South Korean Government. As it happened the Soviet permanent representative on the Security Council was boycotting meetings of the Council at this time – in protest – otherwise he could have vetoed the formation of a United Nations force. In fact this was largely American (with some Commonwealth forces) and led by the American commander – General Douglas MacArthur.

MacArthur was an outstanding and original commander. Instead of just reinforcing the troops caught in the Pusan perimeter zone (see map), he made a landing at Inchon, near Seoul, 300 kilometres inside enemy-occupied territory. Caught off guard, the North Koreans fell back as the soldiers inside the Pusan perimeter linked up with the Inchon landing forces. Together they drove the North Koreans behind the 38th parallel and back into their own Republic.

Instead of staying in South Korea, having forced the North Koreans to obey the UN demand (that they withdraw their troops), MacArthur advanced into North Korea, ignoring Chinese Communist warnings that they would intervene if he did so. China had only just turned Communist and her armed forces were as yet unknown, untried and untested. By November the UN forces had nearly completed their task of reunifying the two Koreas.

Then on 24 November 1950 huge Chinese armies crossed the Yalu River between China and North Korea. Their advance southwards was just as rapid

as that of the UN forces northwards. MacArthur suggested taking the war into China itself and even using the atom bomb. This was dangerous talk and Truman took the courageous step of sacking him. Eventually the UN forces managed to hold a line on or about the 38th parallel. After holding virtually the same positions for two years, the two sides signed an Armistice agreement in July 1953.

The significance of the Korean War lay not so much in the fact that the UN forces regained South Korea for the South Koreans, but in the decisive and convincing way in which the Americans rushed troops to defend the victim of an act of aggression. But victory was bought at a terrible cost – over 50,000 American dead and an estimated 3 million Korean civilians. Yet technically the United States had not been at war – as President Truman explained to an interviewer (see below).

Interviewer:
'Mr President, everyone is asking in this country, are we or are we not at war?'
President Truman:
'We are not at war.'
Interviewer:
'Would it be correct to call it a police action under the United Nations?'
President Truman:
'Yes, that is exactly what it amounts to.'

Explanatory Notes

Communists believe that the State should own the means of production, such as farms and factories.
Capitalists believe in a system of free enterprise, in which individuals are free to work for themselves. They believe that competition between individual owners is the best way to ensure that the best products are made as cheaply and as efficiently as possible. Inferior products will not sell as well and their manufacturers will probably go out of business (putting their employees out of work as well).

Communists say that in a truly Communist country there can be no such competition; so workers can feel secure in their jobs. Only one manufacturer, the State, is needed.

Capitalists say this results in inferior products since the employees of the State-run industries have no incentive to improve the quality of the goods they manufacture.

Under a Communist system, people do not have to take responsibility for their own lives. Few people own their own houses and relatively few own cars. But everyone has somewhere to live and public transport is very cheap. There is little unemployment in Communist societies – everyone has a job. Medical services are free. The State takes care of the sick and needy.

So, the State looks after its people. But it also controls them and people do not have the same freedoms they would have if they lived in, for example, the United States.

Freedom in the United States means freedom to say what you like and freedom to go on strike to get more pay. It means freedom to own your own house, farm or factory. But it also means freedom to become desperately poor, and freedom to live in a city slum.

Exercises

1. Explain carefully the circumstances and events which led to the development of the Cold War between the Soviet bloc and that of the West. Who was to blame for this deterioration in the friendly relations which had existed between both sides during the War? Or were both sides as bad as each other?

2. What was the Truman Doctrine? Describe the sequence of events which preceded this important statement of American policy. How did it represent a departure from the peacetime attitude to diplomacy followed by the Americans in the inter-war years? What other developments in the immediate postwar period indicated that there would be no return to the earlier policy?

3. Write a brief definition of each of the following terms, explaining clearly what they mean, and illustrating your answers with an example taken from the history of the postwar period:
(a) Iron curtain
(b) Cold war
(c) Blockade

4. What was the significance of the Berlin Blockade (1948–49) in the development of the Cold War? How were its effects felt far beyond the boundaries of West Berlin and West Germany?

5. Why did the Western Allies form NATO? What was the Soviet response to this military alliance?

6. How did the Communists manage to take over most of the countries of Eastern Europe? How did Stalin consolidate his hold on these satellites?

7. What were the causes of the outbreak of war in Korea in 1950? Trace in outline the main course of the war and explain why American and Commonwealth forces fought there under the United Nations flag. Did the Americans achieve their aims in fighting this war?

Further Activities

1. Is the Cold War still a force to be reckoned with in the world today? Compile a portfolio or scrapbook of cuttings from daily and weekly newspapers which contain items about relations between the countries of the American-dominated Western Alliance on the one hand, and the countries of the Warsaw Pact on the other.

How do the other countries of the world fit into this pattern of relationships, in particular those which are Communist but not consistent supporters of the Soviet Union (for example China) and those which are non-aligned (taking neither side) like India?

CHAPTER 13

East-West Relations after the Death of Stalin

US IMPOSES ARMS BLOCKADE ON CUBA
ON FINDING OFFENSIVE MISSILE SITES;
KENNEDY READY FOR SOVIET SHOWDOWN

SHIPS MUST STOP
Other Action Planned
If Big Rockets Are Not Dismantled

PRESIDENT GRAVE
Asserts Russians Lied and
Put Hemisphere in Great Danger
New York Times

WE BLOCKADE CUBA
WITH 40 WARSHIPS
JFK's Orders: 'Search,
And If Necessary, Sink Any Arms Ship'
New York Mirror

These were the headlines New Yorkers woke up to on Tuesday, 23 October 1962. It was the start of the gravest crisis since the end of the Second World War.

Many people feared the worst; that Kennedy really would sink Russian ships and that the threatened 'Soviet Showdown' was the start of the Third World War. Only this time it would be a nuclear conflict.

Yet the two world leaders who faced each other across the Atlantic and the Arctic Ocean had been acclaimed as peacemakers. Khruschev of Russia had denounced his predecessor, Stalin, and made peace overtures to the West. It looked as if the Cold War might soon be over. People talked of a 'thaw' in East-West relations.

Kennedy was young, virile, charming; a charis-

Right: A Soviet merchant ship carrying missiles bound for Cuba in 1962.
Below: President Kennedy signs the proclamation, imposing a blockade on Cuba.

matic leader, dedicated to the principle of equality for all peoples; a world statesman seeking to lessen international tension so that East and West could live in harmony.

Just when everyone's hopes had been raised they seemed to sink overnight. Why had relations between the two great powers turned sour? And why was the peril of a nuclear war so much closer?

Russia after Stalin

Stalin's successor?

When Stalin died in 1953 the Russian leaders were thrown in confusion. Stalin, 'the man of steel', had ruled the Soviet Union with an iron fist ever since the late 1920s. When he first came to power the Bolshevik Revolution was not yet ten years old. Russia was still weak, her agriculture backward, her communication systems poor, and most of her industrial resources yet to be developed.

By contrast, the year of Stalin's death was marked by the successful testing of the Russian hydrogen bomb. The Soviet Union was now a superpower, second only to the United States.

Who was to succeed Stalin as ruler of this powerful empire – another dictator like Lenin or Stalin? Or would Russia be governed by a

In a Nutshell

* Stalin dies in 1953 and is eventually succeeded by Khruschev.
* When Khruschev denounces Stalin in 1956 and makes peace overtures to the West, people begin to think the Cold War may be over.
* But the Soviet suppression of the Hungarian Uprising in 1956, the building of the Berlin Wall in 1961, and the Cuban Missiles Crisis in 1962, seem to shatter these hopes.
* In the 1950s and early 1960s the United States becomes involved in a civil war in Vietnam between Communists and a right-wing government. Several million American soldiers fight in Vietnam and over 50,000 are killed, fighting for a cause which the Americans eventually lose.
* Khruschev is replaced by Brezhnev; a Soviet statesman who cracks down on 'dissidents' – Russians opposed to the policies of their government.
* When a more liberal Communist government led by Alexander Dubcek attempts to introduce reforms in Czechoslovakia in 1968, the Warsaw Pact countries send in troops.
* But Brezhnev continues the policy of peaceful co-existence or *detente* as it is now called – seeking ways of living in harmony with the West. Talks are held with Western leaders to control the testing, growth and spread of nuclear arms.
* Mao Zedong's China opposes these Russian moves towards friendship with the West; yet when relations between China and the Soviet Union get worse, the Chinese make friends with the United States and the West in the early 1970s.
* But Russian decisions (a) to send in troops in 1979 to support the shaky Government of Afghanistan, and (b) to help the Polish Government clamp down on the newly formed Solidarity Trade Union in the early 1980s, cause East-West relations to deteriorate once more.

committee of leaders, drawn from the *Politburo* (the Russian equivalent of the British Cabinet)?

At first the Russians announced that Georgi Malenkov was to be the new Prime Minister. But Nikita Khruschev, a rival on the Politburo, knew that the real seat of power in the Soviet Union lay in the post of First Secretary of the Communist Party, the position Stalin held at the time of Lenin's death.

Khruschev denounces Stalin

Two years later First Secretary Khruschev ousted Malenkov as the Russian leader, although at first he shared the limelight with the new Russian Prime

Left: Delegates in the Hall of the Great Palace in the Kremlin in Moscow – listening to speeches at the Twentieth Party Congress of the Soviet Communist Party in 1956 (at which Khruschev denounced Stalin).

Right: Angry Hungarian rioters topple a giant statue of Stalin in Budapest in 1956.

Minister, Marshal Bulganin, until he too was demoted. Malenkov was sent to manage a power station and Bulganin the State Bank. Under Stalin both would have been shot; so people in the West could see that things had changed in the Soviet Union, even if not as rapidly as many people hoped.

At the Twentieth Party Congress in 1956 Khruschev astounded the world when he denounced Stalin and the injustices committed during the Purges in the 1930s. He told the Russian people that Stalin had encouraged the 'cult of personality' – of getting too much power for himself and of encouraging the public to think that he alone was the saviour of Russia, a superman to be worshipped rather than criticized.

In the end these criticisms could be, and were, made about Khruschev himself! In particular the Chinese Communist Party accused him of **revisionism** (see the Explanatory Notes).

Peaceful co-existence

People in the West did not quite know what to make of Khruschev. He had a cheerful face and a fiery temper. One minute he seemed to want to be friends, the next moment he was an enemy.

There seems little doubt that Khruschev genuinely believed in peaceful co-existence between East and West. In doing so he made enemies among the hardliners in the Soviet Union. His task was not made any easier by President Eisenhower's Secretary of State, John Foster Dulles, a man who said that Communism should be resisted at all times, even to the brink of war.

Yet Khruschev's support for better relations with the West did not deter him from taking tough action to put down the rebellion in Hungary in 1956 (see below). He was also reported as saying to Western leaders 'We will bury you'!

Khruschev told the Russians that the danger of nuclear war made it impossible to spread Communism by military means. They would have to do it peacefully, showing the rest of the world the advantages of living in a Communist society. He said there was more than one way of attaining this goal. He called it the 'different roads to socialism'.

His agricultural policies led eventually to his downfall, and he was replaced by Leonid Brezhnev as First Secretary of the Soviet Communist Party. Khruschev had ordered the virgin lands of Kazakhstan be ploughed up, but doing so did not raise Russian food production to the levels needed. The confrontation with Kennedy over Cuba may also have caused him to lose face in the eyes of his rivals.

The Hungarian Uprising in 1956

The background to the Uprising

For several years after the War, the repressive regime of the Hungarian Communist dictator, Matyas Rakosi, aided by the brutality of the Hungarian Secret Police, helped to foster resistance to the Government.

The death of Stalin in 1953 and Khruschev's denunciation of Stalin in 1956 encouraged liberal movements in Hungary. Rakosi resigned in July 1956, under pressure from the Soviet Government, now led by Khruschev. They thought a more liberal leader could contain the voices of dissent which could now be heard in Hungary.

Moderate Prime Minister Imre Nagy of Hungary in 1956. He was executed by the Communists in 1958.

The Russian reaction

This was intolerable to the Soviet leaders and they reacted in the same way that Stalin would have done – with force. Russian tanks left Budapest deluding the Hungarians into thinking they had gone for good; but they returned on 4 November. In the street battles which followed about 20,000 Hungarians were killed and many more rounded up and imprisoned. Nagy was treacherously captured (he had been promised his freedom) and later executed. The new Government, led by Janos Kadar (a former colleague of Nagy and ex-enemy of Rakosi), later introduced many reforms and helped to liberalize Hungary.

Janos Kadar – the man who replaced Imre Nagy as Hungarian Prime Minister in November 1956.

Nagy's reforms

On 24 October 1956 Imre Nagy was made Prime Minister. Nagy had been Prime Minister from 1953–55 until Rakosi forced him out of office as a 'right deviationist' (too far to the right politically) and expelled him from the Communist Party.

Nagy's return was greeted therefore with great delight by the Hungarians. A mood of rejoicing led the crowds to smash a huge statue of Stalin in Budapest. This was no crime in Khruschev's eyes but it was an ominous taste of what might happen if the crowds got out of control. For one thing they began to take the law into their own hands and revenged themselves on members of the hated Secret Police.

Free speech briefly flourished and Nagy not only promised free elections, he told the Hungarians that Russian forces would be withdrawn, that Hungary would leave the Warsaw Pact, and that she would seek the status of a neutral power – like nearby Austria.

All free men, wherever they live, are citizens of Berlin. And therefore, as a free man, I take pride in the words, *Ich bin ein Berliner* ('*I am a Berliner*').
John F. Kennedy

President Kennedy takes a close look at the Berlin Wall in 1963 whilst East German border guards take a close look at President Kennedy.

The Berlin Wall

Emigration from East to West
The lesson of Hungary was not lost on the other leaders of the Eastern bloc countries. In East Germany the country was losing thousands of its people every year as refugees fled across the border into West Germany. Living standards were much higher in the West, and increasing; by contrast the East German Government was repressive, and people had every reason to look with envy at their fellow-Germans on the other side of the Iron Curtain.

Before 1961 it was relatively easy for an East German to cross over into West Germany, since there were many crossing points between East and West Berlin. The East German authorities began to find this an intolerable situation, since the loss of thousands of skilled workers depleted their own factories and offices, whilst providing West Germany with the highly trained workforce it needed to sustain its booming economy.

Khruschev's demands
The presence of West Berlin as a prosperous, democratic Western city in the middle of an Iron Curtain country was an embarrassment to the Russians as well as to the East Germans. So in 1958 Khruschev proposed that the occupying powers should leave Berlin. This was rejected by the Western Allies.

For three years the issue simmered. Summit conferences, a visit by Khruschev to the United States and other signs of a thaw in East-West relations prevented Berlin becoming another crisis point. But in 1961 the flood of emigrants from East Germany (over 100,000 in six months) tried the patience of the East German Government for the last time.

The Wall
The Allies still refused to leave Berlin. So in August 1961 the East Germans closed the crossing points and erected a wall sealing off West Berlin from its twin in East Germany. The flood of refugees dwindled to a trickle, a number of East Berliners made daring escapes and some were killed by East German security troops.

The Allies protested. American tanks faced their Russian counterparts across the wall. But there was nothing else they could do – short of declaring war. But equally there was nothing the Russians could do either to get the Allies out of Berlin. Indeed when President Kennedy visited the city in June 1963 he emphasized that the Allies were standing firm on Berlin (see above left).

A bomb attack blows a hole in the Berlin Wall in 1962. US soldiers look on.

Above: Aerial photograph showing a Soviet missile site on Cuba in 1962.
Right: Map of the Cuban Missiles Crisis in 1962.

The Cuban Missiles Crisis

The Cuban Revolution

As you saw in the headlines on page 158, the Cuban Missiles Crisis was probably the nearest the world has yet been to a nuclear confrontation between the two great superpowers.

The story began about six years earlier, when Fidel Castro landed on the island and led a successful revolution against Cuba's dictator, President Batista. Castro formed a left-wing revolutionary government and announced many far-reaching, and much-needed, social and economic reforms. But these also included moves directed at American business activities in Cuba.

The Americans had a special interest in Cuba, since it was only 200 kilometres or so off the coast of Florida. Near the eastern tip of the island they still had a large naval and air base at Guantanamo.

Relations between the United States and Cuba deteriorated; so the Americans broke off diplomatic relations and severed trade links. This pushed Castro into the Communist camp and he signed trade agreements with the Russians.

The Bay of Pigs

Secretly the United States Central Intelligence Agency (the CIA) began to train supporters of President Batista, in preparation for an ill-fated landing at the Bay of Pigs, in Cuba, in April 1961. This fiasco humiliated the American Government. Worse, it forced Castro to look increasingly to the Soviet Union for support.

Russia builds missile sites

In the summer of 1962 American spies on Cuba saw Russian cargo ships unloading unusual objects. Cubans reported seeing long cigar-like objects on lorries. Russian engineers and other experts were also coming ashore in large numbers. What was going on?

At that time the United States used special spy planes flying at high altitudes to take reconnaissance photographs of hostile territory. On Sunday, 14 October 1962, aerial photographs taken in the west of the island showed unmistakeably that the Russians were building missile-launching sites.

Hitherto American defence policy had been based on the assumption that they would have at least 15 minutes warning of a Russian missile attack from land-based missiles in the Soviet Union. But missiles on Cuba would bring all America's cities within range, and with less than three minutes warning of an attack.

Other reconnaissance photographs showed that the construction work in Cuba was proceeding rapidly and that a fleet of Russian cargo ships had been spotted in the Atlantic heading for Cuba.

163

The Blockade

President Kennedy talked with his advisers and generals for a week, debating what to do about the missile sites. The hawks wanted to bomb the sites; but this would have meant killing Russian engineers and would probably have started World War Three immediately.

Kennedy opted instead for what was termed a 'measured response'. It was a plan which allowed Khruschev to climb down without having to admit an out-and-out defeat. The American navy and air force would seal off Cuba. All ships would be searched. Any found carrying arms would be sent back to Russia.

Tension

On Tuesday, 23 October, people throughout the world had to come to terms with the prospect of imminent nuclear war. If Khruschev did not back down there was no knowing what might happen. The anxiety might have been even worse had they known that the American missiles were specially primed and ready to fire at a second's notice.

The Russian ships moved nearer to Cuba. Some were searched and passed through the Blockade. But others were seen to turn back. Khruschev had ordered the ships carrying missiles to return to base. But this did not solve the problem of the missiles already on the island.

Secret talks were held between the two superpowers. Khruschev wanted to trade an agreement on Cuban missile sites with one which stopped the Americans siting missiles in Turkey. Kennedy refused to agree. But he did promise there would be no attack on Cuba. In the end this was enough for Khruschev and on Sunday, 28 October, the crisis was over. The missiles would be removed under United Nations' supervision.

Effects of the crisis

1. In the first place it showed Khruschev and the Soviet Union that the United States was prepared to stand firm on a major issue and that it really did mean business.
2. The inability of the two superpowers to talk directly to one another at a time of great crisis led to the installation of a direct telephone link from the White House in Washington to the Kremlin in Moscow. This was called the *hotline*.
3. It showed the United States that the Russians could be reasonable after all. As a result relations between East and West actually thawed because of the Missiles Crisis instead of getting worse. Russia had shied away from the prospect of a nuclear war. If this was the case then negotiations on nuclear arms limitation might be fruitful.

Nuclear arms talks

In 1963 the two superpowers joined with other nations in signing the Test Ban Treaty banning nuclear tests in the atmosphere, in space or in the sea. Only nuclear explosions deep underground were permitted.

An American warship steams alongside a Soviet freighter bound for Cuba with military equipment.

Five years later the Soviet Union, United States and United Kingdom signed the Non-Proliferation Treaty in 1968. This was designed to stop the spread of atomic weapons to other countries. People feared what might happen if every country had access to nuclear bombs.

In 1972 the Soviet Union and the United States began talks on limiting the actual numbers of missiles held by both sides. These were popularly known as the SALT (Strategic Arms Limitation Treaty) talks. Because there were other talks in 1978 the 1972 agreement was known as SALT 1. The SALT 2 agreement was signed but later suspended by the Americans as a mark of their displeasure after the Russians invaded Afghanistan.

The War in Vietnam

French Indo China

French Indo China was occupied by the Japanese during the War. The Vichy Government had little option but to agree to loan bases to the Japanese Army in 1941. But Communist guerillas, led by Ho Chi Minh, harassed the Japanese forces so successfully that after the War he felt strong enough to found the Democratic Republic of North Vietnam.

But the French returned and fought a long but fruitless war for their former colony. After a massive defeat at Dien Bien Phu in 1954 they gave up their colony and it was partitioned along the 17th parallel (17° North).

The peace conference at Geneva, where this was decided, also stipulated that free elections should be held in 1956 throughout the country, since it was intended that the two Vietnams should eventually merge as one. Instead the North became a Communist republic, based at Hanoi, and the South became a republic governed by a right-wing dictator called Ngo Dinh Diem and based at Saigon.

American involvement

Diem decided not to hold free elections, so Ho Chi Minh, who had expected to win them, trained guerillas to harass the Government forces in the South. By the late 1950s these guerillas (called Vietcong – meaning Vietnamese Communist) controlled large parts of South Vietnam.

President Eisenhower had used his **domino theory** (see Explanatory Notes) to justify armed American support for the French in 1954 and this policy was continued by President Kennedy. By 1963 substantial numbers of American advisers, arms and equipment were involved in the civil war in South Vietnam.

Diem was killed in a coup in 1963 and succeeded by a hardline army general called Nguyen Van Thieu.

Below: A French machine-gun outpost near one of the landing strips at Dien Bien Phu in May 1954.
Left: Map of the war in Vietnam 1954–75.

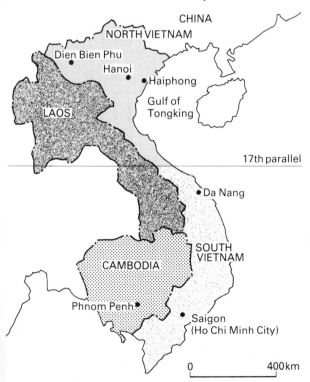

Child victims of the Vietnam War. Nightly television news bulletins brought home the horror of the war to hundreds of millions of people throughout the world.

The war escalates

Lyndon B. Johnson became President of the United States at this time and, believing the Cold War theory that the Communists planned to control the world by stages, he escalated the war by sending in huge numbers of American servicemen; thereby implementing the Truman Doctrine once more.

Johnson used as his excuse an incident in the Gulf of Tongking, in which two American destroyers were said to have been fired upon by North Vietnamese torpedo boats. The United States Congress passed a special motion – the Tongking Gulf Resolution – which gave the President the right 'to take all necessary steps to repel the aggressor'. In the United States, Congress must be asked for its approval before the President can send US armed forces into battle.

Now that Johnson had this approval he widened the conflict by bombing North Vietnamese cities, such as Hanoi and Haiphong.

But this did not seem to halt the advance of the Vietcong and they launched a major campaign in

1968 – the Tet Offensive. By this time there were about half a million American servicemen stationed in Vietnam, compared with about 50,000 or so when Johnson became President.

American protests

Large numbers of American servicemen were killed in the fighting and this, together with the continued escalation of a war which seemed pointless, and none of America's business in the first place, led to riots and demonstrations throughout the United States.

Students taunted Johnson by singing:
'Hey! Hey! LBJ!
How many kids did you kill today?'

Opposition to the war was so bitter that in 1970, four students at Kent State University, Ohio, were killed and many others wounded, when National Guardsmen opened fire during a demonstration against United States involvement in Vietnam and, by then, in Cambodia.

Defeat

By now the United States was ready for peace talks. But the new President, Richard Nixon, tried to bomb the North Vietnamese into submission first and escalated the war by permitting American forces to attack the neighbouring countries of Laos and Cambodia, which were being used by North Vietnam to send supplies and reinforcements to the Vietcong.

The position in the region was further complicated by a civil war in Cambodia between the Communist Khmer Rouge guerillas backed by North Vietnam and the American-backed right-wing government of Lon Nol.

Finally, in 1973, a ceasefire was arranged in South Vietnam and most of the American troops withdrew.

Two years later the North Vietnamese and Vietcong armies seized Saigon and the rest of South Vietnam. At the same time the Cambodian capital city of Phnom-Penh fell to the Khmer Rouge.

The results of the war in Vietnam

1. Thailand, Burma, Malaysia, and other neighbouring states, did not fall to the Communists, contrary to the expectations raised by the domino theory.

2. Nor did the new Vietnam fit neatly into one large Communist empire stretching from East Berlin to Moscow, Beijing, Phnom-Penh and Saigon (now renamed Ho Chi Minh City). Instead war broke out between Communist Cambodia (later renamed Kampuchea) and Communist Vietnam. It seemed

Milwaukee, United States, 1948. The Vietnam War aroused so much opposition in the United States, that many young protestors burnt their draft papers.

clear that the driving force for the Communist guerilla movements had had as much to do with national rivalries as with Communism or Marxist theory.

3. The American people felt entitled to know why vast resources had been spent, nearly 60,000 American lives lost, and over 150,000 servicemen wounded, in a war which had been fought to stop Vietnam turning Communist. What had America gained from the war? In the eyes of many Americans it was the worst war in US history.

Ever since, Congress has been reluctant to endorse any military actions taken by the President which might involve America in a long-drawn-out war against guerillas. Vietnam has become a symbol of how *not* to combat aggression, just as *Munich* has become a warning against appeasement.

4. America lost face with many nations when she withdrew her forces from Vietnam and thus hastened the fall of South Vietnam to the Communists.

But she had earlier been reviled throughout the world for intervening in what many Third World countries regarded as a civil war between rival groups. The Americans saw it differently – as part of a worldwide Communist conspiracy. Either way the Americans lost; so involvement in the Vietnam War cost the United States untold damage in prestige and loss of influence overseas.

Detente

Brezhnev

When Khruschev was removed from office in 1964, his place as First Secretary of the Communist Party was taken by Leonid Brezhnev.

Brezhnev's policies were very similar to those pursued by Khruschev. He sought peaceful co-existence or **detente** (see Explanatory Notes) between East and West.

Even so the superpowers were not prepared to sacrifice their special interests in its cause. The United States claimed a special relationship with the other countries of North or South America. For his part Brezhnev was not prepared to see the USSR lose its control over Eastern Europe.

This was why Brezhnev organized the Warsaw Pact response to the liberal government of Alexander Dubcek in Czechoslovakia in 1968 and why he planned the invasion of Afghanistan in 1979.

He also suppressed opposition to the Soviet regime from within the Soviet Union, imprisoning dissidents, as they were called.

The invasion of Czechoslovakia in 1968

Klement Gottwald, who led the 1948 coup, was succeeded as leader of Czechoslovakia by Antonin Novotny. But strict control of political activities in Czechoslovakia led to student demonstrations and eventually to Novotny's replacement in 1968 by the liberal-minded Communist leader, Alexander Dubcek.

Dubcek introduced a number of reforms, including greater political freedom. This alarmed the Russians and also the leaders of the Warsaw Pact countries. They reasoned with Dubcek but he insisted on going ahead, whilst reassuring them that Czechoslovakia would remain within the Warsaw Pact.

This did not convince Brezhnev and on 20–21 August thousands of Soviet troops, backed by units from Bulgaria, East Germany, Hungary and Poland, entered Czechoslovakia and removed Dubcek from office. There was no armed resistance by the Czech army and less than a hundred people were killed, nor were there the same reprisals by the Russians as in 1956 after the Hungarian Uprising. Dubcek was later released and not replaced as First Secretary of the Czech Communist Party until 1969, although most of his reforms were abandoned.

But the Warsaw Pact invasion of Czechoslovakia provoked a storm of criticism and Brezhnev could be said to have lost as much as he gained:

Prague, Czechoslovakia, August 1968. A Russian tank patrols the streets of Prague to the jeers and cat-calls of scores of angry young Czechs.

* President Ceausescu refused to send Romanian troops to join the invading Warsaw Pact forces. Ever since, Romania has taken a more independent line than the other Communist countries of Eastern Europe.
* Albania did likewise and left the Warsaw Pact.
* China criticized the invasion – not because Mao Zedong approved of Dubcek's reforms but because the Soviet Union used force to bring a fellow Communist state to heel. What could be done with Czechoslovakia could also be done with Communist China.
* Western nations and many Third World countries were appalled, since it was the equivalent of American and NATO forces invading Britain because they disapproved of the policies of a Labour Government.

Ostpolitik

The German Social Democrat leader, Willy Brandt was an outstandingly successful Mayor of West Berlin during the period when the Berlin Wall was built. In 1966 he became the West German Foreign Minister and Chancellor in 1969. He decided to work for detente between East and West Germany

– a policy which was known as *Ostpolitik* – meaning 'eastern policy'.

The main results of this policy were:

(a) treaties with the Soviet Union and Poland, agreeing boundaries and promising not to attack one another;

(b) a lessening of tension between the two Germanies, with West Germany acknowledging the East German Government and accepting the reality of the Oder-Neisse line as the border between Poland and Germany in the east (see Chapter 11).

The Helsinki Agreement

For a time in the early 1970s it looked as if detente could really work and that the superpowers might soon be able to reduce their stocks of arms. President Nixon visited Moscow in 1972 and 1974, whilst President Brezhnev visited Washington in 1973. At about this time, too, the Americans and Chinese began to bury their differences and Nixon visited Beijing in February 1972 to meet Mao Zedong and other Chinese leaders.

In 1975 an international conference held in Helsinki was attended by leaders from 35 countries and they agreed on a number of measures designed to implement the spirit of detente. In particular the conference called on all participating nations, including the Soviet Union, to respect human rights, such as free speech.

But when a group of Soviet dissidents formed the Helsinki Human Rights Group, to monitor Soviet progress on these issues, they were imprisoned by the Russians. This caused a fresh wave of bad feeling between East and West.

German Social Democrat leader Willy Brandt – West German Chancellor from 1969 to 1974.

Above: Afghanistan, 1980. Afghan rebels display their weapons at a mountain hideout near the capital city of Kabul.

Afghanistan

In 1979 the Soviet leaders were faced with the problem of what to do about Afghanistan, a Moslem country on their southern border which had turned Communist, but was threatened from within by tribesmen opposed to the regime.

No one can say what really persuaded the Russians to react as they did, but it seems likely they were worried about the possible effect the strict Islamic movements (which were anti-Communist) in neighbouring Pakistan and Iran might have on the predominantly Moslem people of Afghanistan (and also in the neighbouring Soviet Socialist Republics of the Soviet Union, which were also largely Moslem).

In December 1979 Soviet troops invaded Afghanistan and installed Babrak Karmal as the new Communist leader. But the rebel tribesmen who were hopelessly outnumbered retreated into the mountains and waged a guerilla war, which showed little sign of coming to an end some five years later.

The immediate effect of the invasion was a boycott of the 1980 Moscow Olympics by some Western nations, led by the United States. President Carter imposed a ban (called an embargo) on American grain sales to the Soviet Union. Like other Western leaders he was worried that the Soviet invasion might lead to further Soviet expansion in Central Asia, which would endanger Middle East oil supplies to the Western world.

Solidarity Trade Union in Poland

Poland with 35 million people is easily the largest of the Iron Curtain countries of Eastern Europe (not including the USSR). In 1956 Khruschev allowed the Poles to select a liberal Communist, Wladyslaw Gomulka, as leader. He introduced many reforms, including measures which kept most of the land in private hands instead of in collective farms, as in Russia. But even he could not stop food prices rising and, after a series of food riots, he resigned in 1970. His successors had little better luck and in the late 1970s there was considerable unrest in Poland.

In 1980 a series of strikes in the Polish port of Gdansk (formerly Danzig) led to the formation of a new and independent trade union, which the Polish workers called Solidarity. This was an astonishing departure for a Communist country, since strikes were usually forbidden.

Solidarity, which was led by Lech Walesa, caught the imagination of the Polish people and had the support of the Catholic Church. Strikes spread to many other industries – from coal mines to steel works. There could be no doubting the popular support the movement received.

At first the Polish Government made concessions (including the right to form trade unions) and introduced reforms under the new Communist leader Stanislaw Kania. When these failed to stem the growth of Solidarity and the movement to greater freedom, the Polish Communist Party called for sterner measures to deal with the crisis. The Soviet

Government may well have had a hand in persuading the Polish Communists to replace Kania with another leader – General Jaruzelski.

In 1981 the more extreme Solidarity members demanded reforms which called into question the very existence of the Communist Party in Poland. Soviet army manouevres near the Polish border worried Western leaders, who thought it might be a prelude to a Soviet invasion of Poland. The West warned Brezhnev that any such move would harm East-West relations, despite Brezhnev's denial that any such move was contemplated.

Eventually General Jaruzelski banned Solidarity and placed its leaders in detention camps. Most of them were later released, and the stricter laws relaxed, when the new Government felt it had the situation under control.

The combination of the Soviet invasion of Afghanistan and the suppression of Solidarity in Poland had the effect, however, of bringing back the old atmosphere of mutual distrust and suspicion which characterized the Cold War in the days before detente.

President Reagan later announced a massive increase in American spending on arms. This acceleration of the arms race was matched by the Russians. When the NATO governments of Western Europe agreed to deploy the American Cruise and Pershing Missiles in 1983, the Russians retaliated by deploying their own medium range missiles in Czechoslovakia and other Warsaw Pact countries.

Krakow, Poland. Demonstration by supporters of the banned Solidarity Trade Union at the end of a church service led by Pope John Paul II at Krakow in June 1983.

Explanatory Notes

Revisionism is the term that was used by Communists, notably in China in the 1960s, to describe what they thought were unwarranted modifications to Communist principles. In particular, Khruschev's denunciation of Stalin, and his belief in a policy of peaceful co-existence, were attacked because it was thought they undermined a general belief in the infallibility of Communism.

In fact, no Communist Party can lay claim to being the true (or *orthodox*) party, since all have revised Marxist principles to suit their own needs.

Detente is a French word, which means release from tension. The Cold War had increased tension between East and West, so its opposite – the relaxation of tension – was called detente.

At the height of the Cold War, the Americans were afraid that if one key country in a region turned Communist, then the others might fall as well – like a set of dominoes, each one pushing over its neighbour. This **domino theory** was first used by President Eisenhower in 1954 to describe what might happen if North Vietnam fell into the hands of the Communists.

Exercises

1. Explain the circumstances which led to the rise and fall of Khruschev as leader of the Soviet Union after the death of Stalin.
2. How did Khruschev's policies differ from those of Stalin? What was his importance in the development of international relations between 1953 and 1964?
3. Write brief notes explaining Russian actions on each of the issues listed below:
(a) the Hungarian Uprising in 1956
(b) the building of the Berlin Wall in 1961
(c) the Cuban Missiles Crisis of 1962
(d) the invasion of Czechoslovakia in 1968
(e) peaceful co-existence
(f) the invasion of Afghanistan in 1979
(g) the formation of the Solidarity Trade Union in Poland in 1980
4. What do you understand by the term **detente**? How and why did the superpowers make a determined attempt to end the Cold War after 1953?

5. Trace the origins, and outline what happened, during the Cuban Missiles Crisis of 1962. Why did Kennedy blockade the island and why did Khruschev give way?
6. Explain how and why the United States became involved in the civil war in Vietnam. What were the consequences of this intervention? What was the domino theory and did the aftermath of the Vietnam War prove or disprove it? Did America achieve her objectives by getting involved in the war?
7. Write brief notes commenting on the part played by each of the following statesmen in the development of world affairs in the period after the death of Stalin:
(a) Leonid Brezhnev (USSR)
(b) John F. Kennedy (USA)
(c) Lyndon B. Johnson (USA)
(d) Willy Brandt (Germany)
(e) Fidel Castro (Cuba)
8. What attempts have been made since 1960 to control the spread of nuclear weapons and with what success?

Further Activities

1. Who would you say was the most outstanding and influential leader in world politics since the Second World War? Give reasons for your answer.
2. Berlin has been a focal point of East-West relations since the end of the War. The imposition of the Berlin Blockade and the building of the Berlin Wall were two major flashpoints of the postwar period.

Imagine you are a Berliner. Write an account of what it was like to live in Berlin through the period of 22 years starting from the outbreak of war on 1 September 1939 (the invasion of Poland) to the building of the Berlin Wall in August 1961.

Use information from other chapters in this book to help you depict the period of:
(a) jubilation at the Fall of France in 1940
(b) the destruction of the city in the last weeks of the war
(c) occupation by the Allied forces and the creation of two Berlins
(d) the Blockade 1948–49
(e) the economic miracle of the 1960s
(f) the Berlin Wall 1961

CHAPTER 14

Economic Co-operation in Europe since the War

In October 1943, in the middle of the Second World War, Winston Churchill wrote a note to the British Foreign Secretary, in which he listed the things he wanted to see accomplished after the War.

'We hold strongly to a system of a League of Nations,' he said, 'which will include a Council of Europe, with an International Court and an armed Power capable of enforcing its decisions.'

Seven years later he could point with satisfaction to the United Nations (1945), the Council of Europe (1949), the International Court of Justice (1945) and a United Nations force (in Korea 1950).

Even at the height of the War, many Europeans looked forward to a postwar Europe which would unify nations rather than encourage national rivalries, one of the root causes of both World Wars.

The exiled wartime governments of BElgium, NEtherlands and LUXembourg in London made a start when they agreed that after the War there would be a customs union between them – called BENELUX. This came into effect in 1948, abolishing customs duties on all goods passing between

The European Community's main offices in Brussels. The Berlaymont Building (in the shape of a cross) is the headquarters of the European Commission.

the three member states. Optimists saw it as a preliminary stage in what was hoped would eventually lead to a European **Federation** (see Explanatory Notes).

Postwar Germany

Recovery

The recovery of Germany was crucial to the postwar prosperity of Europe and the eventual creation of a thriving European Community.

But in 1947 things looked bleak. Food was desperately short, there was a flourishing black market and people preferred to barter goods rather than use the existing paper currency.

Something had to be done. Marshall Aid seemed to be one solution, but the Russian delegate would not hear of it being used to help Germany. A new system of currency was badly needed but the Russians would not co-operate with this either.

So the three Western Allies (Britain, France, and the United States) went ahead on their own. The introduction of the new currency, the Deutsche mark, was seen by the Russians as a challenge and they began the Berlin Blockade. This, and the chain of events it set off, finally put Germany on the road to recovery by:
* Giving them a reliable currency they could trust.
* Providing them with financial aid to put industry back on its feet once more.
* Reassuring them, through the Berlin Airlift and the formation of NATO, that they would not be deserted if the Soviet Union attacked.
* Giving them the opportunity to form a democratic government. In 1949 the German parliament was elected with Dr Konrad Adenauer as Chancellor. It was the first free election since 1933.

West Germany was not yet an independent, sovereign nation but this was eventually approved by the

In a Nutshell

* France, Germany, Italy, Belgium, Luxembourg and the Netherlands form the European Coal and Steel Community in 1951 and the European Economic Community in 1957. They hope this will lead to greater unity in Europe and a Federation of European States in the future.
* The United Kingdom is invited to join, but declines, and forms the European Free Trade Association with six other countries instead.
* But the success of the EEC persuades the British Government to change its mind – only to have the UK application for membership vetoed by French President de Gaulle in 1963 and 1967.
* When de Gaulle dies the new French President raises no objections when the UK joins an expanded Common Market in 1973, together with the Irish Republic and Denmark. Greece later joins the EEC in 1981.
* Other movements to greater unity in Europe include the setting up of the Organization for European Economic Co-operation in 1947, and NATO, COMECON and the Council of Europe in 1949.

Western Allies and on 5 May 1955 the Federal Republic of Western Germany was born. West Germany was now on equal terms with the other countries of Western Europe.

Wirtschaftswunder

By 1955 West Germany was already making a remarkable recovery from the effects of the War.

Exactly why German industry should have prospered so swiftly is hard to say. German workers worked hard, there were few strikes and pay rises were kept to a minimum. But the same could also be said of other less prosperous countries at this time. But, few of these started from scratch as in Germany. Not only were many factories in ruins at the end of the War, but Russian demands for war reparations stripped many works of their plant and machinery.

As a result, the new factories took advantage of the latest technology, where their competitors made do with older, less efficient machines. German businesses concentrated on using profits and spare capital to build new factories and install the latest machinery. By 1960 people were talking about the *Wirtschaftswunder* – the 'economic miracle' – for Germany was now the richest country in Europe.

Street in Hamburg in ruins after Allied bombing raids during the Second World War.

173

The Council of Europe

Winston Churchill's hope in 1943 became a fact in 1949 when the three Benelux countries, France, the United Kingdom, the Irish Republic, Italy, Denmark, Norway and Sweden formed the Council of Europe. Austria, West Germany, Greece, Iceland and Turkey joined later in the 1950s and by 1984 the Council included almost all the countries of Western Europe.

The Council meets in Strasbourg in France. Representatives, elected by their own parliaments, form the European Assembly, which meets three times a year. Foreign Ministers, who form a Committee of Ministers, meet about twice a year.

The Council was set up to safeguard Europe's heritage, to strive for greater unity, and to preserve human rights (such as freedom of speech). In 1950 it approved the European Convention on Human Rights and authorized the formation of a Commission to implement this Convention and later a European Court of Human Rights (1959) to decide cases of alleged contravention of these rights.

The European Community

Origins of the Common Market

The Council of Europe was a notable attempt to provide a place where leading Europeans could meet to discuss ways of ensuring that freedom, human rights, and all that was best in the heritage of Europe, would be preserved for all time. But it was not the 'United States of Europe' which Churchill had talked about in 1946.

However, this was also the dream of two French politicians, Robert Schuman and Jean Monnet. They thought that the best way to bring about such a union was through economic co-operation. Accordingly they drew up the Schuman Plan in 1950, which proposed initially to make European industry more efficient by establishing a common policy on coal, iron and steel.

Six countries (Belgium, France, Germany, Italy, Luxembourg and the Netherlands) accepted the plan, signing the Treaty of Paris on 18 April 1951. This created The European Coal and Steel Community, or ECSC, removing restrictions on trade between member countries in coal, iron ore and steel. The Community was given the task of planning the future growth of these basic industries.

The Treaty of Rome

The ECSC was so successful that the member countries could see no good reason why the same idea should not be applied to every item of trade, not

just the raw materials of heavy industry. So they went ahead and signed the Treaty of Rome on 25 March 1957, setting up the European Economic Community.

The EEC or Common Market, as it was usually called, also proved highly successful, making it easier for member nations to export to, and import from, each other. Trade boomed and the industries of the EEC countries prospered.

At the same time the member nations founded Euratom to research and encourage the peaceful uses of atomic energy, and in 1958 they founded the European Investment Bank to finance major projects.

The EEC expands

The United Kingdom was originally invited to join the ECSC and EEC, but declined because British politicians feared the consequences of putting control of the British economy, and ultimately many other aspects of government, in the hands of a supranational organization (ie a body representing several different countries).

In addition they were worried about the effect that Common Market membership might have on trade with the countries of the Commonwealth, since many of these were wholly or partly dependent on Britain as the main market for their goods.

However, the success of the Common Market, and the growing independence of Commonwealth nations, encouraged the United Kingdom to apply for membership in 1961 (together with some of her other trading partners – the Irish Republic, Denmark and Norway). This was welcomed by five of the six members of the EEC but not by France.

The European Community in 1981.

0   500km

Above: Meeting of the fourteen European Commissioners and the President of the European Commission in Brussels.

France's veto

Talks broke down when President de Gaulle of France vetoed the British application in 1963, much to the annoyance of the other members of the EEC.

He used his veto because:

(a) He thought the entry of the United Kingdom would upset existing agreements which had already been accepted by the six founder members of the EEC.

(b) He did not think the British had their hearts set on a united Europe, since their strong and intimate links with both the Commonwealth nations and the United States meant that Europe might well take third place in Britain's priorities.

(c) In any case, he thought that Britain had a weak economy and might therefore weaken rather than strengthen the EEC.

(d) He also knew that British agriculture was extremely efficient compared with that of France, and was likely to gain at the expense of the French farmer.

A further attempt to join the EEC failed in 1967. In the same year the three different communities (ECSC, EEC and Euratom) were merged to form the European Community.

The Six become the Nine and then the Ten

When de Gaulle retired in 1969, the new President (Pompidou) offered no objection when the other five members of 'the Six' invited Britain, Denmark, the Irish Republic and Norway to renew their applications. This was after a summit meeting of EEC leaders at the Hague in December 1969, where the Community made the important decision to expand membership even if this weakened the Community. However, the people of Norway voted in 1972 against joining the Common Market, so in 1973 the Six became the Nine when the United Kingdom, the Irish Republic and Denmark became members.

In Britain there was a lot of opposition to UK membership of the Common Market; so the new Labour Government held a national referendum in 1975 asking the people to vote on whether they wanted to stay in the Common Market or not. They did – by a majority of 2 to 1.

Recognition of the special trading relationship of the former colonial powers to their ex-colonies was established when the Yaounde Convention made special arrangements for 18 French-speaking countries of Africa. This was enlarged to 46 and later 57 countries under the terms of the Lome Convention in 1975 which brought in former countries in the British Empire or Commonwealth. It enabled the developing countries of Africa to sell their goods more easily to the countries of the European Community.

In 1981 Greece became the tenth member of the Community and by 1984 Spain and Portugal were also negotiating to join.

175

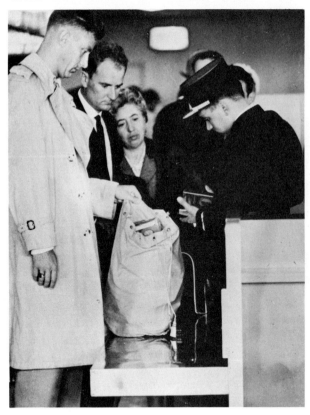

French customs officers at Orly airport, Paris, in August 1961.

How the Common Market Works

Organization

Like the United Nations, or indeed the government of any democratic state, the European Community is organized so that it has:

* An assembly (**The European Parliament**) which meets in Strasbourg and Luxembourg and is representative of the people of the Community as a whole, since the 434 MPs are directly elected, and not selected by their national parliaments (as in the Council of Europe). The Parliament discusses all the important decisions and can dismiss the Commission and refuse to approve the budget.

* An executive committee (**The Council of Ministers**) to make important decisions. Each country takes it in turn to have its leader in the European Parliament serve a term of six months as President of the Council of Ministers.

* A civil service (**The European Commission**) to run the day-to-day business of the Community, and to prepare new laws and regulations. It includes 14 commissioners, two each from France, Germany, Italy and the UK, and one each from the other six member nations. It has its headquarters in the Berlaymont Building in Brussels.

* A law court in Luxembourg (**The European Court of Justice**) to hear cases which infringe the laws of the Community.

Customs and tariffs

The most important change made by the Six in 1957 was their decision that all tariffs and duties were to be phased out over a period of about eleven years. This meant that goods traded inside the Common Market were to be free of customs duties. Goods imported from outside the EEC had to pay a common import duty or tariff of about 6 per cent.

The Common Agricultural Policy

In 1962 the members of the EEC decided they would have a Common Agricultural Policy (CAP) to help the Community's farmers by guaranteeing minimum prices for their produce and putting tariffs on imports to **protect** them from overseas competition (see Explanatory Notes). EEC grants helped farmers to modernize their farms. Special measures were used to help farmers in difficult areas, such as hill farms.

But, by the early 1980s, the success of the Common Agricultural Policy had raised serious problems for the Community. Food prices were kept artificially high because the EEC was committed to buying surplus produce and storing it. These surpluses would have caused prices to fall if sold on the open market. Since the Community's farmers knew they could sell most of their crops and live-stock products, there was little to restrain them from growing as much as possible. So the surpluses got bigger; yet the EEC had to pay out more and more cash to farmers to pay for surpluses it did not want! As a result the Community had yet to solve these problems in 1984:

* What to do with the huge butter, cheese and grain 'mountains' and the large wine 'lake'.

* How to meet the rapidly increasing cost of the CAP, which was taking an undue proportion of the Community's annual budget. This caused the British Government to hold up Community business by insisting that the other nine countries solve these financial problems without calling on member states to pay higher contributions to the annual budget.

Other policies

Other EEC policies include fighting for equal pay for men and women, harmonizing laws in member countries so that all members of the Community enjoy similar rights, and encouraging scientific and technological research.

The EEC 'butter mountain' in July 1984. It was later sold off cheaply to the Soviet Union.

Achievements of the European Community

On balance there seems little reason to doubt that the European Community has been a success. But by 1984 little real progress had been made towards a United States of Europe. The European Parliament had little authority and insufficient power to alter decisions or formulate policy. The Council of Ministers spent too much time squabbling about finance. The high hopes many people had, of the Community as an equal of the USA and the USSR, were dashed.

But there were some achievements:

1. Bitter wartime enemies were now friends: *Axis Powers* (Germany and Italy); *occupied nations* (Belgium, Luxembourg, the Netherlands, France, Greece and Denmark); *Allied power* (the United Kingdom); and *neutral nation* (the Irish Republic).
2. Many barriers to movement between countries had been removed, such as the abolition of customs duties, the introduction of common regulations (for example, Value Added Tax) and the abolition of restrictions on people seeking work in the different countries of the Community.
3. Trade had increased, bringing prosperity to the members of the Community. In particular, the Common Agricultural Policy, for all its faults, stabilized food prices and prevented thousands of farmers from going out of business.
4. On several major world issues, such as the Middle East, the President of the Council of Ministers had been able to speak for the Community as a whole.

EFTA

The European Free Trade Association came into being in 1959 when the countries of the OEEC tried unsuccessfully to link up with the EEC. The OEEC (Organization for European Economic Co-operation) had originally been founded to administer Marshall Aid (see Chapter 12).

The seven original EFTA members were Austria, Denmark, Norway, Portugal, Sweden, Switzerland, and the United Kingdom, but they were later joined by Iceland and Finland, whilst Denmark and the United Kingdom withdrew in 1973 on joining the EEC.

The main work of EFTA has been to remove tariff barriers on industrial goods. It differs from the European Community in that its aims are almost entirely commercial – free trade within the Association, and promoting world trade in general and European trade in particular.

177

COMECON

COMECON or the Council for Mutual Economic Assistance (see also Chapter 12) was originally founded in 1949 as a response to Marshall Aid and the formation of the OEEC in 1947. It was Russia's method of providing assistance for the Communist countries of Eastern Europe.

Since then it has developed into a much larger organization, which aims to further trade between member nations and to assist the planned development of national economies. A large number of commissions have been formed for industries such as iron and steel, food and the peaceful use of atomic energy.

The six original members (USSR, Bulgaria, Czechoslovakia, Hungary, Poland, Romania) were joined by Albania in 1949 (resigned in 1961), East Germany (1950), Mongolia (1962), Cuba (1972) and Vietnam (1978). Interestingly, China did not become a member, nor did Yugoslavia.

De Gaulle

Charles de Gaulle was born in 1890 and joined the French army, serving in the First World War and later rising to the rank of general. He escaped to Britain after the Fall of France in 1940, where he became leader of the Free French.

He became Head of State in the Provisional Government of 1944 but resigned in 1946. Twelve years later he returned as Prime Minister and served as President for ten years – a period made noteworthy by his determination to make France great and prosperous again. He made France an independent nuclear power, resolved the Algerian crisis and took a distinctive and independent line in foreign policy.

Postwar France

The humiliation of defeat in 1940 and the subsequent formation of the Vichy Government, subservient to Hitler, helped to strengthen General de Gaulle's determination to make France strong once again. Yet in the years immediately after the War France saw a return to the pre-war history of weak coalition governments.

A disastrous war in French Indo China (see Chapter 13), and a long and unsuccessful war in Algeria against FLN guerillas (see Chapter 18), undermined confidence in the politicians.

But the postwar years also saw a steady growth in the French economy and the rebuilding of her industries. In particular, the Common Market played an important part in this new-found prosperity.

The inability of the politicians to settle the Algerian crisis eventually brought de Gaulle back to power in 1958. When he died in 1970 he left France one of the strongest powers in Europe, with a thriving economy and a stable political system. Under the former Fourth French Republic, between 1947 and 1959, there were 24 different governments.

President de Gaulle persuaded the French people to accept a new system in which the President assumed a more important role than that of the Prime Minister. In the 25 years after 1959 there were just four Presidents – de Gaulle (1959–69), Pompidou (1969–74), d'Estaing (1974–81) and Mitterand (1981 onwards).

Below: Rebels fighting against the French army in Algeria in the early 1960s.

Explanatory Notes

A **federation** is a union of different governments, such as those of individual states (USA), provinces (Canada), republics (USSR) or nations (Malaysia). A federal government usually takes responsibility for foreign affairs, so that all the states or nations in the federation speak with one voice. It usually has other powers as well; but the constituent units also have their own governments, their own laws, and considerable local independence.

Most countries have adopted ways of **protecting** their farmers against competition from cheap imports, which would otherwise lower prices.

But **protection** like this has drawbacks:
(a) It encourages other countries to protect their industries and farmers, making it more difficult for other nations to export goods;
(b) It keeps food prices higher than they need be, since, without protection, foreign food could be imported at lower prices.

Exercises

1. Define each of the following organizations and explain what it is, and why, and when it was set up:
(a) The EEC
(b) EFTA
(c) Euratom
(d) The Council of Europe
(e) The European Coal and Steel Community
(f) The OEEC
(g) COMECON

2. Outline and explain the different stages by which the countries of Western Europe sought greater political, military and economic unity in the postwar period.
3. Describe carefully the circumstances which led to the founding of the Common Market in 1957. What were its achievements in the 25 years from 1957 to 1982?
4. To what extent is it true to say that de Gaulle's assessment of the consequences of admitting Britain to the EEC has come true?
5. How and why did France and Germany become strong and prosperous again after the War?

Further Activities

1. The Common Market was initially established as a free trade agreement, which the member countries hoped would eventually develop into a United States of Europe, which could meet on equal terms with the United States and the Soviet Union.

By 1984 the peoples of the ten member countries of the European Community elected their own representatives directly to the European Parliament. But the goal of European unity seemed as far off as ever. Member countries still put their own interests first, instead of thinking of the good of the Community as a whole.

Imagine you are the leader of one of the Common Market countries. Which point of view would you hold? Would you be more in favour of a United Europe or of complete independence for your own country? Make a list of the arguments you would use to support your point of view.

CHAPTER 15

The United States in the Postwar Period

Dallas, Texas, 23 November 1963

John Fitzgerald Kennedy, 46, the 34th President of the United States, died this afternoon within half an hour of being shot in the head as he drove through Dallas in an open car. He was on his way to make a speech at a political festival.

The shooting happened as the President's car drove through cheering crowds. Shots rang out and he slumped down in his seat.

Mrs Jacqueline Kennedy, who was also in the car, jumped up and cried 'Oh, no!' She cradled her husband in her arms as the car sped to nearby Parkland Hospital. Police motor-cyclists, with sirens blaring, cleared a path through the crowds and the traffic.

At the hospital President Kennedy was given an immediate blood transfusion and a Roman Catholic priest was called to his bedside to administer the last rites. The President died 25 minutes after being shot.

The quote on the left from the *Daily Telegraph* (London) is how Stephen Barber described the assassination of President Kennedy. It was later said that people throughout the world could remember exactly what they were doing when they heard the news.

Sadly, Kennedy's death, was followed by other assassinations – of the black Civil Rights leader,

The assassination of President Kennedy in November 1963. The President slumped down in his seat leans towards his wife, Jacqueline Kennedy.

Martin Luther King, and Robert Kennedy, President Kennedy's talented younger brother – both in 1968. Four university students were shot in 1970, demonstrating against the war in Vietnam, in which nearly 60,000 Americans lost their lives fighting to prevent Vietnam turning Communist, which it did anyway in 1975. A year earlier, in 1974, President Nixon was forced to resign over the Watergate scandal, which put some of his closest advisers in prison.

The United States, which under Truman, Eisenhower and Kennedy shone as a beacon of freedom and progress, suddenly looked shabby, lawless and vindictive.

Postwar America

President Truman

Harry S. Truman became President when Roosevelt died in 1945. People thought him a modest, unassuming and rather insignificant man. But he made more important decisions than any other postwar President.

Most of these decisions have already been discussed in earlier chapters – the dropping of the atom bomb and the Potsdam Conference in 1945, Marshall Aid and the Truman Doctrine in 1947, the Berlin Blockade in 1948, NATO in 1949, the Korean War in 1950, and then the dismissal of General MacArthur in 1951.

Truman did not flinch from making decisions. He had a sign in his office in the White House which read 'The buck stops here!'

A Fair Deal

American Presidents are often hampered (or restrained) by **Congress** (see Explanatory Notes) if they seek to introduce controversial legislation. Truman was a Democrat but this did not mean that every Democrat in the Senate and in the House of Representatives approved the measures he put before them.

Unemployment, inflation and strikes were problems the American people had to get used to in peacetime. Labour troubles with the trade unions were so serious that Congress passed the Taft-Hartley Bill in 1947, despite Truman's **veto** (see Explanatory Notes) which was substantially overruled by Congress. The Bill was designed to curb the power of the unions.

In the 1948 Presidential election Truman was widely expected to lose, and one newspaper even went to press with a large headline saying that Truman had lost. Instead he won with a comfortable majority. With Democratic majorities in both Houses of Congress, Truman had high hopes of

In a Nutshell

* President Truman's 'Fair Deal' welfare legislation, to improve living standards for the poorest Americans, is blocked by Congress in the 1940s.
* The Cold War causes Americans to start a witch-hunt against suspected Communists and sympathizers working for the Government. The careers of thousands of innocent people are hurt in the Red Scare in the early 1950s, which is led by Senator McCarthy.
* President Eisenhower becomes the new Republican President in 1953 but disappoints his right-wing supporters with moderate policies.
* Eisenhower is succeeded by the young and dynamic President Kennedy in 1961. He alarms and later reassures the world with his handling of the Cuban Missiles Crisis. But at home much of his 'New Frontier' policy is blocked by Congress. He is killed in 1963; the world mourns.
* President Johnson succeeds Kennedy. He is later remembered mainly for his action in escalating the war in Vietnam, rather than for his successful legislative programme in Congress, which includes the Medicare health insurance scheme and civil rights legislation (both originally proposed by Kennedy).
* Civil rights demonstrations, mainly in the South, and serious riots in many large American cities (mostly in the north and west), alert Americans to the plight of black Americans in the 1960s. Civil rights legislation helps to alleviate the problem but not before hundreds have died.
* President Nixon's administration (1969–74) is marked by major achievements, such as the Moon landing, the SALT 1 talks, and visits to Moscow and Beijing in the interests of detente. But he goes down in history as the only American President to resign – in disgrace over the Watergate scandal.
* Nixon is succeeded by Gerald Ford (1974–77), Jimmy Carter (1977–81) – a Southern peanut farmer – and Ronald Reagan (1981) – a former Hollywood film star. All are beset with problems which America has not had to contend with since the 1930s – a slump in industry and widespread unemployment.

pushing through his 'Fair Deal' legislation in 1949.

Some of these laws were approved, such as those guaranteeing farm prices, increased welfare benefits and slum clearance. But Congress turned down Truman's attempt to repeal the Taft-Hartley Bill (one of his election promises), and it turned down a national health insurance scheme and civil rights measures designed to eliminate some of the ways in which black Americans were discriminated against.

Senator Joseph R. McCarthy (left) in conversation with one of his aides at a meeting of the Senate Investigating Committee.

The Red Scare

The Cold War in Europe and the announcement of the Truman Doctrine had unforeseen repercussions in America. Truman ordered that all government employees should be vetted to check their loyalty to the State.

Spy trials (notably that of a diplomat called Alger Hiss in 1948), congressional investigations (such as the House of Representatives Committee on Un-American Activities) and claims by the FBI (Federal Bureau of Investigation) that there were half a million Communist supporters (called fellow-travellers) in the United States, began a witch-hunt against Communism.

Senator McCarthy

In 1950, a relatively unknown Senator from Wisconsin, Joseph McCarthy, claimed that the State Department (the American Foreign Office) was riddled with Communists. In the next four years he was allowed to make a succession of wild accusations against fellow Americans, accusing them of being part of a 'Red' (communist) conspiracy to take over the United States.

This conspiracy, it was said, had even helped the Communists to come to power in China. McCarthy's attacks were rarely supported by any evidence. To their discredit, many prominent Americans believed his accusations, to the extent of sacking employees

and persecuting decent law-abiding citizens. These even included Hollywood film stars, scriptwriters and producers. McCarthy eventually went too far when he attacked President Eisenhower and was censured by the US Senate.

But the damage had been done. The whipping-up of antagonism to Communism at home, undoubtedly had the effect of forcing American statesmen and diplomats to take a tough line against the Soviet Union and China. McCarthy even denounced Winston Churchill's Government in Britain for trading with Communist China.

President Eisenhower

In 1952 General Eisenhower was persuaded to stand for President as a Republican. His supporters carried lapel badges proclaiming 'I like Ike' (Eisenhower's nickname).

Eisenhower was a likeable but rather dull man. His administration was generally moderate in tone but did little that was new. He disappointed right-wing supporters by not reversing earlier decisions on welfare legislation carried out under Roosevelt and Truman. Instead he carried through a number

Below: Campaign slogan for General Eisenhower at the 1952 presidential election.

An armed policeman protects black students at a formerly 'white only' school in Kentucky.

of measures of his own, improving welfare benefits, but failing to get Congress to approve a health insurance scheme.

One of his main problems was what to do about a big drop in farm incomes. Production had increased, so there were food surpluses and this meant lower prices. Under Eisenhower, some farmers were given government assistance if they stopped growing crops on part of their land and left it as a conservation area. This was called a soil bank, since it would keep the land in reserve, yet help the soil to recover from the effects of many years of continuous farming.

Civil Rights

Eisenhower's biggest domestic crisis came when the American Supreme Court ruled, in 1954, that it was unconstitutional to segregate children in schools. Some southern states took steps to obey this ruling, but many dragged their feet. When the State Governor attempted to defy the Supreme Court ruling in Little Rock, Arkansas, President Eisenhower sent a thousand US paratroopers to escort nine black students into Little Rock High School.

Civil rights continued to be a major issue throughout the 1950s and 1960s. Black leaders demanded equal rights. Their leader, Dr Martin Luther King told an audience in 1963:

'I have a dream that one day this nation will rise up and live out the true meaning of its creed: "We hold these truths to be self-evident, that all men are created equal".'

He was quoting from the Declaration of Independence in 1776, but in the Deep South at this time there were still black-only schools, white-only swimming pools and white-only seats on buses. Blacks were segregated (kept apart) from whites and discriminated against in jobs, housing, the armed forces, even in church.

Martin Luther King believed that black Americans could get equality if they used peaceful, non-violent protests, like those used by Gandhi in India (see Chapter 18). He was supported in this by many white Americans as well as black.

In 1955 Mrs Rosa Parkes was arrested in Montgomery, Alabama, for the crime of not giving up her seat in a bus to a white man. The black population was indignant and 26-year old Martin Luther King, one of the city's Baptist ministers, helped to organize a successful black boycott of the city's

Martin Luther King at a massive demonstration in Washington, D.C. on 28 August 1963.

public transport system. A Federal Court later ruled that segregation on the buses was unconstitutional. In 1960, when four black students were refused service in a restaurant in Greensboro, North Carolina, over 70,000 black, and white, students took part in organized sit-ins, in Greensboro's shops and restaurants.

Slowly the tide turned in favour of the civil rights movement. The Supreme Court made a number of rulings, declaring that different forms of segregation and discrimination were unconstitutional. The US Government slowly made progress in Congress, although Southern opposition always made it difficult to make sweeping changes.

The Civil Rights Acts were:
* 1957 [Eisenhower]: Set up a Civil Rights Commission to investigate cases of discrimination against blacks at elections.
* 1960 [Eisenhower]: Protected black voting rights in the southern states.
* 1964 [Johnson]: Banned segregation and racial discrimination at elections, at work, and in hotels, shops, etc. Kennedy originally proposed this Bill but Congress delayed its passage for two years and it was only through Johnson's skill, as a former Senate leader, that the measure became law.
* 1965 [Johnson]: A further Bill to protect black voters against discrimination.
* 1968 [Johnson]: Made it illegal to discriminate against blacks with regard to renting, selling or buying houses and most types of property.

But progresss did not come fast enough for many militant black Americans (for example, the Black Panthers), oppressed by poverty, poor slum conditions, unemployment and the failure of many states to implement the new civil rights laws or to obey the rulings of the Supreme Court. Martin Luther King was criticized for being too soft. 'We want black power', said one of the new black leaders.

Between 1965 and 1968 there were serious riots in the black suburbs of over a hundred American cities. About $200 million worth of damage was done in the Los Angeles suburb of Watts in 1965, and 35 people were killed. The death roll continued and, in 1967, 26 people died in Newark (near New York) and 43 in Detroit.

By the 1970s black Americans had achieved their goal of equality in the eyes of the law but there was still much racial discrimination in the north, as well as in the South.

President Kennedy

People throughout the world welcomed the election of President Kennedy in 1960. They saw him as an energetic, intelligent and courageous leader, who later inspired thousands of young Americans to join the Peace Corps (volunteers working in Third World countries).

Kennedy initiated a lot of much needed legislation on civil rights, welfare measures for the poor and other social reforms. He called this the 'New Frontier'. But he had difficulty getting these radical new proposals accepted by Congress, suspicious, as always, of anything which went against the deep-felt

American belief in self-help. As you will see, it was his successor, Lyndon Johnson, who actually managed to get Congress to accept these new laws.

You have seen in earlier chapters how Kennedy gained respect for his handling of the Cuban Missiles Crisis and the subsequent easing of tension between East and West – with the installation of a hotline between the White House and the Kremlin, and the Test Ban Treaty. Less commendable was Kennedy's involvement in the Bay of Pigs fiasco and his escalation of the Vietnam war.

Kennedy

John Fitzgerald Kennedy was born in 1917. He joined the American navy in the Second World War and became a war hero in the Pacific, where he was wounded.

In 1952 he was elected a senator for his home state of Massachusetts and eight years later was nominated as the Democratic candidate for the Presidency. At the time he was thought to have many disadvantages, being young (only 42), a member of one of America's top families, Catholic and a millionaire. But he narrowly defeated Richard Nixon, then the Republican Vice-President, with the promise of a new and better America.

He was killed in 1963 when a lone gunman, Lee Harvey Oswald, shot the President with a marksman's rifle from the top of a building overlooking the route of the Kennedy motorcade in Dallas, Texas.

President John F. Kennedy and his wife Jacqueline Kennedy.

After Kennedy

President Johnson

Lyndon B. Johnson became President the day Kennedy was assassinated. Although he had none of Kennedy's lustre he achieved much more, because he was able to get Congress to work with him. His period as President saw the passage of many notable measures to improve the lot of the average American.

As you have seen there were the Civil Rights Acts in 1964, 1965 and 1968. Johnson earlier got Congress to approve the 1957 and 1960 Civil Rights Acts, when he was leader of the Democratic majority in the US Senate. Since Congress can block the best laid plans of a President, or pass legislation in the face of a Presidential veto, the wise President will try to ensure that the White House has many allies in Congress. Johnson had many friends in the Senate and was a past master at getting Congress to approve controversial measures.

This is why he was able to secure the passage of the Medicare Bill in 1965, another measure originally proposed by President Kennedy. But this seemed like 'Socialism' to right-wing Americans, since it helped to pay the costs incurred by senior citizens when in hospital or visiting a doctor.

Below: A rare sight in the United States – a free medical clinic. This one is in Baltimore, Maryland.

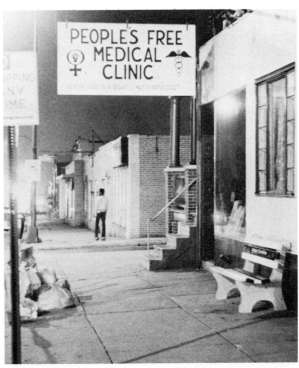

Johnson wanted a 'Great Society', and recognizing that poverty could play no part in such a dream, introduced other legislation, such as a request to Congress for a grant of over $200 million to help the underprivileged people living in the Appalachian Mountains region. The Higher Education Act of 1965 provided Federal scholarships for students (again contrary to American ideas of self-help) whilst other legislation raised minimum wages for the lowest paid workers.

But President Johnson's concern for the underprivileged took place against a violent backcloth – the race riots (1965–68), assassinations (the two Kennedy brothers and Martin Luther King), the spiralling loss of life in Vietnam and violent student demonstrations. His loss of popularity in 1968 made him decide against running for President for a second term.

President Nixon

So in 1969 a Republican was elected. The new President, Richard Nixon, was a Californian lawyer, who first achieved prominence as an anti-Communist member of the House of Representatives Committee on Un-American Activities in the 1940s, and later as a Senator. In the 1950s he served eight years as Vice President under President Eisenhower, and in 1960 only just lost to Kennedy in the Presidential election.

His years as President were marred by the war in Vietnam, but enhanced by the moves he took to reach agreement with both China and the Soviet Union. He also reaped the benefit of President Kennedy's pledge to put a man on the Moon before the end of the decade.

He was re-elected President by a colossal margin in 1972 but fell from grace when Americans learned about the Watergate scandal which implicated Nixon himself and many of his colleagues, some of whom were sent to prison. Five men had broken into the headquarters of the Democratic Party in the Watergate Building in Washington, to try to discover the election plans of President Nixon's rival, Democratic Senator George McGovern.

After Nixon

Gerald Ford became President when Nixon resigned. This was at a time when inflation and unemployment were causing serious problems in the United States in the wake of the 1973 energy crisis (see page 216). As a Republican he stood little chance of being re-elected so soon after the Watergate scandal, and it came as no real surprise when he was beaten in 1976 by a relatively unknown peanut farmer called Jimmy Carter, a former Governor of the State of Georgia.

Carter adopted a high moral tone in his work as President, condemning the abuse of human rights in many countries throughout the world; but he was unable to solve America's economic problems back at home. His foreign policy was noteworthy for his striking achievement in persuading Israel and Egypt to make peace and his SALT 2 agreement with the Soviet Union. Unluckily he found himself powerless to free 52 American hostages when they were taken prisoner by Iranian Revolutionary Guards in 1979, and he had no effective answer when the Soviet Union invaded Afghanistan in December 1979.

President Richard Nixon makes his resignation speech on American television in August 1974.

Explanatory Notes

The American system of government is controlled by a written constitution, which lays down the specific powers granted to the Federal Government in Washington. All other powers are the prerogative of the fifty States of the Union, which elect their own state governments to enact their own state laws, and elect their own state governors to carry them out.

The work of the Federal Government is divided between three main arms or branches:

(a) the *Executive* arm – the elected **President** – who actually carries out the policies.

(b) the *Legislative* arm – **Congress** – which passes the laws. It consists of a **Senate** of two elected senators from each of the fifty states in the Union, and a **House of Representatives** of 435 elected representatives, divided among the different states in proportion to their population.

(c) the *Judicial* arm – the law courts of the land, headed by the **Supreme Court** – which can declare that acts of the President, and laws passed by Congress and the state governments, are **unconstitutional** and therefore unlawful. All bills (laws) must be approved by Congress. Having passed through the Senate and the House of Representatives they are sent to the President. If he (the American constitution assumes that the President is male) signs a bill then it becomes law. If he objects (the President's veto) then the bill is returned to Congress for reconsideration.

If, however, both the Senate and the House of Representatives each then approves the bill by a two-thirds majority, it becomes law, despite the President's objections.

Although the **Republican Party** is mainly supported by big business and the **Democratic Party** by the trade unions, they each include within their ranks, men and women whose policies on social issues, such as welfare benefits, or foreign policy can range widely – from extreme right to well to the left of centre.

Exercises

1. Which American President since Roosevelt do you think achieved the greatest success, both with his domestic policy (at home) and in foreign affairs?

2. Write briefly about the following topics in postwar American history:
(a) Senator McCarthy and the Red Scare
(b) The assassination of President Kennedy
(c) The 'Fair Deal', the 'New Frontier' and the 'Great Society'

3. President Kennedy promised much but actually fulfilled very few of his campaign promises. His successor, President Johnson, promised less but seemed to achieve more. Why was this? What did he achieve? Examine the records of both Presidents, and compare their achievements and failures both at home and abroad.

4. The issue of civil rights in America was primarily a protest movement of American blacks objecting to the laws (mainly in the South) which discriminated against black people. What were the grievances of American blacks at this time? What did the supporters of civil rights hope to achieve? How far were they successful?

Further Activities

1. Start a project to show how the everyday life of Americans changed in the postwar years. Use reference books, magazine articles, television programmes, and other sources to help you find out about topics, such as:

hippies, drug abuse, rock and roll, the Watergate scandal, supermarkets, alternative life styles, Hollywood, computers, robots, automation, technological progress, missile developments, the space race, anti-Communist witch-hunts, racial discrimination.

CHAPTER 16

The United Nations

In October 1977, officials of the World Health Organization (known simply as WHO) discovered a case of smallpox in the East African state of Somalia. It proved to be the last known case of

World Health Organization (WHO) officials vaccinating villagers against smallpox in the African state of Mali.

smallpox found anywhere in the world (apart from cases caused by exposure to the smallpox virus in a medical laboratory).

For the first time in the history of the human race, a terrible disease had been made extinct. This phenomenal achievement was due entirely to the patience of a team of WHO workers, who painstakingly eliminated the disease, region by region, until

188

by 1971 it was confined to the countries of the Horn of Africa (Ethiopia and Somalia).

Smallpox is a contagious disease (one spread by contact with a sufferer). It is often fatal and two hundred years ago was a major cause of death throughout the world. It was checked in the industrial societies soon after 1796, when the technique of vaccination was demonstrated by Edward Jenner.

But the disease lingered on in the more remote corners of the world, wherever medical care was primitive and infants were not vaccinated as a routine precaution.

In Ethiopia and Somalia, the WHO workers vaccinated people, isolated suspected cases to stop the disease spreading and cared for the sick.

Yet this remarkable achievement has gone unremarked by critics of the United Nations, who point instead to the much-publicized failure of the UN to bring peace to the world.

The World Health Organization is just one of many UN success stories which owe their common origin to the determination of wartime statesmen to build a better world after the War. Some of these hopes and aspirations have yet to be fulfilled, some have been dashed. But, unlike the League of Nations (effective for only 19 years at most), the United Nations is still flourishing, forty years after it was founded in 1945.

Origins

The League of Nations

When Churchill and Roosevelt spoke of the need for 'a wider and more permanent system of general security' at the Atlantic Charter summit conference in 1941, they had in mind the failure of the League of Nations to provide any such security in the years before the War.

In actual fact the League of Nations was still functioning and was not finally disbanded until April 1946, when its assets and property were transferred to the United Nations.

But the United States never became a member of the League and by 1941 the only great power still technically a member was the United Kingdom. The Soviet Union had been expelled in 1939, Italy, Germany and Japan resigned in the 1930s and Vichy France was no longer a great power. It was obvious that any future world organization could only work if it included the United States and the Soviet Union. So the League of Nations was dead.

But this did not mean that it had little influence on the shaping of the United Nations. Far from it. The structure of the UN – with its Secretariat, Security Council, General Assembly, International

In a Nutshell

* Churchill and Roosevelt talk of the need for 'a wider and more permanent system of general security' when they draw up the Atlantic Charter in 1941.
* The structure such a system will take is first discussed at a meeting of Allied Foreign Ministers in Moscow in October 1943.
* These proposals are endorsed, and the need for a world organization of nations, is confirmed by Churchill, Roosevelt and Stalin when they meet at the Teheran Conference in November 1943.
* In the autumn of 1944, delegates at the Dumbarton Oaks Conference (near Washington DC) draw up concrete proposals for the United Nations Organization.
* The UN Charter is signed by representatives of fifty Allied nations on 26 June 1945 at San Francisco.
* Much of the UN's most effective work is done through its specialized agencies. These include the World Health Organization (WHO), the United Nations Educational, Scientific and Cultural Organization (UNESCO) and the Food and Agriculture Organization (FAO).
* But the eyes of the world centre on the ability or failure of the United Nations to keep the peace. There are successes, when the UN mediates between warring sides, arranges partition lines and sends peace-keeping forces to keep belligerents apart.
* There are also much-publicized failures, where UN intervention is rejected or ignored. Superpower confrontation between East and West often holds up the deliberations of the Security Council.
* The fact that the five big powers have the power of veto over Security Council decisions is used by them to block UN action which threatens their interests.
* Big power rivalry draws the non-aligned nations together. Increasingly they wield influence as the Third World, numerically a much larger group than either the US-dominated countries of the West or the Soviet-dominated countries of the East.

Court of Justice and specialized agencies – bears more than a strong resemblance to that of the old League of Nations – with its Secretariat, Council, Assembly, Court of International Justice and specialized organizations. The Covenant setting up the League of Nations also influenced the officials who drew up the UN Charter. But the United Nations was much more than a League of Nations, as you will see.

The United Nations

In January 1942, Britain and America were joined by 24 other nations in confirming the principles enshrined in the Atlantic Charter. They included the Soviet Union, China, the Commonwealth Dominions, and most of the exiled governments of the occupied countries of Europe. Roosevelt called them the United Nations.

The Allied Foreign Ministers, Molotov (USSR), Eden (UK) and Hull (USA), took the first step forward when they met in Moscow in October 1943, a month before the Teheran Conference. At both discussions, all three great powers agreed on the desirability of setting up a United Nations Organization.

The Dumbarton Oaks Conference

Accordingly a special conference to draw up a Charter and decide the structure of the United Nations, was called for the autumn of 1944. It met at Dumbarton Oaks near Washington DC, where it was decided that the United Nations would have a General Assembly and a Security Council, consisting of permanent representatives (the great powers) and other representatives appointed for a fixed term from the other member-countries of the UN.

Only the United States, the United Kingdom and the Soviet Union met initially to draw up the Charter; so these were the three great powers, originally envisaged as being permanent representatives on the Security Council. China took part in discussions later ·on with the United Kingdom and the United States but not with the Soviet Union – then neutral in the War between the Allies and Japan.

Although much of the Dumbarton Oaks Conference went well, there was one crucial sticking point. This was the proposed right of the great powers to veto proposals affecting their own interests. The Soviet Union was adamant that they should have that right. The British delegates were equally determined that no one should have that right, arguing that no other country in the world would agree to the great powers having privileges not shared by the others. Without such agreement, there would be no United Nations, they warned. The United States took the Soviet standpoint at first but changed to the British view later.

The San Francisco Conference

The same issue dominated the San Francisco Conference in May and June 1945, attended now by forty other nations besides the Big Four – Britain, the United States, Soviet Union and China. Later on in the Conference it became the Big Five with the addition of France.

There were also discussions over rights to membership. At one stage the Soviet Union insisted that all of the sixteen Socialist Soviet Republics should each have a representative and a vote in the General Assembly! This was because the countries of the British Commonwealth would all be represented separately. In the end the Soviet Union agreed to compromise with three delegations – from the Soviet Union, the Ukraine and Byelorussia.

The debate about the role of the veto showed clearly, long *before* the first meeting of the United Nations, that great power rivalry would dominate its proceedings, and that without great power support and agreement the UN would be just as helpless as the League.

Far left: Soviet Foreign Minister, Vyacheslav Molotov, attending the Conference of Foreign Ministers in Moscow in October 1943.

Left: The San Francisco Conference, April–June 1945, which helped to set up the United Nations.

Right: The San Francisco Conference 26 June 1945. The Earl of Halifax signs the United Nations Charter on behalf of Great Britain.

The United Nations Charter

The UN Charter was signed by representatives of fifty Allied nations on 26 June 1945 at San Francisco. It came into being officially on 24 October 1945 – later known as 'United Nations Day'.

The Charter stated clearly the purposes of the United Nations as being:

1. To maintain international peace and security by acting collectively to deter aggressors and to settle disputes peacefully.

2. To develop friendly relations among nations based on respect for the principle of equal rights and self-determination of peoples.

3. To achieve international co-operation in solving economic, social, cultural and humanitarian problems.

4. To be a centre for harmonizing the actions of nations in the attainment of these common ends.

UNITED NATIONS CHARTER

San Francisco, 26 June 1945

We, the peoples of the United Nations, determined –

to save succeeding generations from the scourge of war, which twice in our lifetime has brought untold sorrow to mankind, and

to re-affirm faith in fundamental human rights, in the dignity and worth of the human person, in the equal rights of men and women and of nations large and small, and

to establish conditions under which justice and respect for the obligations arising from treaties and other sources of international law can be maintained, and

to promote social progress and better standards of life in larger freedom, and for these ends:

to practise tolerance and live together in peace with one another as good neighbours, and

to unite our strength to maintain international peace and security, and

to ensure, by the acceptance of principles and the institution of methods, that armed force shall not be used, save in the common interest, and

to employ international machinery for the promotion of the economic and social advancement of all peoples,

have resolved to combine our efforts to accomplish these aims.

Accordingly, our respective Governments, through representatives assembled in the city of San Francisco, who have exhibited their full powers found to be in good and due form, have agreed to the present charter of the United Nations and do hereby establish an international organization to be known as the United Nations.

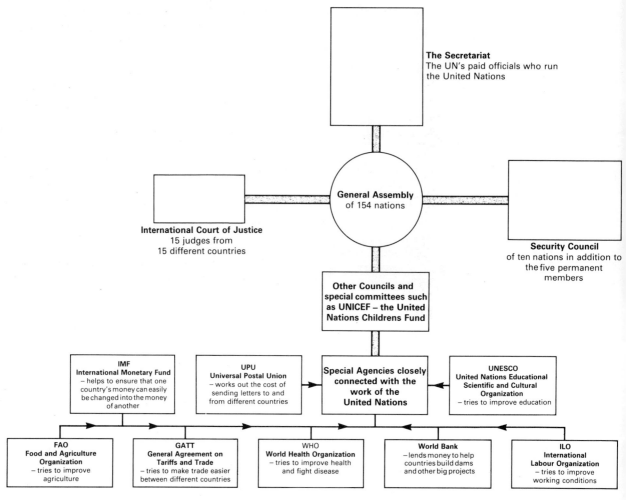

The Secretariat
The UN's paid officials who run the United Nations

General Assembly
of 154 nations

International Court of Justice
15 judges from
15 different countries

Security Council
of ten nations in addition to the five permanent members

Other Councils and special committees such as UNICEF – the United Nations Childrens Fund

IMF
International Monetary Fund
– helps to ensure that one country's money can easily be changed into the money of another

UPU
Universal Postal Union
– works out the cost of sending letters to and from different countries

Special Agencies closely connected with the work of the United Nations

UNESCO
United Nations Educational Scientific and Cultural Organization
– tries to improve education

FAO
Food and Agriculture Organization
– tries to improve agriculture

GATT
General Agreement on Tariffs and Trade
– tries to make trade easier between different countries

WHO
World Health Organization
– tries to improve health and fight disease

World Bank
– lends money to help countries build dams and other big projects

ILO
International Labour Organization
– tries to improve working conditions

How the United Nations is Organized

Membership

Membership of the United Nations is continually changing, as new countries gain their independence and apply for membership, or when countries merge to form a union or federation (eg Tanzania in 1964). By 1981 there were 154 member states, from Afghanistan and Albania to Zambia and Zimbabwe.

Of the major countries of the world only Switzerland, North Korea and South Korea are not in membership. South African membership was suspended in 1974; Indonesia resigned in 1965 but returned in 1966; and the Nationalist Chinese Government on Taiwan was expelled in 1971 and the Communist Chinese Government based in Beijing took its place.

Chinese membership had been a matter of long dispute in the United Nations. Indeed, the reason why the Soviet Union was unable to prevent UN involvement in the Korean War, was simply because its delegate was boycotting the Security Council at the time – in protest at the American refusal to agree to the admission of Red China to the United Nations. For over twenty years, the United States vetoed proposals to admit the world's largest country! It was only when relations between Red China and the USA thawed in 1971 that China gained her rightful place in the General Assembly and as one of the five permanent representatives on the Security Council.

The General Assembly

Each member country can be represented in the General Assembly by up to five delegates. The General Assembly is the parliament of the United Nations, and meets to discuss and debate issues brought before it and to send proposals to the Security Council for approval.

Each country has one vote in the General

Assembly, so China with 1000 million people has the same vote as Grenada with 100,000. A simple majority is sufficient to decide most issues, except where a matter of crucial importance is discussed. Then a two-thirds majority is needed.

The General Assembly meets once a year in the third week of September, but special meetings can also be held in an emergency. Much of its work is carried on in seven special committees, on which every member country is entitled to be represented.

The Security Council
The Security Council is authorized to take immediate action on behalf of the General Assembly and has 15 members, each with the right to send one delegate, armed with one vote.

The five permanent members are the United States, United Kingdom, Soviet Union, China and France. The ten other members are elected from the General Assembly for a period of two years.

Unlike decisions taken in the General Assembly by a simple majority, the rules of the Security Council require that a motion can only be carried if nine of the 15 members vote *for* the motion and *if* none of the five permanent members on the Council votes *against*. A single *no* vote (called the veto) from any one of the Big Five is sufficient to stop a proposal going through.

This great-power veto was used by the Soviet Union, in particular, to block many proposals made by the General Assembly. So in 1950 the General Assembly approved the 'Uniting for Peace' Resolution, which now enables it to take emergency action to override a Security Council veto, provided an emergency meeting is called within 24 hours and approves the vetoed motion by a two-thirds majority.

For instance, on 19 September 1960, the Soviet Union vetoed a resolution approving Dag Hammarskjold's policy on the Congo. But within 24 hours a meeting of the General Assembly was called and an emergency resolution was passed overriding the Soviet veto by 70 votes to nil – the Iron Curtain countries abstained.

The Secretariat
The Secretary General has ultimate responsibility for the smooth functioning of the United Nations Organization, aided by officials drawn from the different member countries. Since its foundation in 1945 there have only been five Secretary Generals:
* Trygve Lie (Norway) 1946–53: Helped to organize the UN forces sent to South Korea in 1950.
* Dag Hammarskjold (Sweden) 1953–61: Probably the most influential of all the UN Secretary Generals; sent a UN peace-keeping force to help dampen down the Suez Crisis in 1956 (see page 196); was killed on UN business, trying to bring peace to the Congo (now Zaire) in 1961.
* U Thant (Burma) 1961–71: Sent a UN peace-keeping force to Cyprus in 1964, but his withdrawal of the UN peace-keeping force in the Sinai Peninsula in Egypt helped to start the Six Day War between Egypt and Israel in 1967. Helped to arrange a ceasefire between India and Pakistan in Kashmir in 1965.
* Kurt Waldheim (Austria) 1972–81: Played little part in resolving the crises of the 1970s, as, progressively, the major powers settled disputes outside the United Nations (eg the Camp David agreement between Israel and Egypt).
* Perez de Cuellar (Peru) 1981– : Tried to prevent the United Kingdom and Argentina going to war in 1982, but without success; his reported aim as Secretary-General is to 'Negotiate, negotiate, negotiate'.

The International Court of Justice
The International Court of Justice is a direct descendant of the pre-war League of Nations Court of International Justice, both based at The Hague in the Netherlands. It consists of 15 judges, each elected to serve for a nine-year term, no more than one judge from any one country.

The Court is unusual in that it can only hear cases brought by member states, not by individuals. Decisions of the Court are by a simple majority. In its first decision in 1949 the Court awarded damages to Britain over a complaint about Albanian explosions in the Corfu Channel.

The Trusteeship Council
This committee of the Big Five was set up to administer territories, not yet independent, which were placed under the control of the United Nations at the end of the Second World War. By 1980 only the Trust Territory of the Pacific Islands, administered by the United States, was left.

South West Africa, a former German colony, was handed over to South Africa as a League of Nations mandate, but South Africa has refused to accept the authority of the Trusteeship Council as successor to the League.

The Economic and Social Council
This is a committee of 54 members elected by the General Assembly, who serve for three years, and have the responsibility of supervising the work of the United Nations specialized agencies in health, education, welfare, economic, and social affairs and other areas of similar concern.

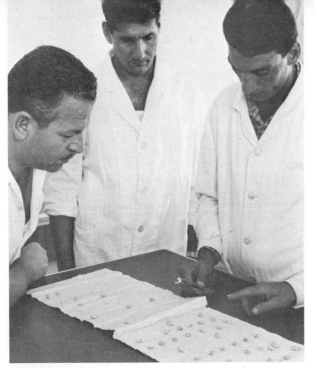

The Food and Agriculture Organization (FAO) –
testing seed grain (wheat and barley) in Iraq.

The Specialized International Agencies

The World Health Organization [WHO] was formed to raise health standards throughout the world by controlling epidemics, evaluating new drugs and medicines, promoting positive health measures such as better diets, child care, health education, etc.

The Food and Agriculture Organization [FAO] was founded to help farmers (particularly those in the **Third World** – see Explanatory Notes) grow more food, through the proper use of fertilizers, crop sprays and other forms of pest control; agricultural education, etc. It is also concerned to promote healthier diets, combat famine, and raise living standards among the world's rural populations.

The United Nations Educational, Scientific and Cultural Organization [UNESCO] was founded to implement the UN Charter's call to 'to re-affirm faith in fundamental human rights, in the dignity and worth of the human person, in the equal rights of men and women'. It does this through its work in promoting higher educational standards, scientific research and cultural exchanges. UNESCO has been particularly concerned to eradicate illiteracy by helping to train teachers and facilitate the exchange of ideas between member countries.

The International Labour Organization [ILO] was founded by the League of Nations in 1919. Its main function is to improve working conditions throughout the world by encouraging member states to insist on minimum safety standards, good labour relations, sound management methods, vocational training, etc.

The International Monetary Fund [IMF] was founded to make it easier to exchange one currency for another.

Universal Postal Union [UPU] was founded to co-ordinate and improve the world's postal services.

The General Agreement on Tariffs and Trade [GATT] was founded to promote and develop world trade, and to settle disputes between trading nations.

Other UN agencies include the World Meteorological Organization; the International Telecommunications Union; the International Civil Aviation Organization; the International Finance Corporation; the World Bank; the International Atomic Energy Agency.

UNESCO at work – a discussion group in Bombay (India) after listening to a radio programme.

Peace-keeping. Dutch volunteers learning how to use new automatic weapons, as members of the United Nations forces in Korea in 1951.

Keeping the Peace

The great power squabbling over the right of veto when the United Nations was founded showed clearly that neither the Soviet Union nor the United States was prepared to allow the UN to intervene where its own vital interests were at stake.

Although the United Kingdom argued against the veto, she later used it when the occasion suited, such as joining with France in vetoing the Security Council motion condemning the use of force during the Suez Crisis in 1956. This was later carried by a huge majority in the General Assembly.

However, the newly independent countries of the Third World, who joined the United Nations in the 1950s and 1960s, changed the pattern of voting in favour of the non-aligned nations, seriously weakening the position of the great powers in the General Assembly, if not in the Security Council.

Inevitably it is the peace-keeping role of the United Nations which has come in for the greatest criticism. The League of Nations failed, not for the excellent work it did in improving public health and working conditions throughout the world, but because it failed to stop the Japanese invading Manchuria and the Italians seizing Abyssinia.

Most of the failures of the UN can be attributed to the unhelpful attitude adopted by the great powers and, in particular, to the inability of member countries to see beyond their own regional or power groupings (Communist bloc, the Western Alliance, or the Third World).

Nonetheless supporters of the United Nations can point to some solid achievements during the first forty years in the history of the organization, and to some valiant, if unsuccessful, efforts to preserve the peace in trying circumstances.

Palestine 1947–48

The UN sent a commission to Palestine, which reported back, recommending the partition of Palestine into two states – one Arab, one Jewish. This was passed by the General Assembly in 1947 but the proposals were rejected by the Arabs. The UN tried to mediate in the Arab-Israeli war which followed, but the Chief UN Mediator, Count Bernadotte, was assassinated in 1948 by Jewish terrorists. The UN later played a part in supervising a ceasefire.

Indonesia 1947–49

The UN intervened in the war between Dutch troops and Indonesian nationalists, calling for a peaceful settlement. Much later U Thant successfully intervened over Dutch and Indonesian claims to West Irian (New Guinea) in 1962.

Kashmir 1949

There was a dispute between Pakistan and India over Kashmir. The United Nations arranged an armistice which ended the fighting.

Korea 1950–53

The Security Council voted by seven to one (at a time when the Soviet delegate was boycotting Security Council meetings) to intervene in South Korea against North Korean aggression. The UN armies (token forces from 16 countries, otherwise mainly American soldiers) drove the North Koreans back across the border and, but for Chinese intervention, would have reunited the whole of Korea.

Nicosia, Cyprus, August 1974. Canadian troops manning an official Observation Post as members of the United Nations peace-keeping force.

Suez 1956

British, French and Israeli forces seized the Suez Canal in a campaign which was overwhelmingly condemned by the United Nations. In November a large peace-keeping force of 6000 from ten different nations was sent to separate the two sides.

Congo 1960–64

A large peace-keeping force (mainly African) was sent to keep law and order in the Congo, which had only just been given its independence by Belgium.

Cyprus 1964

War between the Greek and Turkish people on the island of Cyprus led to UN intervention. The UN Secretary General, U Thant, sent a peace-keeping force to separate the two sides.

Other successful ventures included the imposition of sanctions against Rhodesia in 1966 (see Chapter 18) and intervention in the Lebanon in 1968. But for every successful intervention there were failures. The United Nations was powerless to intervene (apart from passing votes of censure):
* when the Soviet Union invaded Hungary in 1956 (see page 160);
* during the Cuban Missiles Crisis in 1962 (see page 163);
* in the war in Vietnam 1964–75 (see pages 165–7);
* when the Warsaw Pact nations invaded Czechoslovakia in 1968 (see page 168);
* in the India-Pakistan war 1971–72;
* when American hostages were seized in Iran in 1979 (see page 186);
* when the Russians invaded Afghanistan in 1979 (see page 169);
* during the war between Iraq and Iran which started in 1981;
* to stop the war between the UK and Argentina over the Falkland Isles in 1982.

The League of Nations and the United Nations

The United Nations closely resembles the old League of Nations but there are a number of important differences:
* The UN has been able to send peace-keeping forces, drawn from the forces of member nations, to separate belligerents.
* Almost all the countries of the world are members of the UN, including the two superpowers – the United States and the Soviet Union. Indeed, the United States provided the site for the UN building in New York City (through the generosity of John D. Rockefeller) and has always provided the lion's share (25 per cent) of the cost of running the UN.
* There are more specialized agencies in the UN than there were under the auspices of the League.
* The UN Secretary General has more power, and more scope for initiative, than had the Secretary General of the League of Nations.
* The ability of the General Assembly to override the veto of the permanent representatives in the Security Council has given its discussions greater significance.

Nonetheless, it is still disturbing that very few nations seem to have been able to accept United Nations' criticism, and many have simply ignored or rejected its proposals.

Explanatory Notes

The **Third World** is the name given to those countries which do not have Western-type governments, and which are not members of the Soviet bloc. In practice it usually refers to the countries of the **developing world**, who for various reasons (for example, poverty, illiteracy, low life-expectancy, diet, etc), have yet to attain the same high living standards as countries in the **developed world**, such as the United States or the Soviet Union.

Third World can also be used to describe those countries which prefer to remain neutral in the war of words between the two superpowers. The term **non-aligned** is often used to describe nations in this category. But note that many non-aligned countries are not necessarily developing countries (for example Switzerland and Yugoslavia), nor are all Soviet bloc countries fully developed (for example, Vietnam).

Exercises

1. Explain carefully the circumstances which led to the formation of the United Nations Organization. How, why, when and where was it founded?

2. Describe the structure and organization of (a) the UN General Assembly, (b) the UN Security Council. Who are the members of these organizations, how are they elected or nominated, what powers do they have?

3. In what ways is the structure of the United Nations different from that of the League of Nations? Is it more or less representative of the world's peoples? Has it proved more or less effective in resolving the world's crises? Give detailed examples to illustrate your answer.

4. Write brief notes outlining the achievements of the following United Nations Secretary Generals:
(a) Dag Hammarskjold
(b) U Thant

5. Write brief notes saying why the United Nations was involved in:
(a) Palestine 1947
(b) Korea 1950
(c) Suez 1956
(d) Congo 1960
(e) Cyprus 1964

6. Describe the structure and organization of each of the following and say what its functions are:
(a) The International Court of Justice
(b) The Trusteeship Council
(c) The Economic and Social Council

7. Many people throughout the world only really come into contact with the work of the United Nations through its specialized agencies. Choose any one of those listed below and outline and explain its main achievements:
(a) WHO – World Health Organization
(b) UNESCO – United Nations Educational, Scientific and Cultural Organization
(c) FAO – Food and Agriculture Organization
(d) ILO – International Labour Organization

Further Activities

1. Read the aims and objectives of the United Nations as defined in the Preamble to the UN Charter which you can see printed on page 191. Make a list of what you think are the ten most important aims and objectives.

Against each of the statements on your list write down whether you think the United Nations has successfully achieved its intended objectives or not.

CHAPTER 17

The Chinese Revolution

China's 800 million people, a quarter of the world's population, will stand to attention for three minutes a week tomorrow in mourning for Chairman Mao Tse-Tung who died yesterday aged 82.

Peking accepted with quiet sorrow the announcement of the death of the god-like symbol of the Chinese Communist Revolution.

Several hundred mourners, some sobbing openly, gathered in the Square of Heavenly Peace within minutes of the announcement.

The red flag of China was soon flying at half mast on buildings across the city. People standing around the flagpole in the square stared at the flag and a huge portrait of Mao on the wall of the Forbidden City.

The report on the left, by Nigel Wade in the *Daily Telegraph* on 10 September 1976, told people in Britain how the death of Mao Zedong, China's greatest leader, had been received in Beijing.

For nearly fifty years Mao led the Chinese Revolution. He made many grave mistakes but few can doubt his success. In 1976 China had a strong unified government, something Chiang Kaishek and Sun Yixian had been unable to achieve; and, by any standards, China was an industrial and agricultural giant, ranking alongside the United States and the Soviet Union in the production of coal and grain.

The Civil War

The Japanese surrender

Although Mao Zedong's Communists and Chiang Kaishek's Guomindang were allies during the War against Japan, they distrusted each other. In 1941 there were 25,000 casualties in a clash between the two Chinese sides.

However, neither made much of a dent in the Japanese front line during the War, although the Red Army did infiltrate Japanese lines throughout China, destroying war materials and ambushing units of the Japanese army.

In 1945 the Japanese still held a large part of China, when the War suddenly ended in August 1945. The Japanese were ordered to surrender to the Guomindang *not* the Communists. The Americans used ships and aircraft to take half a million

Beijing, China, 18 September 1976. Chinese party and state leaders stand in silence before the body of Mao Zedong.

In a Nutshell

* The Guomindang and the Chinese Communists renew the Civil War after the defeat of Japan.
* The Red Army crushes Chiang Kaishek's armies in Manchuria and northern China. When they march into southern China, Chiang Kaishek and the Guomindang are forced to flee to Taiwan.
* As a first stage in the creation of a Communist China, the peasants take over the land whilst the first Five Year Plan concentrates on heavy industry.
* In 1953 the peasants are encouraged to form collectives. These are merged in 1958 to form huge self-supporting communes during the Great Leap Forward.
* But the Great Leap Forward is not an immediate success. Disastrous harvests contribute to severe food shortages. Industrial production does not rise as fast as had been hoped. Party workers begin to question Mao's leadership.
* Meanwhile relations with the Soviet Union deteriorate and lead to serious border clashes in the 1960s.
* In 1965 Mao Zedong encourages young Chinese to form Red Guards to root out 'false thinkers'. So begins the Cultural Revolution. It throws China into turmoil but strengthens Mao's position as leader.
* Increasing distrust of the Soviet Union leads China to seek friendship with the West. When Mao dies in 1976 the trend continues.
* China's new leader, Deng Xiaoping, introduces the Responsibility System which gives peasants greater freedom on the land.

Guomindang troops to different parts of China to accept the Japanese surrender.

Mao Zedong, believing the key to the control of China lay with the peasants, took control of the countryside instead. He did this by gaining the trust of the peasants, who were usually treated badly by the Guomindang soldiers.

American involvement in the Civil War

Manchuria had been occupied by the Russian army in the last weeks of the War. Although it was returned to Chiang Kaishek in 1946, units of Mao Zedong's forces were able to use the delay to seize items of Japanese military equipment which had been left behind, and to strengthen their forces in the Manchurian mountains and villages.

Renewal of the Civil War prompted the Americans to try a peace initiative led by General Marshall, but it failed. Chiang Kaishek thought that his much larger army was bound to win, whilst Mao Zedong sensed the weakness of the Guomindang who were now thinly spread across China.

Victory for the Red Army

The main Communist effort, however, was in Manchuria. Early in 1948, Lin Biao, the Red Army commander, led a brilliant offensive which drove the Guomindang forces into the towns. In October 1948 his Communist troops severed the links between the 300,000 Guomindang soldiers in Manchuria and Chiang Kaishek's forces in the rest of China. On 29 October the Red Army took Shenyang, the Manchurian capital.

It was the beginning of the end for Chiang Kaishek, since it gave the Red Army enormous confidence, destroyed Guomindang morale, and gave Mao Zedong control of a rich industrial and grain-growing region. After consolidating their position in northern China the Communists turned to the south, capturing Beijing and winning a crucial battle north of Nanjing in January 1949.

The southern city of Guangzhou fell nine months later and Chiang Kaishek's armies were forced out of China, most of them going to the island of Taiwan, off the Chinese coast.

In Beijing, on 1 October 1949, Mao Zedong was able at long last to read the official proclamation announcing the new People's Republic of China.

But China's involvement in the Korean War in 1950 prevented the Red Army from following up their victory by invading Taiwan. The United States, at war with Chinese troops in Korea, was no longer prepared to take a semi-neutral stand in the conflict between Chiang Kaishek and Mao Zedong. American warships patrolled the seas and the American Government stepped up military aid to the Taiwan Government.

Despite American aid, the Guomindang forces were soon on the defensive. Chiang Kaishek had difficulty co-ordinating his forces, and was hampered by the inefficiency of corrupt officials. The Communists cleverly avoided open conflict in the south, where they were outnumbered. Instead they used guerilla tactics to build up their strength in the countryside in the north.

Above: Chinese Communist soldiers march in triumph through yet another captured city in October 1949.

Right: An artist's impression of the proclamation of the People's Republic of China by Mao Zedong on 1 October 1949.

Xizang (Tibet) 1950.
Above: Chinese soldiers reading mail from home.
Right: Refugees crossing the border into India.

The People's Republic

Relations with other countries

Now, Mao had the problem of how to bring Communism to a country with over 600 million people and a land area of nearly 10 million square kilometres, the third largest country in the world.

It was a formidable task; not made any easier when many foreign governments refused to recognize (accept) the People's Republic as the legitimate government of China. However, the Soviet Union did so, on 2 October 1949. This action was soon followed by other countries as well, such as the United Kingdom in 1950. But France only did so in 1964 and the United States waited until 1978.

The Soviet Union offered material support, signing a thirty-year treaty of 'friendship, alliance and mutual assistance' on 15 February 1950. As a result, thousands of Soviet engineers, agricultural scientists and other technicians and experts went to China to help Mao rebuild a country which had been shattered by war.

American hostility to the Communist regime, and friendship for the Guomindang, continued. This was at the time of the 'Red Scare' in the United States, when politicians and diplomats could not afford to be thought 'soft' on Communism.

The Korean War did nothing to reassure China when General MacArthur drove the North Korean forces back to the Chinese border. For its part, the US Government suspected the Chinese of having encouraged the North Korean aggression in the first place.

Tensions were also heightened when Chinese forces invaded Xizang (Tibet) in October 1950 and later occupied the whole of the region in 1959. Because it was a relatively uninhabited mountainous region, boundaries between the countries were indeterminate. The Chinese claimed territory from Burma (the Wa district which was ceded to China in 1960) and the Aksai region of Kashmir. This later led to a border war with India in 1962.

Land reform

Mao Zedong's immediate problem was to reform the system by which the peasants held land. In the past, rich landlords were said to have extorted high rents from their tenant farmers. Many poor peasant families had starved. One peasant on a commune near Beijing told a Western visitor 'By the time I was ten, five of my brothers and sisters had died of starvation and exposure.'

At first the Communist authorities told the peasants to set up tribunals to punish the landlords and to redistribute the land, giving everyone an equal share. Many of the richer peasants and the landlords were executed or imprisoned when they resisted the forcible seizure of their land.

But providing the peasants with small farms was not Communism. So in 1953 the Communist authorities began to persuade groups of peasants to co-operate with one another, stressing the benefits that mutual aid could bring.

This was but a short step to the introduction of collective farms; except that under collectivization the peasants were employees not landowners.

The First Five Year Plan

Stalin's reforms of 1928 also provided Mao with another model – the Five Year Plan. The first of these was introduced in 1953 and, like Stalin's 1928 Plan, was designed to put most of the Chinese effort into the development of heavy industry, power supplies and railways.

'A Hundred Flowers'

Mao Zedong believed in the idea of a permanent revolution. He did not want to see Party officials becoming complacent, settling down into routines and losing touch with the peasants and workers of China. Needless to say, this was resented by many members of the Chinese Communist Party.

Complaints had already been made about the high-handed behaviour of some Party workers. So in May 1956 he initiated a campaign to let the people challenge the work and attitudes of Party officials. 'Let a hundred flowers blossom and a hundred schools of thought compete', he told them.

But the 'Hundred Flowers' campaign back-fired. Mao and his colleagues were surprised at the scale of the response and alarmed at the strength of the opposition. The 'Hundred Flowers' policy was quickly abandoned.

The Great Leap Forward

The communes

However, Mao had another plan to revitalize China and strengthen the grip of the Party on the countryside. This was 'The Great Leap Forward' in 1958. Progress under the first Five Year Plan (1953–58) was disappointing. The Second Five Year Plan would take a leap forward bringing a new form of Communism to the countryside.

Accordingly, the collective farms were merged into super-collectives, called **communes** (see Explanatory Notes) which were not only responsible for growing farm produce but also for building dams, weaving cloth and running other local industries, even making iron. But the idea had not been properly thought out and the Great Leap Forward ran into trouble.

Paper tigers

To make matters worse many of the technical experts returned to Russia and the Soviet Union cut its aid programme to China.

The Chinese leaders had accused the Russians of 'revisionism' – of tampering with Marxist-Leninist ideas. The Russians, for their part, distrusted Mao Zedong's insistence that the mainspring for the Chinese Revolution should come from the peasants, rather than from the urban working class – the orthodox Marxist belief.

The Chinese disapproved of Khruschev's attack on Stalin in 1956 and Russia's desire for 'peaceful co-existence' with the West. Nor did Mao Zedong take the threat of nuclear war as reason for abandoning Leninist-Marxist principles, as Khruschev did (see page 160). He was reported in 1960 as saying:

'The atom bomb is a paper tiger which the American imperialists use to frighten people. It looks horrific, but isn't.'

Temporary setback

Unhappily for Mao these tensions coincided with two extremely poor harvests. Food production fell sharply and millions of Chinese were close to starvation. Nor did industrial output improve at anything like the rate demanded by the Five Year Plan.

So in the end the Great Leap Forward was modified and the Chinese reverted to less radical ways of increasing output. The larger communes were reduced in size and greater concentration on food production, not industry, was made their top priority.

Mao was unrepentant. He thought the exercise had shaken up the Communist Party and taught the country 'a lesson'.

But the failure of the Great Leap Forward seriously damaged his position in China. His opponents were growing in number and were successful in getting Liu Shaoqi to replace him as Chairman of the People's Republic, although Mao, nonetheless, retained the top post of Chairman of the Chinese Communist Party.

The Cultural Revolution, Beijing, February 1967. Red Guards humiliate a number of Chinese accused of being anti-revolutionaries. As you can see they have been forced to wear dunces' caps.

Liu Shaoqi was now the likely successor to Mao Zedong. He wanted to emphasize the role that industrial workers would have to play in bringing Communism to China. He was backed by many city officials, thinkers, writers and lecturers. But Mao Zedong always took the view that real power in China, unlike the Soviet Union, lay in the hands of the peasants.

The Cultural Revolution

Purification
Mao Zedong set out to overthrow Liu Shaoqi and to 'purify' the Party and the Government. 'False thinkers' were to be weeded out; those who put their own interests and those of officials and city workers before the peasants and the Party.

His supporters urged the young people of China to go back to the basic principles of the Communist Party. What was wanted was a new revolution, a Cultural Revolution, designed to give fresh impetus to Chinese Communism and to question the beliefs of philosophers and intellectuals. It was to be a revolution of the peasants and workers.

The Red Guards
Mao's supporters formed the Red Guards from hundreds of thousands of university, college and high school students. They used propaganda to carry the message across China.

Gangs of youths stormed the offices of Party officials, commune headquarters, schools and universities, denouncing and humiliating their seniors and sending many of them to work on the land. Red Guards were to be seen everywhere, travelling by lorry, van or bus, attending mass rallies and hanging on to Mao's words with religious zeal and rapt attention.

All Red Guards, without exception, carried a little red book containing the thoughts of Chairman Mao. These were committed to memory, chanted by enthusiastic crowds and read out to workers in the fields.

The Army takes control
In October 1968 Liu Shaoqi was dismissed from his posts, following thousands of others who had been justly or unjustly purged.

But the Cultural Revolution got out of hand. Red Guards fought pitched battles with peasants and many people were killed. So Mao used the Red Army under Marshal Lin Biao to curb the Red Guards. China went back to normal once more.

Foreign Relations

The Soviet Union
By now relations with the Soviet Union had fallen to their lowest point yet. The reason had little to do with squabbles about Marxism and much more to do with nationalism. The Chinese claimed a border zone in Siberia which had been acquired by Russia in the days of the Czars. In 1969 Chinese and Russian troops even exchanged fire along the Ussuri River on the border between the two countries.

After the Cultural Revolution Marshal Lin Biao was made heir-apparent to Mao. But, in a curious incident in 1971, he was killed in an air crash – escaping to the Soviet Union – after attempting to seize power.

Former US President, Richard Nixon, chatting with Acting Chinese Premier, Hua Guofeng, in Beijing in 1976.

The United States

Fear of Soviet intentions caused the Chinese leaders to rethink their policy on defence. China was now a nuclear power, having successfully tested an atomic bomb in 1964 and a hydrogen bomb in 1967.

Instead of approaching the United States directly, the Chinese let it be known that they would welcome a visit by an American table tennis team! This unexpected gesture of friendship was repaid when the Americans decided not to oppose the admission of Communist China to the United Nations in 1971, in place of Chiang Kaishek's government on Taiwan.

In 1972 President Nixon made a widely publicized visit to China, meeting Mao Zedong, Zhou Enlai and other leaders. Tension between the two countries lessened and trade links multiplied.

In 1976 Mao Zedong died; a year which also saw the deaths of two of his oldest colleagues – Zhou Enlai and Chu De. Who would be China's new leaders and what would be their relations with the rest of the world?

China After the Death of Mao Zedong

Deng Xiaoping

In 1976 Hua Guofeng became first the Prime Minister (when Zhou Enlai died) and then Party Chairman (when Mao died). The influence of the Cultural Revolution was still much in evidence in China. For instance, Zhou Enlai's Deputy Prime Minister, Deng Xiaoping, was purged and sacked from all his posts in the Government and in the Party at this time.

But a year later Deng Xiaoping was restored to power and by 1984 had become China's new leader. His policies were still those of a convinced Communist, but he was also a pragmatist. This means someone who is usually more concerned to make sure something works, rather than insisting that everything be done exactly according to a set of existing principles.

The Responsibility System

This was well illustrated when the Chinese introduced the Responsibility System in the early 1980s. Although the commune system worked well, it had the disadvantage of not giving workers and peasants an incentive to work to their maximum capacity. It was easy for hard workers to feel they were supporting the lazy workers as well.

Under the commune system the peasants had been given small plots of land, to grow vegetables and rear pigs and poultry. These provided a small income to supplement the wages paid by the commune.

Now under the Responsibility System the peasants were given the responsibility of planning and cultivating their own individual holdings under the overall supervision of the commune's committees.

Explanatory Notes

The **communes** were groups of fifty to sixty villages, each with a combined population, on average, of about 20,000 to 30,000 people. By the end of 1960 there were about 25,000 of these communes throughout China. Some were even as large as 70,000 or 80,000 people.

Each commune was divided into brigades and each brigade into work units. These brigades were run by committees of the workers themselves and given the responsibility of determining what crops should be grown and when.

Each commune was also expected to build its own schools, hospitals, stores and machine shops (where machinery could be repaired).

Each commune was expected to try to become self-sufficient for most of its needs, in addition to food. Dams were to be built for irrigation purposes, using local stones and clay as raw materials and the manual labour of thousands of peasants to build them, instead of using trucks and machinery.

The most controversial idea was the plan to build backyard blast furnaces to smelt iron ore. This proved a disastrous failure since the quality of the iron produced in these homemade furnaces was poor and unsuitable for most normal uses.

The emphasis was on peasants helping each other to rebuild the economy, not expecting the initiative to come from the Government – the new landlord.

Exercises

1. Why did Chiang Kaishek lose control of China after 1945? Trace the course of events which led to his exile in Taiwan.

2. Describe carefully the changes which Mao Zedong and the Communists made in China after 1949.

3. How did Mao Zedong consolidate his power over China? Trace the stages which ensured there would be no counter-revolution.

4. Write detailed notes explaining the circumstances which led to each of the undermentioned events or happenings in recent Chinese history. Critically examine their effect on China and on the Chinese people.
(a) Letting 'a hundred flowers blossom'
(b) The Great Leap Forward
(c) The Cultural Revolution
(d) The Responsibility System

5. Examine the relationship between (a) the Soviet Union and Communist China (b) the United States and Communist China in the period between 1949 and 1984. Account for any hostility and show how Communist China has changed its conception of which one is its friend and which its enemy.

Further Activities

1. Many people would argue that Mao Zedong was probably the greatest leader of the twentieth century.

Write a biography of Chairman Mao under a title of your own choosing, such as 'A Life of Mao'. Trace the early stages of his life, when and where he was born, how he was educated, his early career and how he became a Communist. But devote most of your time to Mao's work as leader of China from 1949 to 1976.

CHAPTER 18

Nationalism and the Developing World

'The wind of change is blowing through the continent . . . this tide of national consciousness which is now arising in Africa is a political fact and we must accept it as such.'

The British Prime Minister, Harold Macmillan, used these famous words when he addressed the South African parliament in 1960. He was warning the South Africans that Africa was changing fast and that the old empires would soon be broken up.

Midnight, 5 March 1957. Prime Minister Nkrumah of Ghana celebrates the arrival of independence.

The pace of these changes was remarkably rapid. In 1955 the independent countries in Africa could be counted on the fingers of one hand – South Africa, Liberia, Libya, Egypt and Ethiopia. In the next ten years no less than 33 other African states had achieved independence from their colonial rulers in Europe and formed their own governments. Ten years after that (ie by 1975) only three countries had still to gain that freedom.

Some gained independence the hard way, through revolution, terrorism and guerilla warfare. Others came by it peacefully, without conflict and without acrimony.

Movements to Independence

The British Commonwealth of Nations
When Britain declared war on Germany in 1914, she did so in the name of the British Empire as well, automatically involving countries such as Australia and New Zealand in a European war which was of very little concern to the people of those lands.

The start of the Second World War was different. Britain made no automatic declaration of war on their behalf, though in practice the Dominions rose valiantly to the occasion.

What had happened was simply that, at the Imperial Conference in 1926, the United Kingdom and the Dominions (Canada, Australia, New Zealand, South Africa, Newfoundland and the Irish Free State) had agreed they were all:

'. . . autonomous (self-governing) Communities, equal in status, in no way subordinate one to another in any aspect of their domestic or external affairs, though united by a common allegiance to the Crown, and free association as members of the British Commonwealth of Nations.'

These principles were put into law in 1931 in The Statute of Westminster.

The Commonwealth
This is still the accepted definition of a member of the Commonwealth (the 'British' was dropped in the mid-1950s) but 'common allegiance to the Crown' no longer applies, since over twenty of the Commonwealth countries are republics. When India became a republic in 1949 she retained her membership of the Commonwealth by accepting the British monarch (then King George VI) as Head of the Commonwealth.

The Second World War
The Statute of Westminster only applied to the 'white' Dominions before 1939. The situation with regard to other parts of the British Empire was

In a Nutshell

* The Mahatma Gandhi leads a campaign of 'civil disobedience' to try to force the British Government to grant independence to the peoples of India.
* When the British are ready at last to agree to this, Hindu and Moslem leaders are unable to agree on forming a government; so India is divided into two countries – India and Pakistan.
* When India, Burma, Indonesia and other Asian countries gain their independence after the War, they pave the way for other colonies to gain theirs as well; particularly since the War itself was fought in the name of freedom.
* But the colonial powers are reluctant to grant independence, initially at least. France fights to regain control of French Indo China but without success. The Dutch fight unsuccessfully for the Dutch East Indies.
* A long war of liberation is fought in Algeria against the French, in Kenya against the British, and in Angola and Mozambique against the Portuguese.
* Independence comes eventually to almost every African state, the principal exception being South Africa, where a large white minority retains power and subjugates its large black population through a policy of segregation known as apartheid.
* In the Middle East the British promise, in 1917, that Jews can settle in Palestine, leads to unforeseen problems, aggravated when Hitler begins to persecute the Jews in Central Europe.
* Antagonism between Jews and Arabs flares again after the War. When Britain pulls out of Palestine in 1948, the State of Israel is proclaimed by the Jewish leader David Ben Gurion. A day later five Arab countries attack Israel but with little success. Instead Israel wins territory from her Arab neighbours.
* A succession of wars is fought between Israel and her Arab neighbours. The Camp David Peace Agreement (1978) promises peace between Egypt and Israel but in 1984 there are few signs that the conflict is over for good.

different. Here the only significant movement towards independence came from the Indian nationalists (see below). But the Second World War changed that.

In 1942 Churchill boasted that he had 'not become the King's First Minister in order to preside over the liquidation of the British Empire'. In fact he had no choice. It was not the intention of the leaders of his Soviet or American allies to fight to preserve an empire.

The Atlantic Charter

In 1941 Churchill and Roosevelt signed the Atlantic Charter and declared (clause 3):

> 'They respect the right of all peoples to choose the form of government under which they wish to live; and they wish to see sovereign rights and self-government restored to those who have been forcibly deprived of them.'

If this meant anything at all, it clearly indicated that the peoples of India and of other countries (such as Kenya) had the right to *choose* their own governments and to have their right to self-government restored to them.

In fact Churchill had opposed the granting of independence to India before 1939. But the War changed his mind. He had already promised (in 1940) that India would decide the nature of her own constitution after the War. In 1942 he told the King that all the political parties were agreed that India would be given its independence after the War.

Ideas of freedom

The War also put ideas into the heads of the thousands of Commonwealth soldiers who fought for the freedom of Poland and liberated Paris and Rangoon. A small minority even turned to the Axis Powers. The Indian National Army, founded by an Indian nationalist leader, Subhas Chandra Bose, fought with the Japanese against Allied forces in Burma.

The fall of Singapore

Probably the most significant event was the fall of Singapore – 'the worst disaster and largest capitulation in British history' (Churchill). In February 1942 a Japanese army forced the Singapore garrison of 130,000 British and Commonwealth soldiers to surrender a supposedly impregnable fort.

February 1942. The British Commander surrenders Singapore to the Japanese.
Below: The British Empire after the First World War.

British Possessions

British Mandates

An Asiatic army had humiliated the might of the British Empire. What was clear was that the British authorities had grossly underestimated their opponents. Two months earlier the Japanese had sunk the only significant British warships in south-east Asia – *Prince of Wales* and *Repulse*.

This massive blow to the prestige of the British Empire was followed by the fall of Burma. Soon Japanese forces were threatening Australia in the Coral Sea and India on the Burmese border.

After the War

After the War it was only a matter of time before people in all the countries of the British Empire would seek independence.

Many of the Commonwealth leaders, who demanded independence, had been educated at British universities. There they had been taught the virtues of democracy, such as freedom of speech, freedom to vote, freedom to choose a government.

Men like Jomo Kenyatta of Kenya and Kwame Nkrumah of Ghana, who both went to the London School of Economics, Julius Nyerere of Tanzania, who studied at Edinburgh University, Lee Kuan Yew of Singapore and Jawaharlal Nehru of India, who both went to Cambridge, could see no reason why their countries should not enjoy these same basic freedoms.

India and Pakistan

Gandhi

In 1919 British soldiers fired on a crowd of Indians demonstrating peacefully in Amritsar. The massacre – of 379 people – added fuel to the campaign of the leaders of the Indian National Congress Party who sought independence for their country, the second largest in the world.

The leader of their campaign was known as the Mahatma Gandhi, a lawyer who had worked in South Africa. His method of protest was very simple and effective. He chose passive resistance (civil disobedience) *not* violence. The Indian people were to boycott the British and have nothing to do with them.

Gandhi was imprisoned many times but the British authorities found no adequate way to counter these peaceful protests. So, the Mahatma ('wise man') became a symbol of resistance to the British Empire and an example to other subject peoples.

The Mahatma Gandhi in New Delhi in July 1947.

209

Right: Calcutta, April 1947. Rioters stoning trams in the streets of the city.

Independence

Some progress towards independence had been made before the War, with the granting of self-government to the different provinces of India. But these were dominated by the Hindu majority. The Moslems, who formed a very substantial minority, were worried about what might happen if India later became independent with a Hindu-dominated government. Their leader, Mohammed Ali Jinnah, demanded that when independence came, it should take the form of partition, with two governments – Hindu India and Moslem Pakistan.

After the War the British Labour Government speeded up moves to give India independence. They tried to get the two sides to agree to a system of government which would allow India to remain as one country. But the situation in India deteriorated when riots broke out. Thousands were killed when Moslems and Hindus fought in the streets of Calcutta.

Partition

The British Viceroy in India, Lord Mountbatten, advised that the immediate granting of independence was the only way to avoid further bloodshed and the possibility of full scale civil war. The British Government agreed and on 15 August 1947 Moslem Pakistan and Hindu India became two independent countries.

Instead of an orderly, planned progression to independence, this massive sub-continent had been partitioned off in a hurry. Millions of Moslems were left in India and millions of Hindus in Pakistan, to say nothing of Sikhs, Parsees and other substantial religious minorities in both countries. So the bloodshed continued, with massacres on both sides of the frontiers and long streams of refugees crossing the borders in both directions. Half a million people are believed to have died in the killings.

Gandhi, the man of peace, was appalled, and openly deplored the violence; but was himself assassinated by a Hindu fanatic in 1948.

The Decolonization of Asia

The granting of independence to India and Pakistan was followed in 1948 with the creation of the independent states of Ceylon (later Sri Lanka) and Burma. The floodgates had been opened. This process is usually called **decolonization** (see Explanatory Notes).

The Dutch East Indies: The Indonesian Nationalist Party was formed before the War but its leaders were suppressed by the Dutch. When the Japanese invaded the Dutch East Indies in 1942 they were welcomed by the Nationalists. After the Japanese surrender, and before the Dutch could return to reclaim their colony, Achmad Sukarno declared Indonesia an independent republic. A bitter war followed, which ended in 1949 when UN intervention secured Indonesian independence.

French Indo China: Nationalist movements in this French colony before the War, were led by Ho Chi Minh, and gained prominence during the Japanese occupation between 1941 and 1945. Instead of regarding the Japanese as liberators, Ho Chi Minh organized a successful campaign by Viet-Minh guerillas against the invaders.

At the end of the War, Ho established the independent republic of Vietnam centred on Hanoi in the north. When the French returned to reclaim their colonies they tried to make the new republic part of an Indo-Chinese federation. This led to a war of independence, which terminated with French withdrawal in 1954 (see page 165).

Malaya and Singapore: British settlements on the Malay Peninsula were overrun by the Japanese when they fought their way through the jungle to Singapore. After the War the British successfully reclaimed these territories and formed them into a federation. In 1948 Communist guerillas began a ten-year war against the British occupying forces. Although they were defeated, the 'Emergency' stimulated demands for independence, which was granted in 1957. Six years later the Federation

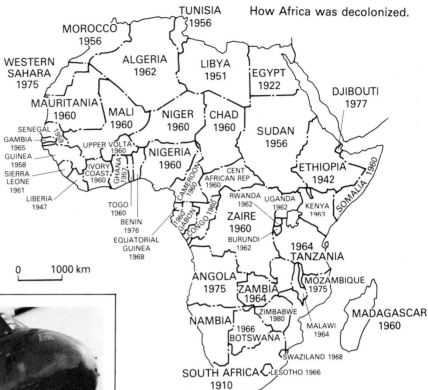

How Africa was decolonized.

TUNISIA 1956
MOROCCO 1956
WESTERN SAHARA 1975
ALGERIA 1962
LIBYA 1951
EGYPT 1922
DJIBOUTI 1977
MAURITANIA 1960
MALI 1960
NIGER 1960
CHAD 1960
SUDAN 1956
SENEGAL 1960
GAMBIA 1965
GUINEA 1958
SIERRA LEONE 1961
LIBERIA 1947
UPPER VOLTA 1960
IVORY COAST 1960
GHANA 1957
NIGERIA 1960
TOGO 1960
BENIN 1976
EQUATORIAL GUINEA 1968
CAMEROON 1960
CENT AFRICAN REP 1960
GABON 1960
CONGO 1960
ETHIOPIA 1942
RWANDA 1962
UGANDA 1962
KENYA 1963
SOMALIA 1960
ZAIRE 1960
BURUNDI 1962
1964 TANZANIA
ANGOLA 1975
ZAMBIA 1964
MOZAMBIQUE 1975
NAMBIA
ZIMBABWE 1980
1966 BOTSWANA
MALAWI 1964
MADAGASCAR 1960
SWAZILAND 1968
SOUTH AFRICA 1910
LESOTHO 1966

0   1000 km

Supplying British troops during the 'Emergency'.

joined Sabah and Sarawak (both in north Borneo) and Singapore to form the federation of Malaysia in 1963. But Singapore left two years later when her largely Chinese population found it impossible to reconcile their differences with the Malays.

The Wind of Change

As you have seen the 'wind of change' blew rapidly through Africa in the 1950s and 1960s. The different methods of gaining independence, which had been demonstrated by the countries of south-east Asia and the Indian sub-continent in the 1940s and 1950s, were not lost on African nationalists.

Some, like the British colonies of the Gold Coast (Ghana), Nigeria, Uganda, Tanganyika (Tanzania with Zanzibar) and Northern Rhodesia (Zambia), followed the constitutional path – mainly peaceful protests, civil disobedience and stage-by-stage progression through elections and local self-government to full independence.

Others chose a violent confrontation between guerillas and settlers to force through early independence. These included the British colonies of Kenya, where the Kikuyu tribe formed the Mau-Mau terrorists to fight against British rule in the 1950s, and Southern Rhodesia (Zimbabwe), where Joshua Nkomo and Robert Mugabe led black guerilla attacks in the 1970s on white settlers and forces controlled by Ian Smith's white government. Smith had already illegally declared Rhodesia independent of Britain in 1965 (called UDI – unilateral declaration of independence).

In Algeria the FLN (National Liberation Front) fought an eight-year war against the French. In Angola several different guerilla groups fought against the Portuguese from 1961 to 1974. Other long guerilla wars were fought by Frelimo guerillas against the Portuguese in Mozambique and by Swapo against South Africa in Namibia.

In 1960 the Belgians, like the British in India, were pressured into granting independence in a hurry to the Congo (Zaire). In the chaos which followed, the Prime Minister, Patrice Lumumba, was murdered and the richest province, Katanga, claimed independence from the rest of the country. United Nations forces were sent in to intervene and eventually helped to restore order. The Congo, like many other newly independent states, was later taken over by the army, under its leader General Mobutu.

Apartheid

In general the most violent independence movements have been in countries where there are, or were, substantial numbers of European settlers (eg Kenya, Zimbabwe, Algeria). After independence many settlers stayed behind and co-operated with the new governments.

But in South Africa the white population forms a substantial minority (roughly one person in every five) and has had control of the independent government of the country since 1910.

In 1948 Malan's Nationalist Party introduced the

June 1976. Rioters in Soweto (a township near Johannesburg, South Africa). Police opened fire killing many students.

policy of *apartheid* to the country. This means 'keeping apart' and has been implemented by segregating whites from blacks (and also from Asians and from coloureds – these of mixed race). Schools, ambulances, buses, beaches and even hospitals are reserved for whites or blacks only.

In 1959 the ruling Nationalist Party introduced a new plan – of creating independent black homelands for the peoples of different tribal groups. So those who speak the Xhosa language belong to the Transkei. These new homelands are self-governing independent republics, although in practice most black people continue to live and work outside their homelands, simply because this is where they can find work. Without these black workers the South African gold and coal mines, the farms, the transport system and the whole economy would grind to a halt.

Apartheid has been accompanied by much-resented laws, such as those which require blacks, but not whites, to carry pass books.

Until the 1970s, black protests in South Africa were generally peaceful although they sometimes ended in bloodshed, as in 1960 when 67 Africans were killed by police at Sharpeville. But serious riots, in 1976 over the proposal to make Afrikaans the official language in black schools, resulted in the deaths of over five hundred people.

Israel

Israel also gained its independence when the British left Palestine in 1948. But unlike the other newly independent countries since the War, this led immediately to war with her neighbours. Since then the Israelis have fought three other major wars (see below) and many other campaigns, clashes and skirmishes with their Arab neighbours.

The origin of this unhappy state of affairs goes back to the nineteenth century in the origins of **Zionism** (see Explanatory Notes) and the events which immediately followed the end of the First World War.

The Balfour Declaration

In 1917 A. J. Balfour, the British Foreign Secretary, told a leader of the Zionist movement that Britain supported the idea of 'a national home for the Jewish people' in Palestine, since it had been their traditional home.

When Palestine was made a British mandate in 1920, Jewish settlers were encouraged to continue setting up communal farm settlements (*kibbutzim*) which they had been allowed to do when Palestine was part of the Turkish Empire.

Friction

Inevitably, this meant that the ratio of Jews to Arabs would increase, from less than one in ten in 1920 (80,000) to one in three in 1940 (460,000). Consequently, there were serious clashes between the two sides in 1929 (when a hundred Arabs and a hundred Jews were killed) and again in 1936. It was then that Arab nationalists began to organize demonstrations and strikes.

The problem was aggravated when Hitler's persecution of the Jews in the 1930s increased the numbers of those who wanted to settle in Palestine.

Partition

The difficulty of reconciling the differences between the two peoples caused the British authorities to think seriously of partition in 1937 but the report of the Peel Commission which recommended this step was rejected by the majority of Jews and Arabs.

Britain was in a cleft stick, since trouble caused by Arabs was matched by the actions of Jewish activists, who began to demonstrate against the restrictions the British authorities had placed on further Jewish immigration.

Britain was torn between the humane wish to accommodate Jews fleeing from tyranny and the desire to placate the Arabs whose homeland it now was. The problem became almost insoluble after the War when thousands of Jews fled from Europe, where their relatives had been systematically put to death. But the British authorities, under pressure from the neighbouring Arab states, and fearing an explosive civil war, refused them entry. Jewish terrorist groups (the Stern Gang and Irgun) then tried to force the British out of Palestine.

The United Nations

The British Government, pleasing neither Jew nor Arab, turned to the United Nations for a solution. The General Assembly voted to partition Palestine despite the violent opposition of the Arabs. But by this time Britain had had enough. The mandate was ended on 14 May 1948 and the Palestinian Jews, under their leader David Ben Gurion, immediately proclaimed the state of Israel.

1947 – a Jewish refugee ship crammed with Jews seeking a home in Israel.

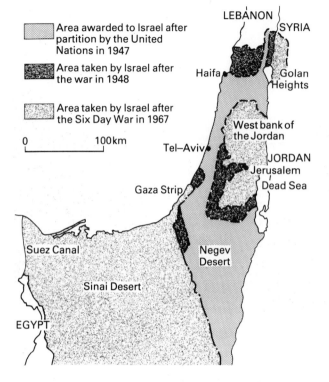

Above: Israel's conquests 1948–67.
Below: September 1956. Egyptian President, Gamal Abdel Nasser, tells a huge crowd in Alexandria that Egypt has nationalized the Suez Canal Company.

Independence

The following day, 15 May 1948, the Arab armies of Jordan, Iraq, Syria, Lebanon and Egypt attacked. However, the Israelis had prepared for the conflict. With their superior equipment and training, and the financial support of American Jews, they not only held on to the land awarded to them under the UN partition plan, they seized other territory which made their country seem less fragmented than before (as you can see from the map).

After the war

But during the fighting many Arabs were killed, including civilians. This frightened many of the Arabs living in Israel or in parts of Palestine under threat from the advancing Israeli armies. Their flight created a mammoth refugee problem. They were housed in temporary camps and as their resentment grew, the refugee camps became training grounds for terrorists seeking to return to their homeland. Israel's Arab neighbours licked their wounds but were not prepared to let the matter rest. There were fresh wars in 1956, 1967 and 1973 (see below) and the only hope of compromise came in 1978 when Israel and Egypt signed the Camp David Peace Agreement.

War in the Middle East

Suez 1956

The Suez Canal, long regarded as a vital link between Britain and India, runs through Egypt. After a revolt there in 1882 the British stationed troops to protect the Canal. This privilege was continued after 1922 when Egypt became an independent kingdom. After the War arrangements were made to reduce the British presence in Egypt and the last troops left in June 1956.

By this time nationalist feeling in Egypt was running high and the army had staged a coup, first deposing King Farouk in 1952 and then President Neguib in 1954. The new leader of Egypt was a dynamic young army officer called Colonel Nasser.

Gamal Abdel Nasser was a controversial figure and in 1956 nationalized the Suez Canal when the Western nations refused to grant a loan to build the Aswan High Dam. The news outraged the British Government. The Prime Minister, Sir Anthony Eden, likened Nasser to Hitler and quoted the Munich Crisis of 1938 as an example of what might happen if a dictator was allowed to get away with an act of aggression of this kind.

To the Egyptians, of course, it seemed a perfectly logical thing to do, since the canal ran through Egypt and the revenues from the shipping companies using

The Six Day War, June 1967. Israeli tanks moving out into the desert to counter an Egyptian attack.

the canal could be used to finance the dam they wanted.

Nonetheless, Britain and France were provoked into action and they planned a joint venture with Israel. Israel had been threatened by Egypt and there were numerous border incidents. So in October 1956 she launched a sudden attack on Egypt. This gave France and the United Kingdom the excuse to intervene, saying they were sending in troops to protect the Canal.

But they were immediately condemned for this action by the United Nations, the Soviet Union, the United States, many Commonwealth nations and the British Labour Party. Britain and France had to climb down, United Nations troops were sent in to keep the peace between Israel and Egypt and Nasser got his canal and eventually his dam (with the aid of a Russian loan and Russian technology).

The Six Day War

After the Suez War, President Nasser turned increasingly to the Soviet Union for help. By the mid 1960s Israel was ringed by hostile forces. At one stage Egypt and Syria united to form the United Arab Republic (1958–61).

Egypt's increasingly aggressive stance alerted the Israelis to the likelihood of a new war. This seemed imminent when Nasser told U Thant to remove the UN peace-keeping force from the border zone on 18 May 1967 and followed this by closing the Gulf of Aqaba to Israeli ships. This cut off Israel's access from the port of Eilat to the Red Sea and the Indian Ocean. Israel called up her army.

Then suddenly on 5 June 1967, without warning and without a declaration of war, Israeli planes destroyed the Arab air forces on the ground and launched a massive attack on several fronts, seizing the whole of the Sinai Peninsula (thus protecting her Gulf of Aqaba shipping route), occupying the west bank of the Jordan, and capturing Jerusalem and the Golan Heights in Syria.

The United Nations Security Council (Soviet Union, United States, United Kingdom and France therefore concurring) demanded that Israel withdraw from these territories whilst asking the Arab nations to respect Israel's rights to exist as an independent nation. This, neither side was prepared to do.

The Yom Kippur War

Instead the Arab countries re-equipped their armed forces, mainly with Soviet help. Now it was their turn to catch the Israelis off guard. On Saturday 6 October 1973 most Israelis were busy observing Yom Kippur (the Day of Atonement). This is the holiest day of the Jewish year.

Egyptian tanks crossed the Suez Canal and started to advance across the Sinai Peninsula towards Israel. Simultaneously, Syrian forces launched an attack on the Golan Heights.

But once again Israel's commanders lived up to their reputation for military daring. Israeli troops crossed the Suez Canal and trapped the Egyptian Third Army. The United Nations arranged a ceasefire and sent a peace-keeping force to patrol the border between Israel and Syria.

215

The oil weapon

The Yom Kippur War caused much heart-searching in Israel. Over 2000 soldiers had been killed. Although this seems negligible it has to be related to Israel's population of under four million people. If a similar proportion of the American people had been killed in Vietnam or Korea then casualties would have been doubled to 110,000.

The Arab armies had acquitted themselves well. Israel could not count on a swift military victory in future.

The Arab oil producers exerted pressure when they banned all oil exports to the United States at a meeting on 19–21 October. This was in retaliation for the massive US airlift of weapons which re-supplied the Israeli forces. The resultant oil crisis had dramatic side effects. Oil prices increased so sharply they caused a steep rise in inflation in the industrial countries, a drop in output, and a rise in unemployment.

Other effects of the war included an increase in the numbers of terrorist attacks on Israeli targets throughout the world and a disastrous rise in Israel's rate of inflation.

Camp David

The high cost of the war had also affected the Egyptians. Their President, Anwar Sadat, took the courageous step of suggesting peace talks with Israel. The resulting negotiations, culminating in a series of meetings arranged by US President Carter, at Camp David near Washington DC, produced a peace agreement which was signed on 26 March 1979. It brought to an end the long on-and-off conflict between Israel and her largest neighbour, Egypt. By its terms the Israelis agreed to withdraw from the Sinai Peninsula to the pre-1967 frontier.

At the time it seemed to offer hope that peace might come at last to the Middle East. For in no other part of the world has the likelihood of major conflict seemed greater than in the countries surrounding Israel.

Since then hopes of lasting peace have faded. In 1979 American hostages were seized in Iran, soon after the Ayatollah Khomeini replaced the Shah as leader and brought the **Islamic Revolution** to Iran (see Explanatory Notes). In 1980 war broke out between Iraq and Iran, in 1981 President Sadat was assassinated and in 1982 Israel invaded the Lebanon.

The war in Lebanon, 1982. Israeli troops carry a wounded colleague on a stretcher in south Beirut.

Explanatory Notes

Decolonization is the name given to the process by which the former colonies of the great European empires were given up and granted independence. Sometimes this was achieved after a long and hard-fought period of guerilla activity (as in Algeria). In other cases it came about as the result of peaceful negotiation.

Zionism is the name given to the movement initiated by European Jews in the late nineteenth century to try to establish a homeland for the Jewish people. The Jews originally lived in Palestine but had been expelled by the Romans. By the late nineteenth century many of them lived in western Russia.

Most Jews at that time thought they could be assimilated into the life of the countries where they lived. They did not think of themselves as a separate nation but simply as the people of a country who happened to have their own religion. But examples of discrimination against the Jews (such as the Dreyfus case in France) and the pogroms (persecutions) of the Russian Jews in the 1880s convinced many Jews that the only safe and adequate solution lay in a Jewish homeland. Since Palestine was the original homeland of the Jews – some 2000 years earlier – they hoped to make Palestine their homeland again. Zion was the name given to the people of Israel in the Bible.

The **Islamic Revolution** is the name given to the resurgence of Moslem feeling in some of the countries of the Middle East. Countries like Pakistan and Iran re-introduced traditional Islamic laws, many of them prescribing grave penalties, such as flogging and stoning, for criminal offences. In Iran the fervour was stimulated by the Moslem leaders (called Mullahs) led by the Ayatollah Khomeini.

Exercises

1. What do you understand by the term decolonization? Use examples from recent history, chosen from different continents, to illustrate your answer.
2. Explain the circumstances which led the British Prime Minister, Harold Macmillan, to talk about a 'wind of change' blowing through the African continent.

3. What do you understand by the policy of apartheid? Outline the nature of this policy and examine its effects on the people of South Africa, black, coloured and white.
4. Describe the long struggle to achieve independence for India. Why was Britain reluctant to grant independence at first but over-anxious to settle the question in 1947? What were the tragic consequences of that decision?
5. Outline and examine carefully the stages by which the old white-dominated British Empire has been transformed into a multi-racial Commonwealth of independent nations. What problems has the Commonwealth had to face during the last 25 years?
6. Write brief notes explaining the significance of each of the following in the history of Palestine and Israel:
(a) The Balfour Declaration of 1917
(b) The building of kibbutzim in Palestine
(c) The Zionist movement
(d) Hitler's rise to power in Nazi Germany
(e) The Stern Gang and Irgun terrorist movements
7. Examine in detail the circumstances and the events which led to the founding of the independent state of Israel in 1948.
8. Write notes commenting on the significance of each of the following Middle Eastern wars:
(a) Palestine 1948
(b) Suez 1956
(c) Six Day War 1967
(d) Yom Kippur 1973

Further Activities

1. Draw a large map of Africa and the Middle East. Mark in the boundaries of each separate nation and print the date on which it became independent. Add comments or annotations to describe the recent history of each country 'in a nutshell'.
2. Examine the problems listed below and use reference books to find examples which show how they have affected the developing nations:
(a) Tribalism. Social, cultural and racial differences. Language differences
(b) Religious differences
(c) Lack of preparation for the responsibilities of government
(d) The presence of large numbers of European settlers

Reading List

Bayne-Jardine, C.C., *Mussolini and Italy*, Longman, 1966.

Bayne-Jardine, C.C., *World War Two*, Longman, 1968.

Clement, H.A., *Story of Modern Europe*, Harrap, 1974.

Cobban, Alfred, *A History of Modern France (3) 1871–1962*, Penguin, 1965.

Cowie, L.W., *Europe 1789–1939*, Nelson, 1969.

Criswell, C.N., *Far East History 1860–1952*, Longman, 1975.

Derry, T.K. and Jarman, T.L., *The European World 1870–1975*, Bell, 1977.

Elliott, B.J., *Hitler and Germany*, Longman, 1966.

Isaac, M.L.R., *A History of Europe since 1870*, Arnold, 1970.

Jones, W.R.D., *Nazi Germany*, Macmillan Education, 1970.

Kochan, Lionel, *The Making of Modern Russia*, Cape, 1962.

Larkin, P.J., *Europe and World Affairs*, Hulton, 1969.

Larkin, P.J., *European History for Certificate Classes*, Hulton, 1969.

Larkin, P.J., *U.S.A. and Russia*, Hulton, 1968.

Larkin, P.J., *The Far East and India*, Hulton, 1968.

Larkin, P.J., *The Middle East and Africa*, Hulton, 1968.

Liddell-Hart, Basil, *History of the Second World War*, Cassell, 1970.

Morales, A.C., *Europe The Last Hundred Years*, Macmillan Education, 1979.

O'Callaghan, D.B., *Roosevelt and the United States*, Longman, 1966.

Peacock, H.L., *A History of Modern Europe 1789–1939*, Heinemann, 1958.

Robottom, John, *Modern China*, Longman, 1967.

Sauvain, Philip, *History Mapbooks: The Modern World since 1917*, Basil Blackwell, 1983.

Snellgrove, L.E., *Franco and the Spanish Civil War*, Longman, 1965.

Snellgrove, L.E., *Hitler*, Longman, 1974.

Snellgrove, L.E., *The Modern World since 1870*, Longman, 1968.

Speed, P.F., *A Course Book in Modern World History*, Wheaton, 1982.

Storry, R., *A History of Modern Japan*, Penguin, 1967.

Thomson, David, *Europe since Napoleon*, Pelican, 1966.

Walker, A., *Modern Commonwealth*, Longman, 1975.

Williams, Barry, *Modern Africa 1870–1970*, Longman, 1970.

Williams, Barry, *Modern Japan*, Longman, 1969.

Wood, Anthony, *Europe 1815 to 1945*, Longman, 1964.

Wood, S.H., *World Affairs, 1900 to the Present Day*, Oliver and Boyd, 1970.

Reference books

ed Breach, R.W., *Documents and descriptions : The World since 1914*, Oxford, 1966.

ed Clark, Michael and Teed, Peter, *Portraits and Documents: 1906–60*, Hutchinson, 1972.

Cook, Chris and Stevenson, John, *The Atlas of Modern Warfare*, Putnam's, 1978.

ed Hook, Brian, *The Cambridge Encyclopaedia of China*, Cambridge, 1982.

ed Mitchell, James, *The Illustrated Reference Book of Modern History*, Windward, 1982.

ed Moore, R.I., *The Hamlyn Historical Atlas*, Hamlyn, 1981.

Natkiel, Richard, *Atlas of Twentieth Century History*, Hamlyn, 1982.

Penguin Atlas of World History Volume Two, Penguin, 1978.

ed Barraclough, G., *The Times Atlas of World History*, Times Books, 1978.

TIME LINE

Date	Events in EUROPE	Events in the WORLD
1917	Bolshevik Revolution; battle of Passchendaele	Guomindang revolutionary government in Guangzhou; Balfour Declaration on Palestine
1918	End of First World War; Communist uprising in Berlin	Prohibition in America
1919	Treaty of Versailles; rise of Fascist Party in Italy; Weimar Republic in Germany	Amritsar massacre in India
1920	Nazi Party formed in Germany	League of Nations founded
1921	Mutiny at Kronstadt in Russia	
1922	The March on Rome; Mussolini in power in Italy	
1923	French troops occupy the Ruhr; inflation in Germany; Hitler's Munich Putsch	
1924	Death of Lenin; Corfu incident; Italians occupy Fiume	Dawes Plan – American loan to help Germany
1925	Mussolini becomes a dictator	Death of Sun Yixian
1926	General Strike in Britain	
1927	First Nuremberg Rally; Stalin becomes leader of USSR	
1928	First Five Year Plan in Russia	
1929	Lateran Treaty and Concordat	Wall Street Crash
1930		
1931		Japanese seize Manchuria
1932		Manchuria becomes Manchukuo
1933	Hitler becomes dictator in Germany; Germany leaves the League of Nations	Roosevelt's New Deal; Japan leaves the League of Nations
1934	USSR joins the League of Nations	Long March by Communists led by Mao Zedong
1935	Italy invades Abyssinia	
1936	Purges in the USSR; Spanish Civil War; Hitler marches troops into the Rhineland	
1937	Anti-Comintern Pact; Italy leaves the League of Nations	Japan invades China

Date	Events in EUROPE	Events in the WORLD
1938	Anschluss (union between Austria and Germany); Munich Crisis	
1939	Start of Second World War; German Blitzkrieg on Poland	
1940	Dunkirk; Fall of France	
1941	Operation 'Barbarossa'; Siege of Leningrad	Pearl Harbor; fall of Hong Kong
1942	El Alamein; Stalingrad	Fall of Singapore and the Philippines; Midway
1943	Kursk; Allied invasion of Italy	Capture of Tarawa; Teheran Conference
1944	D-Day landings; battle of the Bulge; V1 and V2 missiles	Battle of Leyte Gulf
1945	End of Second World War; Yalta and Potsdam conferences; deaths of Hitler and Mussolini	Iwo Jima; Okinawa; Hiroshima; death of Roosevelt; founding of United Nations
1946		Civil war in China; Churchill makes Iron Curtain speech
1947	Cominform; Marshall Aid to Europe	Truman Doctrine; India and Pakistan gain independence
1948	Berlin Blockade; Tito breaks with the Soviet bloc	Israel founded; Kashmir crisis; assassination of Gandhi
1949	Comecon and NATO founded; USSR tests A-bomb; Dr. Adenauer Chancellor of Germany	Chinese People's Republic founded
1950		Xizang (Tibet) annexed by China; start of the Korean War
1951	European Coal and Steel Community	
1952	British atomic bomb	
1953	Death of Stalin	Peace in Korea
1954		Fall of Dien Bien Phu in Vietnam; Algerian revolution
1955	Warsaw Pact	
1956	Khruschev denounces Stalin; Russia puts down revolt in Hungary	Suez Crisis
1957	Russia launches 'Sputnik'; Treaty of Rome founds EEC	Mao Zedong's 'Let a Hundred flowers blossom' speech
1958	de Gaulle takes over in France	Great Leap Forward in China
1959	EFTA formed	Castro seizes power in Cuba

Date	Events in EUROPE	Events in the WORLD
1960	French atomic bomb	Congo crisis; Macmillan makes 'Wind of change' speech
1961	Berlin Wall; Russia launches Gagarin – world's first astronaut in space	Bay of Pigs fiasco; India seizes Goa; South Africa leaves Commonwealth
1962		Cuban Missiles Crisis; de Gaulle brings peace to Algeria
1963		Test Ban Treaty; Kennedy assassinated
1964	Khruschev replaced by Brezhnev; UN intervention in Cyprus	Chinese atomic bomb; US more deeply involved in Vietnam
1965		Cultural Revolution in China
1966		UN sanctions against Rhodesia
1967		Six Day War between Egypt and Israel
1968	Warsaw Pact countries invade Czechoslovakia; Albania leaves Warsaw Pact in protest	Non-Proliferation Treaty; Tet Offensive in Vietnam; Martin Luther King killed
1969		Moon landing; Gaddafi seizes power in Libya; Russian-Chinese frontier dispute
1970	Death of de Gaulle	
1971		India and Pakistan at war; Communist China admitted to the United Nations
1972	Arab terrorist kill 11 Israeli athletes at Munich	SALT 1
1973	UK, Ireland and Denmark join the Common Market	The Yom Kippur War
1974		India explodes atomic bomb; Nixon resigns over Watergate
1975		End of the Vietnam War
1976		Death of Mao Zedong
1977		
1978		SALT 2; Camp David Peace Agreement
1979		Ayatollah Khomeini in Iran; American hostages imprisoned; Russians invade Afghanistan
1980	Solidarity Trade Union in Poland	Iraq and Iran at war
1981		President Sadat of Egypt is assassinated
1982		Falklands War; Israel invades Lebanon

INDEX – Modern World History 1919 onwards